Gabriel García Márquez's

One Hundred Years of Solitude
New Edition

Edited and with an introduction by
Harold Bloom
Sterling Professor of the Humanities
Yale University

BLOOM'S
LITERARY CRITICISM
An imprint of Infobase Publishing

**Bloom's Modern Critical Interpretations:
One Hundred Years of Solitude—New Edition**

Copyright © 2009 by Infobase Publishing
Introduction © 2009 by Harold Bloom

Bloom's Literary Criticism
An imprint of Infobase Publishing
132 West 31st Street
New York NY 10001

Library of Congress Cataloging-in-Publication Data
Gabriel García Márquez's One hundred years of solitude / edited and with an introduction by Harold Bloom. — New ed.
    p. cm. — (Bloom's modern critical interpretations)
 Includes bibliographical references and index.
 ISBN 978-1-60413-391-2
 1. García Márquez, Gabriel, 1928– Cien años de soledad. I. Bloom, Harold. II. Title. III. Series.

 PQ8180.17.A73C53233 2009
 863'.64—dc22   2008050534

Contributing editor: Pamela Loos
Cover design by Takeshi Takahashi

Printed in the United States of America
IBT EJB 10 9 8 7 6 5 4 3 2 1

This book is printed on acid-free paper.

All links and Web addresses were checked and verified to be correct at the time of publication. Because of the dynamic nature of the Web, some addresses and links may have changed since publication and may no longer be valid.

Contents

Editor's Note

My only slightly disenchanted introduction suggests a few reservations while admiring the over-rich textures of García Márquez's epic narrative.

Ralph Ellison's *Invisible Man* and *One Hundred Years of Solitude* are brought together by Michael Cooke, who finds their greatest affinity to be nostalgia for a canonical text that will not fail.

The curious dialectic of imperialism and apocalyptic in *One Hundred Years* is expounded by Brian Conniff, after which Gene H. Bell-Villada gives a broad overview of the novel's family chronicle.

Allied egoism and incest is traced by James Higgins in the saga of the Buendías, while Ariel Dorfman reflects on the relation between incest and fratricide in the book's violent cosmos.

Cervantes, as dangerous an analogue as Shakespeare, is invoked by Michael Bell as a structural guide to *One Hundred Years*, after which Florence Delay and Jacqueline de Labriolle attempt the almost-as-dangerous comparison of Gabriel García Márquez with William Faulkner.

André Brink focuses on how language itself leads the characters (and the reader) to death, while John Krapp refreshingly reads *One Hundred Years* as an implicit critique of identity politics.

In this volume's final essay, Shannin Schroeder sums up the book's visionary alchemy.

HAROLD BLOOM

Introduction

Macondo, according to Carlos Fuentes, "begins to proliferate with the rich-ness of a Colombian Yoknapatawpha." Faulkner, crossed by Kafka, is the literary origins of Gabriel García Márquez. So pervasive is the Faulknerian influence that at times one hears Joyce and Conrad, Faulkner's masters, echoed in García Márquez, yet almost always as mediated by Faulkner. *The Autumn of the Patriarch* may be too pervaded by Faulkner, but *One Hundred Years of Solitude* absorbs Faulkner, as it does all other influences, into a phan-tasmagoria so powerful and self-consistent that the reader never questions the authority of García Márquez. Perhaps, as Reinard Argas suggested, Faulkner is replaced by Carpentier and Kafka by Borges in *One Hundred Years of Solitude*, so that the imagination of García Márquez domesticates itself within its own language. Macondo, visionary realm, is an Indian and Hispanic act of consciousness, very remote from Oxford, Mississippi, and from the Jewish cemetery in Prague. In his subsequent work, García Márquez went back to Faulkner and Kafka, but then *One Hundred Years of Solitude* is a miracle and could only happen once, if only because it is less a novel than it is a Scripture, the Bible of Macondo; Melquíades the Magus, who writes in Sanskrit, may be more a mask for Borges than for the author himself, and yet the Gypsy storyteller also connects García Márquez to the archaic Hebrew storyteller, the Yahwist, at once the greatest of realists and the greatest of fantasists but above all the only true rival of Homer and Tolstoy as a storyteller.

My primary impression, in the act of rereading *One Hundred Years of Solitude*, is a kind of aesthetic battle fatigue, since every page is rammed full of life beyond the capacity of any single reader to absorb. Whether the

1

impacted quality of this novel's texture is finally a virtue I am not sure, since sometimes I feel like a man invited to dinner who has been served nothing but an enormous platter of Turkish Delight. Yet it is all story, where everything conceivable and inconceivable is happening at once, from creation to apocalypse, birth to death. Roberto González Echevarría has gone so far as to surmise that in some sense it is the reader who must die at the end of the story, and perhaps it is the sheer richness of the text that serves to destroy us. Joyce half-seriously envisioned an ideal reader cursed with insomnia who would spend her life in unpacking *Finnegans Wake*. The reader need not translate *One Hundred Years of Solitude*, a novel that deserves its popularity as it has no surface difficulties whatsoever. And yet, a new dimension is added to reading by this book. Its ideal reader has to be like its most memorable personage, the sublimely outrageous Colonel Aureliano Buendía, who "had wept in his mother's womb and been born with his eyes open." There are no wasted sentences, no mere transitions, in this novel, and you must notice everything at the moment you read it. It will all cohere, at least as myth and metaphor if not always as literary meaning.

In the presence of an extraordinary actuality, consciousness takes the place of imagination. That Emersonian maxim is Wallace Stevens's and is worthy of the visionary of *Notes Toward a Supreme Fiction* and *An Ordinary Evening in New Haven*. Macondo is a supreme fiction, and there are no ordinary evenings within its boundaries. Satire, even parody, and most fantasy—these are now scarcely possible in the United States. How can you satirize Ronald Reagan or Jerry Falwell? Pynchon's *The Crying of Lot 49* ceases to seem fantasy whenever I visit Southern California, and a ride on the New York City subway tends to reduce all literary realism to an idealizing projection. Some aspects of Latin American existence transcend even the inventions of García Márquez. I am informed, on good authority, that the older of the Duvalier dictators of Haiti, the illustrious Papa Doc, commanded that all black dogs in his nation be destroyed when he came to believe that a principal enemy had transformed himself into a black dog. Much that is fantastic in *One Hundred Years of Solitude* would be fantastic anywhere, but much that seems unlikely to a North American critic may well be a representation of reality.

Emir Monegal emphasized that García Márquez's masterwork was unique among Latin American novels, being radically different from the diverse achievements of Julio Cortázar, Carlos Fuentes, Lezama Lima, Mario Vargas Llosa, Miguel Angel Asturias, Manuel Puig, Guillermo Cabrera Infante, and so many more. The affinities to Borges and to Carpentier were noted by Monegal as by Arenas, but Monegal's dialectical point seemed to be that García Márquez was representative only by joining all his colleagues in not being representative. Yet it is now true that, for most

North American readers, *One Hundred Years of Solitude* comes first to mind when they think of the Hispanic novel in America. Alejo Carpentier's *Explosion in a Cathedral* may be an even stronger book, but only Borges has dominated the North American literary imagination as García Márquez has with his grand fantasy. It is inevitable that we are fated to identify *One Hundred Years of Solitude* with an entire culture, almost as though it were a new *Don Quixote*, which it most definitely is not. Comparisons to Balzac and even to Faulkner are also not very fair to García Márquez. The titanic inventiveness of Balzac dwarfs the later visionary, and nothing even in Macondo is as much a negative Sublime as the fearsome quest of the Bundrens in *As I Lay Dying*. *One Hundred Years of Solitude* is more of the stature of Nabokov's *Pale Fire* and Pynchon's *Gravity's Rainbow*, latecomers' fantasies, strong inheritors of waning traditions.

Whatever its limitations may or may not be, García Márquez's major narrative now enjoys canonical status as well as a representative function. Its cultural status continues to be enhanced, and it would be foolish to quarrel with so large a phenomenon. I wish to address myself only to the question of how seriously, as readers, we need to receive the book's scriptural aspect. The novel's third sentence is: "The world was so recent that things lacked names, and in order to indicate them it was necessary to point," and the third sentence from the end is long and beautiful:

> Macondo was already a fearful whirlwind of dust and rubble being spun about by the wrath of the biblical hurricane when Aureliano skipped eleven pages so as not to lose time with facts he knew only too well, and he began to decipher the instant that he was living, deciphering it as he lived it, prophesying himself in the act of deciphering the last page of the parchment, as if he were looking into a speaking mirror.

The time span between this Genesis and this Apocalypse is six generations, so that José Arcadio Buendía, the line's founder, is the grandfather of the last Aureliano's grandfather. The grandfather of Dante's grandfather, the crusader Cassaguida, tells his descendant Dante that the poet perceives the truth because he gazes into that mirror in which the great and small of this life, before they think, behold their thought. Aureliano, at the end, reads the Sanskrit parchment of the gypsy, Borges-like Magus, and looks into a speaking mirror, beholding his thought before he thinks it. But does he, like Dante, behold the truth? Was Florence, like Macondo, a city of mirrors (or mirages) in contrast to the realities of the Inferno, the Purgatorio, the Paradiso? Is *One Hundred Years of Solitude* only a speaking mirror? Or does it contain, somehow within it, an Inferno, a Purgatorio, a Paradiso?

Only the experience and disciplined reflections of a great many more strong readers will serve to answer those questions with any conclusiveness. The final eminence of *One Hundred Years of Solitude* for now remains undecided. What is clear to the book's contemporaries is that García Márquez has given contemporary culture, in North America and Europe, as much as in Latin America, one of its double handful of necessary narratives, without which we will understand neither one another nor our own selves.

MICHAEL G. COOKE

Ellison and García Márquez: Nostalgia and the Destruction of "Text"

The speaker in Ralph Ellison's *Invisible Man* himself urges us to take his story as one of revitalization. He is returning from hibernation to a fresh expression of sociopolitical purpose and force. Certainly critics have obliged. Tony Tanner says the invisible man is at last ready to act and think effectively on his own;[1] and Robert Stepto has taken the image of hibernation, with its promise of awakening, as the cardinal one not only for Ellison but for modern Afro-American literature.[2] But it is easier for a beaver to tell what a bear will do in the spring than for the most discerning critic to figure out what career "invisible man," or Jack-the-Bear, will follow once he leaves his manhole. That is, if he ever actually does so.

What does this indeterminacy of the future mean to our overall reading of Ellison's text? Does it reflect only a quirk of the protagonist's temperament, as passing is a personal maneuver and signal of temperament in J. W. Johnson's *The Autobiography of an Ex-Colored Man*? Or is it an inevitable result of the way the novel's action is structured and conceived?

It is striking that a very different novel, out of a very different tradition, gives rise to virtually identical questions. I refer to Gabriel García Márquez's *Cien años de soledad*. It may afford an illuminating perspective on both works that they should coincide so, representing as they do the most prominent single achievements in two burgeoning literary traditions, the Afro-American and the Latin American.

From *The Yale Journal of Criticism* 1, no. 1 (Fall 1987): 87–106. © 1987 by Yale University.

5

The fundamental points at which *Cien años* converges with *Invisible Man* may be readily noted: the action recapitulates, on a historical rather than an autobiographical scale, a dismal course of misguided aspiration, deceit, folly, cruelty, and sensuality, and this action culminates in a cataclysmic episode marked by two separate but convergent strains. First, we may understand that some escape is effected from the labyrinthine state (explicitly in *Cien años*, subliminally in *Invisible Man*); and second, we may infer that a clue into the redeemed air, out of the miasma and the maze of the past, has been identified.

Given the fact that *Cien años* does not have a first-person narrator, can personal temperament play any role here in creating the indeterminacy of the future? But *Cien años* does have what may be termed a first-person or subjective bias. Individual characters by the score are given their heads, their own way; the force and values exerted by these various characters in turn establish the force and values of the text at that point.[3]

Remedios the Beauty makes a good illustration; her solipsistic self-will seems winsome and right, and almost too late do we see the havoc her outlook breeds. In like manner, as soon as we recognize that Aureliano Babilonia recapitulates and fuses the traits of various of the founding characters in the novel, that is, those of the first two generations, we are in a position to infer that his story, because of the prevailing subjective bias, is as much a consummation for *Cien años* as the manhole experience is for Ellison's invisible man.

And Aureliano Babilonia, like Jack-the-Bear, clears away clichés and misconceptions, comes upon the truth, and makes a distinctive new commitment in his life. *His* sense of where he stands must be taken to be positive, while the narrator's rather plangent (and gratuitous) declaration that "las estirpes condenadas a cien años de soledad no tenían una segunda oportunidad sobre la tierra" (races doomed to one hundred years of solitude didn't use to have a second chance on earth) need be no more than the equivalent of the invisible man's failure to move in fact into a new order, into a second chance. García Márquez's use of physical annihilation is only another way of achieving the same effect as Ellison's psychic paralysis.

Here again the critics have tended to take Aureliano Babilonia's position as straightforward and validating for the text. Suzanne Jill Levine declares that the "dominant obsession" of love between Babilonia and Amaranta Úrsula (who herself gives us a reprise of earlier female characters)[4] both overpowers present difficulties and anchors the novel as a whole.[5] And David William Foster sees the novel as embodying "an eschatological vision of Latin America: the end of the cyclical process of feudal repression that destroys both Macondo and the prophetic text itself."[6] The theme of love would have for *Cien años* the force that the theme of justice does for *Invisible Man*.

It is a revelatory and redemptive light, a light that proves at once material and metaphysical in each of the novels. In the context of self-imprisonment that seems necessary to revelation, Jack-the-Bear engineers a world of material light and wants not only the man under the street lamp but all of us to see him as a man metaphysically, to see the light of human and political values he has seen. In like manner, on the material level in *Cien años* we see the "inner fire" (fuego interior) of a self-consuming wedding ring, the sublunary explosions of ants, and the luminous discs in the sky before the apocalyptic wind rounds out Aureliano Babilonia's life, just as he sees, metaphysically, the meaning of the entire past in Melquíades's parchments.

Even as we acknowledge the richness and momentum of these novels, however, it becomes necessary to take account of a quizzical undercurrent of opinion about them. Foster, after praising the eschatological vision of *Cien años*, calls it a disappointment, "in that it does not fulfill the pattern demanded" by the interplay of the written text and the sociocultural matrix it both springs from and returns to (5). Larry Neal makes an almost identical complaint about *Invisible Man*, finding that the protagonist remains in a "ritualistic" scheme, without bearing on the "secular" world, for all his claims of new vision and new goals.[7]

One cannot lightly dismiss such criticism. The texts make a strong representation of the end of an evil and a strong intimation that it is the turn of a new and better order to occupy the fields of time. When nothing happens or seems likely to happen, dissatisfaction will ensue. The dissatisfaction we feel here is interwoven with a sense that the invisible man, who speaks for us, and Aureliano Babilonia, who acts as the representative figure in the text, personally let us down. That is to say, we infer a defect of temperament in the crucial characters. This reaction is natural but proves in that respect similar to envy: natural and hard to justify.

The fact is that evidence of the destruction of the old order remains strictly confined to the state of the individual characters. The evidence and the characters are neutral, if not irrelevant, to change in the larger world, which goes on though Macondo does not; indeed it is clear that Macondo has been turning into a ghost town, on demographic and economic grounds, before the "biblical hurricane." The thirty-two wars that the abandoned offspring of Aureliano Babilonia and Amaranta Úrsula might properly have won *will still be fought* though the fated boy has not survived even to take part in them. By the same token neither the college nor the Brotherhood ceases to thrive because Jack-the-Bear ceases to believe in them. Mr. Norton may have personally fallen upon evil days, but specious philanthropy and spiritual repression and moral pollution doubtless continue in other exemplars.

Nothing in the prevailing action bears toward even the slightest change in the order of life. The change occurs in the feelings and conceptions and values of a single character, however outstanding among the total panorama of the text. For the rest, the wayward and distorting play of life goes on.

This leads back to the question of the structure of the novels. For despite their plethora of dramatic episodes, their basic action is so structured as to engender not a refined state of action but a fixated state of consciousness. The real interest, to put it in other terms, lies in the way the focal characters come to see the inner data and mechanisms of the imposing world that has contained and controlled them. Given the suddenness of this coming-to-consciousness in both Aureliano Babilonia and the invisible man, it is no wonder that they go into a total absorption, the one reading and the other writing, in the manner psychiatrists identify as cathexis. Enlightenment proves self-obsessive.

If consciousness itself is not axiomatically of the past, the consciousness of the protagonists in *Cien años* and *Invisible Man* is simply and strictly geared to the past. For that reason I would contend that these are essentially paradoxical novels. They are novels of nostalgia that debunk nostalgia. They seduce us into thinking of them as works of prophecy, when they prophesy nothing in particular, but only stimulate an abstract feeling for the future. We cannot come to terms with this paradoxicality without delving into the status of the two texts and into their internal treatment of the idea of texts.

Both narratives are devoted to the past, vitally invested and steeped in the past, and above all spiritually dependent on the past. Why, then, is the text that preserves the past destroyed? Why does the invisible man burn the contents of his briefcase, when they symbolize the past he is, on this reading, incapable of letting go? And why does Melquíades's parchment crumble and blow away in the annihilating wind, when Aureliano Babilonia is so caught up in reading it? Certainly we are not in a Dantesque situation, where a reliable Vergil has reached the limit of his capacity, and now useless leaves blow away in the wind. Here the guiding texts cannot afford clear, let alone true, guidance, but then again no other guidance comes readily to hand.

One thing is clear: Jack-the-Bear recreates what he burns, and more; and the narrator of *Cien años* effectively restores the cryptic parchment in a commonly available tongue. The question then arises: is the content of the recreated text a mere semantic reproduction, a recovery-by-displacement of the original events and conditions? We have also a corollary question: as long as the original matter stood to be recreated, why destroy it in the first place?

But consider the sheer phenomenon of destroying "text." Ishmael Reed has a case of it in *Mumbo Jumbo*, and Alice Walker a case of repressing texts of letters in *The Color Purple*, that is, the effect of the text is destroyed (it is well to recall Parson Adams's accidental immolation of his Aeschylus in *Joseph Andrews*). But even if it is not unheard of among us, destroying a text is unexpected. The way John Washington pores over and carefully perpetuates a text in David Bradley's *The Chaneysville Incident* strikes us as nearer to the tradition of literate and sensitive people. Book-burning, to use a blunt term, smacks of inquisitions, fanaticism, and tyranny. But in fact there exists a minor tradition of noninquisitional destroying of texts, and it sheds important light on what Ellison and García Márquez are doing.

In book 5 of *The Prelude*, Wordsworth reports "perusing" Cervantes's *Don Quixote* and then falling asleep, whereupon he has a dream in which an Arab is seen racing ahead of oceanic waters with a shell and a stone. This stark and complex image is the indisputable but also mutant offspring of his reading. Critics have shown its value in the immediate context of articulating "the growth of the poet's mind" but have tended to ignore a special resonance the scene has outside of its established frame. The Arab dream presents an early form of a pseudocritical phenomenon that at once arises and departs from concern with a text. The reader-figure makes a devout engagement with the text-object, and then, breaking off into his private occupations, carries an image (provoked but not given by the text) as a significant force in the personal organization of his life. In effect, the text dissolves and becomes recrystallized in a private stream, or scheme, in the reader's mind. And there is about that recrystallization a peculiar chemistry that makes it impossible to recover or rediscover the text in its original form; a basic change has occurred.

The reader's situation absorbs and reclassifies the reading act.[8] Though I call this a pseudocritical phenomenon, I would stress that it occurs without deviousness or treachery. No pretense is made at "fair" reading, nor even at a definite response or reader-response. The text is actually accorded a singular force, but not as itself, and not even as a displaced, concentrated message (such as a preacher might produce, or as readers of *Jude the Obscure* or *The Possessed*, say, might entertain in carrying the text as a crushing revelation of the nature of life). The text's, that is, the *Quixote*'s force proves at best occasional. It serves as a timely catalyst or counterweight for the reader's, that is, the poet Wordsworth's, ongoing practical business. There is no room even for a ruse like misprision.[9] The *Quixote* is first focused, then abandoned. In its status as text it ceases to count, save as an inarticulate, submerged prompting. It stands essentially as a pre-amble.

With the episode of the Arab dream, *The Prelude* initiates the late nineteenth-century's search for a new manner of text and a new relationship of *reader-as-actor* to it. This search effectively extends to the story of the Grand Inquisitor in Dostoevski's *The Brothers Karamazov*, to Browning's *The Ring and the Book*, Arnold's *The Scholar Gypsy*, and Gosse's *Father and Son*. All four depend on a text that is at once orthodox and nullified. The tyrannical nihilism of Ivan Karamazov's "text," the irresoluteness of Browning's multiform "text," the deadly contagion of the "text" of Arnold's world, and the frank repudiation in Gosse's "text" of Christianity and science converge at one point: the basic text must be dismissed, like a sandbar which allows for moment's perspective but from which the flow of life and the swimmer's energy intrinsically depart.

Two of the more interesting developments of the Arab dream complex occur in the widely celebrated novels we are scrutinizing, Ellison's *Invisible Man* and García Márquez's *Cien años de soledad*. These works make overt the political intimations of the Wordsworthian context, where the quixotic romance of chivalry comes out, in the truth of dreams, as a promise of disaster;[10] they give a social cast to Wordsworth's symbolic conversion of an original text into practical action; and they absorb into the literal level Wordsworth's dream-ridden concern with destruction not just for *Don Quixote* (or Milton or Shakespeare) but for anything with cultural form, any text. The functional "text" in Ellison and García Márquez ends in destruction.

The action of both novels stems from a text that is unintelligible and/or unheeded, while at the same time something unidentifiable in the text precipitates images and responses in the ongoing action. A significant difference between Wordsworth and the modern novelists would seem to arise with the fact that the Arab dream is an isolated episode, whereas the whole of Ellison's work is affected by the grandfather's portentous sentence and Bledsoe's secret message, and the whole of García Márquez's work becomes identical with Melquíades's mystical text. In both novels, too, there is an element of prophecy or fatal control not only in the overall action but also in the separate episodes, as character after character seeks knowledge and domination of others; in the Arab dream prophecy appears to have no place.

But such differences do not take away from the basic parallelism between nineteenth-century poet and twentieth-century novelists. In fact, the Arab dream does carry forward subtly through *The Prelude*. It enables the action to pivot from a condition of authorial anxiety to a conviction of authorial mission; it intimates that Wordsworth is more than the latter-day heir, he is the current guardian and champion of the tradition that, far from looming dauntingly over him like the mountain in the rowboat episode, is only "frail" and in flight from enveloping waters.

That phenomenon of flight calls for special attention. The flight is taken not with the precipitating text but more truly away from it, away from anything definite, concrete, constant. The text has virtually dissolved into the waters, and there remain only cryptic symbols that have neither specific function nor positive force. The usual interpretation of the Arab's stone and shell as mathematics and poetry (inertly inspired by Wordsworth's remark about musing on "poetry and geometric truth") may not be wholly satisfactory.

The dreaming Wordsworth is convinced that the Arab has come to him as a guide "through the desert," but as in all cases where a guide is nominated in *The Prelude*, disappointment ensues; "he left me," Wordsworth intones. In a sense Wordsworth is left not simply vacant, but with something unstated, obscure. The Arab calls the stone and the shell books, identifying the stone as Euclid's Elements and the shell as having even "more worth." But the shell turns out to be a book that one must listen to, not read, and in "an unknown tongue / Which yet [Wordsworth] understood." What guidance can constitute itself from such unorthodox turns?

It strikes me that guidance is greatest where it is least specific, or that Wordsworth is being guided into a state of paradox that defies the very idea of a "guide" book. The shell, for example, specifically prophesies doom, but it is being protected from destruction in the waters; and again the shell belongs in the waters and should not need protection from them. The Arab furthermore is going to bury the stone and shell to preserve their existence. We can elude the trap of paradox by recognizing two planes of text in the Arab's scheme: the objects he carries as books, and the language he uses about them. The former are free in themselves, but the construction he puts upon them has singular authority in light of the desperate mood and need of the dreamer. In fact, a principle may emerge here, to the effect that the authority of a text increases in proportion to the user's need.

And Wordsworth, instead of running the risk of writing, is seeking a guarantee against time, and failing to see (1) that his ability to understand an "unknown tongue" is already a promise for the future, and (2) that the future is destruction for those who hold on to the past and, worse, its symbols and for those who dwell on thoughts of destruction.

The Arab—or Wordsworth's dream—is doing something less systematic and simple than any one-to-one formula of correspondences would suggest. He is acting in primary terms of preserving the stone as a housing of the soul (that is what the stone represented in megalithic cultures),[11] and conserving the form of a past life, which the shell represents in containing the sound of an absent, unreal sea.

The stone and the shell are in conflict, moreover. If they do not stand for masculine and feminine forms, they do show divergent, and defective, characters. The stone offers power without functional embodiment, the shell articulation without distinct life. Though the Arab may escape the flood, he could fall and the stone might smash the shell or the stone might break or both might be destroyed. That would leave, respectively, a spiritual potential without tradition, a tradition without capacity for renovation, or nothing at all. In this light it may be plausible to see the waters as the bearer of unevacuated shells, that is, living things in carapace, and the Arab as fleeing because of a blind devotion to the inadequate forms of stone and shell and out of ignorance of the fact that the waters bear toward him all stages of things in solution. The conversion of the desert, the Arab's ordinary milieu, into the sea suggests such a reformation of values.[12]

Both Ellison and García Márquez make central use of flight in a mode that, like the Arab's, proves at once purposive and addled. Typically, too, they make literal and political what Wordsworth leaves as an oneiric image. Ellison's invisible man is identified with the idea of running, that is, finding himself perpetually on the move without a trustworthy sense of motive or direction. More profligate than to focus on a single central figure, *Cien años* begins with a Vergilian scene of seeking a new homeland, but accident and arbitrary impulse have more to do with the settlement than national destiny or communal purpose. It proves much the same with other instances of travel, whether the character in question is hoping to bring the railroad to Macondo or struggling to bring justice and equality to the entire nation, or is "un abuelo concupiscente que se dejaba arrastrar por la frivolidad a través de un páramo alucinado, en busca de una mujer hermosa a quien no haría feliz" (a concupiscent grandfather who let himself be frivolously dragged along over a hallucinated plain in search of a beautiful woman whom he would not make happy).

While great prominence is given to the way other people keep the invisible man running, his chronic state of flight or dislocation is not all imposed from without. It happens that, before the despotic educator, Bledsoe, sets him running, he shows ready capacity for random and dangerous turns. That is how he comes to take the VIP Mr. Norton down the forbidden road to the incestuous straw-man, Trueblood, and the zany subworld of the Golden Day. His slip of the tongue in the speech before "the town's leading white citizens"—he blurts "equality" instead of "social responsibility"—also gives evidence of this capacity.

The invisible man grows from rank materialism—scrounging for supposed "gold" in the Battle Royal—to the hortatory idealism of the passages on the Bill of Rights at novel's end: his grandfather "*must* have meant the principle . . . on which the country was built." He does so without getting away from a basic disconnection and instability. He wants higher things; he has no sure means of attaining them. In a measure he has traded victimization for illusion, as we can see if we compare his seduction at the hands of the Brotherhood bigwig's wife in midnovel and his nonseduction of Sybil at the end. To live by his new perception, he would have to get into a difficult candor and a volatile connection with Sybil. He would have to spell from Sybil's confused leaves. Instead he is looking for easy assurance and control. His inability to erase his deceitful lipstick message from Sybil's stomach significantly reminds us of Pilate's difficulty in cleansing his hands of the sign of his unprincipled course. The invisible man not only will not make sacrifices for his newfound principles, he shies away from them.

That shying away is represented in the image of hibernation, with its promise of a return to the central field of endeavor. But there is neither social nor psychic nor physiological ecology within which hibernation would prove intelligible. Hibernation has the aspect of frozen flight. In action and in spirit the protagonist has divorced himself from the world of "running," from the inscrutable "text" of his grandfather and the treacherous "text" of Bledsoe. But he spends his energy, paradoxically, recreating that world. *Invisible Man* is a text of ambivalence or unconsummated transition. It embodies retrospect but professes anticipation; it rejects the protagonist's original "text" while having no substantial alternative.

We may recognize two sorts of "text" here: the eventual or principal text (text-n), the one the speaker makes to sum up his history, enunciate his critique of society, and portend his escape from both; and the original or precipitating texts (text-o). Text-n is oddly self-thwarting. At incidental moments, such as the description of Mr. Norton's daughter seen in a photograph, text-n exhibits a positive dynamic judgment that can do honor to the original impact of felt life and still correct it in light of eventual reflection and knowledge. What first captivates the speaker as "delicate, dreamy features" in the girl come to be judged as merely "ordinary" and "machine-tooled." No comparable development occurs in the fundamental levels of the action.

The suggestion arises that only the tacit favor and collaboration of the reader ("Who knows but that . . . I speak for you") could bring about a substantial vision of a new order in the face of general failure in the old. The invisible man recognizes that he can no more generate a new order singlehandedly than he can singlehandedly do in the Monopolated Light and Power Company. Hence what his story embodies is what his values repudiate: the world of Bledsoe and Norton, Jack and Ras and Rinehart. Like the original texts (text-o), the principal text (or text-n) might appear fit only for repudiation, in that it instructs only in its outmoded teleology. The difference between the protagonist's speeches at the Battle Royal or the eviction scene or for the Brotherhood, on the one hand, and his speaking-for-us which is text-n becomes important here. In the topical speeches, he is looking for a special personal effect and advantage. In retrospect he is looking for the communal possibility of the good. But still practically looking in vain.

It has been customary to emphasize the way the idyllic and nostalgic description of the college at the beginning of chapter 2 of *Invisible Man* takes a "sudden forking" and leads "off to the insane asylum." The dexterity of the movement and its ironic finish is worthy of Byron himself. But Byron's narration is above all current. Ellison takes on the posture of a Wordsworthian narrator, dwelling in memory and scouring it for value. His satire works as the flip side of a spontaneous and deep nostalgia. The burning of his briefcase of mementos and talismans clarifies his history without releasing him from it. His voice ultimately registers with a kind of volatile nostalgia; his story assumes the air of a perverse elegy, not only by virtue of its tone of hilarious misery (as in the Trueblood episode), but also because of its preservation of a past that the speaker himself wishes annihilated.

What does it mean that preservation and destruction equally attend the precipitating texts and the principal one? Essentially, I think, an unenforceable preference for the deep integrity and resonance of civilized action over the superficial, automatic authority of words. The text, as dynamic social summons, in that sense desires the end of texts as rigid political authority. Even the invocation of the Bill of Rights does not go counter to this bias. The revolt against Supercargo in the Golden Day, the riot that Ras leads which leads to the narrator's plunge into the manhole, and the narrator's own burst of violence under the streetlight have one thing in common: a refusal to be taken in, or even to be indefinitely put off, by uncorresponding words. But anarchy in action is as bad as fixed words. Both must yield, ideally, to an evolving correspondence between words and states.

Invisible Man tacitly demands that the Bill of Rights and the Constitution be realized in society, or their real irrelevance admitted. In either case action, actuality determines the status of words in a way that does not work in reverse; that is to say, words do not determine the status of actuality, but only the status of belief, and they do that most successfully where the dimensions of actuality remain unknown. When we see the narrator unable to enact his vision, it becomes clear that regenerative action fails not only on the national but also on the personal plane.

Jack-the-Bear's hibernation corresponds to the society's incoherence and inefficacy. In proclaiming his hibernation, he surpasses his totem animal and arises from animality to language. But in staying in hibernation, he sacrifices action and even a form of actuality for language. The rejection of rigid form and invalid authority that is implied in the rejection of text falters before the amorphousness of his final position. He becomes a reluctant and resentful reflection of his society, consuming its light to recreate its story, rather than getting on with a new life-plan. Thus text reasserts itself not because it is more complex, more permanent, or truer than action, but because it is easier.

Many of the elements we have been scrutinizing in *Invisible Man* appear again in a central position in García Márquez's *Cien años de soledad*. Though this novel pivots around multifarious failures of love rather than of justice (as in *Invisible Man*), it too takes on the character of a perverse elegy and carries as a primary freight the conflict between text and action, between the permanence and the emptiness of text. *Cien años*, like *Invisible Man*, involves the actual destruction of a text, Colonel Aureliano Buendía's peripatetic poems being the analog of the contents of Jack-the-Bear's briefcase. García Márquez, however, goes far beyond Ellison in actually wiping out text and central setting with an apocalyptic wind, at the end of *Cien años*; *Invisible Man* only intimates its radical dissatisfaction with the abstraction of texts, itself included. But by the same token the elegiac temper of the Colombian novel is deepened.

Ellison ends with the wistful, quizzical universality of "Who knows but that, on the lower frequencies, I speak for you?" García Márquez ends with the dread apocalyptic finality of

> ya había comprendido que no saldría jamás de ese cuarto, pues estaba previsto que la ciudad de los espejos (o los espejismos) sería arrasada por el viento y desterrada de la memoria de los hombres ... , y que todo lo escrito ... era irrepetible desde siempre y para siempre, porque las estirpes condenadas a cien años de soledad no tenían una segunda oportunidad sobre la tierra.

> [already he had understood that he would never leave that room, since it was foreseen that the city of mirrors (or mirages) would be laid waste by the wind and banished from the memory of mankind ... , and that all that was written ... was unrepeatable from all eternity and for all eternity, because races doomed to one hundred years of solitude didn't use to have a second chance on earth.]

But if the wind's effect is to lay them waste, its inner voice and freight do just the opposite. The wind of destruction is equally the wind of nostalgia and elegy:

> Entonces empezó el viento, tibio, incipiente, lleno de voces del pasado, de murmullos de geranios antiguos, de suspiros de desengaños anteriores a las nostalgias más tenaces.

> [Then the wind commenced, lukewarm, uncradling, full of voices from the past, of murmurs of age-old geraniums, of sighs of disenchantments reaching farther back than the most tenacious nostalgias.]

Ellison turns *us* into secret coauthors; García Márquez gives authorship over entirely, if also dwindlingly, to the wind, with its voices turning to murmurs and those murmurs to sighs. But both novels make authorship only a summons to readership. The issue is less whether writing is possible than how it can be legitimate and fruitful. It would not seem implausible to take both novels as devoted to the issue of learning to read.[13] Certainly both abound in "texts" of astonishing formal variety.

But the texts also include a devastating practical critique of learning to read. The plethora of internal texts may be seen to have one essential feature in common: to master reading is to find reading useless. Infallibly, reading comes later and cannot ever catch up with life. Its failure to catch up applies not just where the text pretends to the status of a comprehensive schema, but even in the case where the text is frankly a partitive feature of life, for the understanding of the part is by definition posthumous and in that degree useless.

The opposition of text and action is nowhere clearer than in the accumulating sheaf of poetry by the rebel commander, Colonel Aureliano Buendía, in *Cien años*. The novel, which is structurally an infinite series of beginnings with one end, devastation, begins with the colonel facing a firing squad and/or, in interfusing time, going as a stripling boy to "get acquainted [conocer] with ice." The capacity for wonder and accurate observation the child displays, if it remains at all, remains only in the colonel's penning never-to-be-seen poems as he pursues a doomed campaign. The poems constitute their own form of incongruous nostalgia, while the warfare that should stand as their antithesis represents at equally idle animation and goal.

The maker vs. the doer in the colonel's nature had been anticipated in his production of gold fishes, which were to him artifacts, but to his mother commerce, survival. The fish and the poetry suggest the same things: on the one hand, a potential spirituality that remains mechanical, repetitious, and unaware; and on the other hand a blind animal energy reproducing itself (as the colonel blindly makes sons in his military tent) to nobody's benefit or satisfaction.

The poetry—and the fishes, and the spawning of sons—must carry then a secondary value. They represent an impulse to put a certain stamp on matter, and on time. The colonel's ten-foot circle, within which no one may come, is less important as a mark of his cutting himself off from people than as a proof of his purpose to make life around him consistent and sure. The inaccessibility of the physical text of his poetry does not rule out understanding of their paradoxical existence, any more than the forbidden circle keeps the secrets of the colonel's heart.

It is the colonel, the maker of the "text," who does not know the secrets of his own heart or, as the debacle of the attempted suicide shows, even its location. His burning of his poems works exactly as does the invisible man's burning of his talismans: to express a disinterest and disconnection bordering on nihilism. There is no past, for him, no present and no future; and it would be wholly out of place to have a record or text of any kind.

The destruction of the poems is, of course, part of a larger pattern in *Cien años de soledad*. It corresponds to José Arcadio Buendía's attempt to destroy the alchemical laboratory he had instituted in his home. And it anticipates, in the personal scale, the comprehensive destruction that overtakes Macondo at the novel's end. The laboratory, let us recall, contained Melquíades's parchments, which—finally deciphered—Aureliano Babilonia is reading as the nostalgic/apocalyptic wind arises. In each case the text is secret, like Ellison's, and inescapable, and ineligible for any good. Its immolation entails a sort of truculence, a brutal serving of the moment's needs and impulses. But that moment of brutality entails an uncanny argument against the promise of sustained stability and achievement that the abstract idea of a text holds up. We cannot rely on a text in actuality, as the final text of the banana company massacre shows, with its total, cynical invention of history.

In the case of *Cien años*, truculence gets into the realm of downright vindictiveness: "Porque las estirpes condenadas a cien años de soledad no tenían una segunda oportunidad sobre la tierra." (Because races doomed to one hundred years of solitude didn't use to have a second chance on earth.) The principle of vindictiveness is less readily apparent in the case of *Invisible Man*, but surely the wanton beating of the unwitting white man under the streetlight is in the same vein. The protagonist is paying back all who have made him invisible, who have missed centuries, not just one century of chances to make manifest his humanity, and their own. No further chance remains, he says with his fists.

But vindictiveness, even as it destroys its object, builds on a supposed ideal that seems impossible of realization. What or where is that ideal for Gabriel García Márquez and Ralph Waldo Ellison? In a word, the ideal is diffused through, and must be distilled from, the New World adventure. Differences in the forms that the New World adventure took in Latin America and in the United States notwithstanding, both novelists make it a background, or rather a foundation image in the works in question, and show it as a slipping, vicious foundation. The ultimate text is, then, Western Culture, which came mysteriously to Macondo and to which the African slave was as mysteriously brought. Exploration, religion, political missionism (or messianism), capitalist expansion, technological sleight of hand: these are the instruments of Western culture both novelists deal with, and sardonically so.

This brings us squarely up against the question of whether the texts of the two novels (designated here text-*n*) are different in character or merit from the text of Western culture (text-*w/c*). Is not one as much an imposition as the other? And we may hark back to the question of how to evaluate the recreation of the events and conditions of autobiography and history in text-*n*, when text-*n* is at pains to destroy the texts of experience (text-*e*) on which it is based.

To take these questions in order, I would recognize a major difference between text-*n* and text-*w/c* in the respect that text-*n* is not a credulous recounting but a probing, challenging one; text-*n* proceeds as if on a simple

narrative footing, but with continual, indeed increasing critical interpola-
tions. Text-*n* thus becomes an explication of the mystery of text-*w/c* and
perhaps of its exorcism.

The answer to the second question follows readily in the train of this
recognition, for text-*n* is destroying the automatic, ancient authority of text-*e*
while holding text-*e* up to a wider audience and under a sharper light, to create at least the impossibility of any recurrence. This stands as a major value in
both Ellison and García Márquez.

But at bottom do the facts of the novels justify the pervasive condemnation of the New World adventure? Is the real culprit the adventurer or
the capacity, almost the eagerness of his victims for victimization? After
all, the narrator's deference to Mr. Norton, as *Invisible Man* begins, comes
unforced from the depths of his being and sets up complex levels of satisfaction (while his mockery at the end seems merely reactionary and leaves him
radically unsatisfied). From another perspective, Jack-the-Bear's complaint
in the Trueblood scene has nothing to do with revulsion or even racial em-
barrassment; in fact he seems blithely unaware that Norton himself is spiritually implicated in Trueblood's state of incest. He flings two exclamations
at Trueblood, and whatever possible virtue the first one suggests is wholly
wiped out by the second: "You no-good bastard! *You* get a hundred-dollar
bill!" He plays systematically into the hands of his exploiters. His own need
to survive and prosper does him in.

The picture in *Cien años de soledad* is much the same. The sense of wonder at the magnet or at the materialization of the banana company arises
from a deep vein. If "innocents" are being "imposed upon," it is with their
own exaggerated collusion. It is not insignificant that the gypsies, the transitional figures between Western development and regional integrity, should
have "first . . . brought the magnet" [primero Ilevaron el imán] to the isolated
town of Macondo. The magnet works ostensibly on metal, intrinsically on
the people. They are magnetized, and the magnet, the argument might run,
should no more be blamed for its effect on metal than the New World adventure for its effect on the New World.

Such an argument breaks down in both novels, though, and seemingly
of its own weight. Ellison presents us the obligatory scene in which Jack-
the-Bear runs across Norton again, in the subway. The latter, as the invisible
man pointedly observes, is lost. This fact leads to the following reflection:
"Perhaps to lose a sense of *where* you are implies the danger of losing a sense
of *who* you are. That must be it . . . —to lose your direction is to lose your
face. So here he comes to ask his direction from the lost, the invisible." When
it turns out that Mr. Norton is seeking "the way to Centre Street," the personal import of the scene becomes general and overwhelming. Norton, the
man of eminence and authority, builder and benefactor and leader, does not

know where the "centre" is. He does not know, by extension, anything about the circle or the world in which he so influentially operates. Illness, indeed moral illness, took him to the Golden Day (with its poignant implications of paradise), and that moral illness carried to its extreme enables him to declare at last: "I have lived too long in the world to be ashamed of anything."[14] From the Golden Day to the subway there is a blistering indictment of the aimless and shameless arrogance and veneer, as of a whited sepulchre, that is the New World adventure.[15]

The shameless sense of not being "ashamed of anything," and not responsible to and for anything, and not to be located or identified in or with any place, in short, the Norton syndrome, occurs in magnified, institutionalized form in the massacre episode of *Cien años*. The banana company, whose impenetrable fences suggest that it is not in or part of the community but a weirdly detached presence, is behind the massacre. The company never comes forward, never takes a position; in fact, the harsher the activities undertaken on its behalf become, the more the company recedes from attention, until it is as though the massacre never occurred, the victims never existed, the company itself never had been there. This disappearing act comes about by dint of propaganda (again, the "text" overwhelming the authenticity of the "action"), and by reason of the company's freedom—financial, social, cultural, moral—to dissolve and abscond at will. The sudden apparition of the company and its sudden vanishing resonate in areas quite distinct from the people's susceptibility to the company's so-called goods. Its lack of stability and of substantial identity, its randomness of movement go to its very character and being. The New World adventure in this form may be summarized as spastic, gorging, and wasting alike to express little more than gross restlessness and greed.

The indictment of the New World adventure is only incidentally related to issues like capitalist exploitation. The fundamental issue bears on the quality of the human presence, in the adventurers, and on the drastic decay of humanity, in their collaborator-victims. In the titles of the two novels, the ultimate effect of the New World adventure throughout its span manifests itself: solitude and invisibility. These are complementary states, as the solitary has no one to see him and the invisible, being unseen, is in effect solitary. Solitude arises from a desperate, almost pathological obsession with grand goals, like the triumph of alchemy or gluttony or the ambition to be pope. Invisibility arises from a desperate, almost pathological obsession with winning approval within other people's schemes. Together, solitude and invisibility exhaust the options for individual response available to native and slave in the New World scheme. Otherwise, the response must be collective, as in the antic militarism of Ellison's Ras the Destroyer, or in the robot militarism of the lawyers and soldiers who uphold the New World regime in Macondo.

In sum, we can see in the early stages of *Cien años* and *Invisible Man* some justification for Whitman's conclusion that the "variety and freedom" of nature are reflected in New World politics and its sense of progress. But the picture darkens, the flow congeals, and we see at last the justice of the comment Octavio Paz makes in *The Labyrinth of Solitude*: "The founding of Mexico [emblematically, not exclusively] on a general [abstract] notion of man, rather than on the actual situation of our people, sacrificed reality to words and delivered us up to the ravenous appetites of the strong." It is this sacrifice of reality to words that Ellison and García Márquez depict and deplore.

The novels come to distinguish between textual fidelity and textual credulity, between seeing that it is all there and saying that it is all worthwhile. The latter, in the light of the position the novels reach on conclusion, is not so. The available text of the created novels (text-*n*) is the record but also the undermining of the New World adventure. Having the force of actuality, and under the aegis of the law of familiarity, that adventure leads to the elegiac nostalgia of *Invisible Man* and *Cien años de soledad*. In the new light of justice (*Invisible Man*) and of love (*Cien años de soledad*), however, it draws the satirical fire the novels abound in. The principle of nostalgia is itself weakened when the dying Colonel Aureliano Buendía experiences a sense of recollection and nostalgia for something he cannot focus or identify. Nostalgia cannot preserve anything but a ghost of itself. The decay and death of nostalgia are generalized in the merciless wind that wipes out everything at novel's end. Nothing survives, or escapes censure. On the one hand, we see the ironic folly of Aureliano Babilonia hurrying to finish a book whose conclusion entails his own demise. On the other the native population that has conspired in or been the dupes of the New World adventure are pilloried along with their leaders; they too belong to the past.

Perhaps García Márquez's position on nostalgia appears most tellingly in "The Handsomest Drowned Man in the World." Here nostalgia is something of which divers die beyond a certain depth in the water, and yet the society instinctively gravitates toward the drowned man washed ashore in its midst, finding more beauty and power and promise in his figure than in any living man. They even christen him, giving him as it were an independent new life. But his is the life of nostalgia, life-in-death, death-as-life. What saves the society from dying in the depths of its own nostalgia is a connection between the past that the dead Esteban embodies and the future, vague and speculative as it is, that he conjures up in the communal mind: "Everything would be different from now on." The people have a sense of proportion and rhythm that will save them from their superstitious impulses of reverence toward the past, save them, in effect, from nostalgia. They throw Esteban back into the water (and rather unceremoniously at that, heaving his body off a cliff). He could "come back if he wished, and whenever he wished," but he could not stay and certainly would not be enshrined among them. The difference between giving the past or the dead its own time and place, in "The Handsomest Drowned Man," and devoting oneself wholly to recording, recreating, and decoding it in *Cien años* accounts for the tolerance, even indulgence, of nostalgia that we find in the short story, as against the vindictiveness of the novel.

Only the instinct for a renewed New World exists to countervail the forces of the last four centuries in *Cien años*. But it is an instinct without canonical form, without text. The question has to be posed whether the mere recognition of that instinct is ground enough for its development. Neither García Márquez nor Ellison goes so far as to project an answer.

Nor had Wordsworth gone so far, though it seems clear that the question framed itself in his mind. It has been customary, since Hartman's groundbreaking work, to treat Wordsworth as one who canonized the processes of his own mind, vis-à-vis the summons of nature.[16] But perhaps the real opposition occurs between the individual mind and the prevailing culture. For not only did *Don Quixote* "fail" Wordsworth, but so did Cambridge and London and the French Revolution. His attempt to find a new text, in Godwin's *Political Justice*, to cope with wide and deepening disillusionment also comes to naught. Wordsworth himself seems to put the mind against nature, but in view of the fact that nature alone seems to supply solace and lucidity in his life, we may with justice read this as a displacement, a masking synecdoche. Nature only stands for the culture in which it is encountered.[17] Wordsworth precedes Ellison and García Márquez in repudiating a world for which he could realize no alternative, as they join him in writing nostalgic and compelling preludes.

This is not to say that their preludes go no further than Wordsworth's. In fact, we know that Wordsworth, for reasons of his own, envisioned a *Recluse* that he ultimately failed to realize. Paradoxically, Ellison and García Márquez depict a recluse, for that is what the invisible man and Aureliano Babilonia become, but they seem unable to hold to a reclusive position. However erratically, the invisible man does come out and seek communication, even identification with others. And however unhappily, Aureliano Babilonia does the same; finding no one, he bemoans and curses the untrustworthiness of friends. But more than these passing moments, the final gesture, the determining voice of both novels points to the spirit of a prelude. The invisible man suggests that he speaks for us, thus achieving the identification denied him elsewhere. One reason for his saying "perhaps" may be hope, rather than timidity. If he does speak for us, then we too will have learned, without the long and circuitous waste of his journey, not to be taken in and to look for the good; and if that is true, more than a prelude we would have a genuine beginning.[18]

In the case of García Márquez, the same effect comes about. For the reader is also bodily brought into the action in the concluding sentence. Text-*n*, which in this respect clearly differs from Melquíades's parchments, reads, ". . . didn't use to have a second chance on earth."[19] That imperfect tense ("tenían") has many ramifications in context, but the most compelling must be that it raises the question, "What about now, how do things stand today?" And even for a race doomed as indicated the answer would amount to a beginning, in that the reader who is granted this information, this warning, could put the new chance, the new century to better use. Text-*n* for Ellison and García Márquez, then, would become the cause of a beginning in actuality, not a sacred document or virtual juggernaut down the ages. Text-*n* not only has the courage, on this reading, to deconstruct text-*e* and text-*w/c*, but also the creative tact and grace to make itself secure from deconstruction by self-transcendence. Indeed, text-*n* has the genius to transcend itself in the direction of enhanced—if still tentative—actuality.

Notes

1. *City of Words: American Fiction, 1950–1970* (New York: Harper & Row, 1971), 52, 54–55, 60ff.

2. See "Literacy and Hibernation: Ralph Ellison's *Invisible Man*," in *From Behind the Veil: A Study of Afro-American Narrative* (Urbana: University of Illinois Press, 1979).

3. Isabel Paraíso de Leal speaks of "el área lingüística de cada personaje, y el zigzag[u]eo narrativo del autor" and observes that we find "nada en dosis suficiente ni bastante sostenido como para impregnar todo lo demás" (*Explicación de "Cien Años de Soledad*," IV [Añejo I], in *Explicación de Textos Literarios*, ed. Francisco E. Porrata y Fausto Avendano, 209, 211).

4. The earlier characters, of course, come back to them mystically in their final days together.

5. "*One Hundred Years of Solitude* and *Pedro Páramo*: A Parallel," *Books Abroad* 47 (1973): 494.

6. "The Demythification of Buenos Aires in Selected Argentine Novels of the Seventies," *Chasqui* 10 (1980): 5.

7. *Black World* 20 (Dec. 1970): 51.

8. Three interacting but independent dimensions occur here: that of the book, that of the dream, and that of the reader-dreamer in everyday. Wordsworth gives a strong warrant for this division in "Personal Talk," where he speaks of "Dreams" and "books" as "each a world," obviously to be set against the material-social world we live in.

9. See the introduction and chap. 1 of Harold Bloom, *The Anxiety of Influence: A Theory of Poetry* (New York: Oxford University Press, 1973).

10. It is arresting that Edmund Burke, in *Reflections on the Revolution of France*, should have treated chivalry as the cornerstone and sole hope of Western

culture. Matthew Arnold's later discussions of the aristocratic Barbarians in *Culture and Anarchy* also deserves notice.

11. Perhaps the quotidian gravestone preserves a trace of this idea. Wordsworth's interest in epitaphs takes on peculiar interest here, as does Mircea Eliade's observation that the stone stands as a "hierophany," showing "something that is no longer stone" but the "*sacred*, the *ganz andere*" (*The Sacred and the Profane: The Nature of Religion* [New York: Harcourt Brace Jovanovich, 1959], 12). In *Paterson* William Carlos Williams asserts that "The stone lives, the flesh dies" (II.i).

12. A rich and provocative reading of the Arab dream, with emphases differing from my own, has recently been published by Ernest Bernhardt-Kabisch; see "The Stone and the Shell: Wordsworth, Cataclysm, and the Myth of Glaucus," *SIR* 23 (1984): 455–90. We may also note Theresa M. Kelley, "Spirit and Geometric Form: The Stone and the Shell in Wordsworth's Arab Dream," *Studies in English Literature: 1500–1900* 22 (Autumn 1982): 563–82, and J. Hillis Miller, "The Stone and the Shell: The Problem of Poetic Form in Wordsworth's Dream of the Arab," in *Mouvements Premiers: Études critiques offertes à Georges Poulet* (Paris: Librairie José Corti, 1972), 124–47.

13. Birute Ciplijaustaike calls *Cien años* an "account of its [own] reading and interpretation" (*Books Abroad* 47 [1973]: 480). Emir Rodriguez-Monegal speaks tellingly of the text as self-referential and self-enclosed in "García Márquez: The Long Road to the Nobel Prize," in *Contemporary Latin American Culture*, ed. C. Gail Guntermann (Tempe: Center for Latin American Studies, Arizona State University, 1984), 102, 104. In this context, great interest attaches to Robert Stepto's analysis of literacy in Afro-American literature (see chaps. 5 and 6 of *From Behind the Veil*).

14. Shades of *Chinatown*!

15. In this connection, see the chapter entitled "White City" in Alan Trachtenberg, *The Incorporation of America* (New York: Hill and Wang, 1982), 208–34.

16. Recent criticism offers striking perspectives on Wordsworth and history or politics: Kenneth Johnston, *Wordsworth and "The Recluse"* (New Haven and London: Yale University Press, 1984); Jerome McGann, *The Romantic Ideology: A Critical Investigation* (Chicago: University of Chicago Press, 1983), esp. 70–118, 134–60; Alan Liu, "Wordsworth: The History of Imagination," *ELH* 51 (1984): 535; James K. Chandler, *Wordsworth's Second Nature: A Study of the Poetry and Politics* (Chicago: University of Chicago Press, 1984). In their different ways, David Erdman and Paul Sheats stand as significant forerunners of this group, which, allowing for certain differences among them, tend to privilege contemporary events in arriving at critical readings. The issues here are complex enough, but it seems appropriate to note that in *The Ruined Cottage* Wordsworth raises meditation above the most urgent and arresting events and that he balked in bk. 5 of *The Prelude* at a tendency he saw of the authorities to defy the "froward chaos of futurity" and try to pin life's forms down in dogmatic schools.

17. Peter J. Manning demonstrates Wordsworth's drifting away from forthright social and political positions in revising *The Prelude* ("Reading Wordsworth's Revisions: *Othello* and the Drowned Man," *SIR* 22 (Spring 1983): 6–8, 14–17, passim.

18. José David Salazar presents a provocative treatment of "the illusory coherence of the textual surface" and the need for "an affirmative vision of cultural unity" in "The Ideological and the Utopian in Tomas Rivera's *y no se lo tragó*

la tierra and Ron Arias' *The Road to Tamazunchale,*" *Critica: A Journal of Critical Essays* 1 (1985): 100–14.

    19. My translations of passages from *Cien años de soledad* depart from the standard English version by Gregory Rabassa, in an effort to elicit some of the under-resonances of Márquez's language (e.g., the force of "tenían" in the novel's overall scheme).

BRIAN CONNIFF

The Dark Side of Magical Realism: Science, Oppression, and Apocalypse in One Hundred Years of Solitude

In criticism of the Latin American novel, "magical realism" has typically been described as an impulse to create a fictive world that can somehow compete with the "insatiable fount of creation" that is Latin America's actual history.[1] This concept of magical realism received perhaps its most influential endorsement in the Nobel Prize acceptance speech of Gabriel García Márquez. The famous Colombian novelist began this speech, suggestively enough, with an account of the "meticulous log" kept by Magellan's navigator, Antonia Pigafetta. In the course of this fateful exploration of the "Southern American continent," the imaginative Florentine recorded such oddities as "a monstrosity of an animal with the head and ears of a mule, the body of a camel, the hooves of a deer, and the neigh of a horse" (207). In the course of his Nobel speech, García Márquez recorded many less imaginative but equally improbable facts—"in the past eleven years twenty million Latin American children have died before their second birthday. Nearly one hundred and twenty thousand have disappeared as a consequence of repression. . . . A country created from all these Latin Americans in exile or enforced emigration would have a larger population than Norway" ("Solitude of Latin America" 208, 209)—on and on, as if he were trying to combat a plague of amnesia.

From *Modern Fiction Studies* 36, no. 2 (Summer 1990): 167–179. © 1990 by the Purdue Research Foundation.

In such a "disorderly reality," García Márquez explained, the "poets and beggars, musicians and prophets, soldiers and scoundrels" of Colombia had been forced to respond to one of the saddest and most productive challenges in modern literature: "the want of conventional resources to make our life credible" (208–209). Fortunately, conventional resources were not everything. So, according to conventional wisdom, "magical realism" was born, offering the type of hope that García Márquez tried to provide, in that famous speech, when he said that the writer can somehow "bring light to this very chamber with his words" (208). Perhaps magical realism might allow the writer to create in his work a "minor utopia," like the one inhabited by Amaranta Úrsula and the next to last Aureliano at the end of *One Hundred Years of Solitude*, a fictive order that might somehow, like the birth of a child, affirm life in the face of the most brutal oppression. It was a novelistic act analogous to pulling a rabbit, or a child with a tail of a pig, out of a hat. It was magic.

Needless to say, critics have been quick to make use of such a powerful precept. "Magical realism" has typically been seen as the redemption of fiction in the face of a reality that is still becoming progressively more disorderly. But some critics have noted that the term, as it has most often been used, has always lent itself to certain simplifications. Most important, it has sometimes served as "an ideological stratagem to collapse many different kinds of writing, and many different political perspectives, into one single, usually escapist, concept" (Martin 102). Still, the overall optimism needs further qualification. In fact, there is another side of "magical realism," just as there is another side of magic. Not only can the conjuror make rabbits and flowers and crazed revolutionaries appear instantly, but he can also make them disappear, just as instantly. Although critics have not been quick to notice, García Márquez also sensed this darker side of magical realism. Unlike his "master" William Faulkner thirty-two years before, he could not "refuse to admit the end of mankind." Apocalypse, he was forced to admit, had become "for the first time in the history of humanity . . . simply a scientific possibility" ("Solitude of Latin America" 211). By the end of *One Hundred Years of Solitude*, apocalypse had become, perhaps for the first time in the history of the novel, just one more calamity on "this planet of misfortune" (211). When apocalypse does occur, García Márquez suggested, it will be pervaded, like so many events toward the end of *One Hundred Years of Solitude*, by a strange air of eternal repetition. It will be only the logical conclusion of the progress already brought by "advanced" ideas. In the disorderly modern world, magical realism is not merely an expression of hope; it is also a "resource" that can depict such a "scientific possibility." That is, it can depict events strange enough, and oppressive enough, to make apocalypse appear not only credible but inevitable.

On the first page of *One Hundred Years of Solitude*, such a strange event occurs, an event that will recur, over and over, like the ceaseless repetition—of names and incest, solitude and nostalgia, madness and failed revolutions—that haunts the house of Buendía: the gypsies come to Macondo. For a long time, they will come every year, always "with an uproar of pipes and kettledrums," and always with new inventions, until the wars make such trips too dangerous, and the natives become too indifferent; but their first appearance is the most impressive, and the most ominous. They first appear in a distant past, "when the world was so recent that many things lacked names, and in order to indicate them it was necessary to point" (11). Into this "primitive world" the gypsies bring an omen of the future, an invention of great wonder and potential: the magnet.

Melquíades, the "heavy gypsy with the untamed beard," calls this invention "the eighth wonder of the learned alchemists of Macedonia" (11). He drags it around, from house to house so that everyone can see pots and pans fly through the air, nails and screws pull out of the woodwork, long-lost objects reappear. Like any great missionary of progress, Melquíades is concerned with enlightening the natives, so he also provides an explanation: "Things have a life of their own. . . . It's simply a matter of waking up their souls" (11).

But José Arcadio Buendía, the first citizen of Macondo, has an idea of his own. Prophet, patriarch, inventor, and murderer—José Arcadio is not a man to forsake progress. He is, in fact, "the most enterprising man ever to be seen in the village" (18). His "unbridled imagination" often takes him, along with anyone he can convince to follow, "beyond the genius of nature, and even beyond miracles and magic," just as he once led a handful of men and women on an "absurd journey" in search of the sea, the journey that resulted in the founding of their inland village (31–32). Confronted with the marvelous magnet, José Arcadio feels that it is necessary to discover a useful application. Whereas Melquíades is content to mystify the natives, José Arcadio must look, with a wonder of his own, toward the future. He comes up with an idea that is portentious, just as his technological imagination will be fatal. Through a process no one else seems to understand, he calculates that it must be possible to use this marvelous invention "to extract gold from the bowels of the earth" (12). A "brilliant idea," to a man like José Arcadio, should translate into a well-deserved profit.[2] Even though Melquíades is honest and tells him that this idea will not work, José Arcadio begins to search for "gold enough and more to pave the floors of the house." He trades in "his mule and a pair of goats for the two magnetized ingots" and explores "every inch of the region"; but he fails to find anything he considers valuable. All he finds is "a suit of fifteenth-century armor which had all of its pieces soldered together with rust and inside of which there was the hollow resonance of an enormous stone-filled gourd" (12). Searching for gold, José Arcadio finds the remains of Spanish imperialism.

The following March, when the gypsies next appear in Macondo, they bring a telescope and a magnifying glass, "the latest discovery of the Jews of Amsterdam." Once again, Melquíades provides an explanation—"Science has eliminated distance"—and, not surprisingly, he once again mystifies the natives (12). His theory of the elimination of distance, like his theory of magnetic souls, is a fusion of chicanery and "advanced" science—and it is just as prophetic as José Arcadio's accidental discovery of the suit of armor. Even though the natives, José Arcadio in particular, are unable to understand the principles of Melquíades' discoveries, they are all too willing to assume that it is because they are not "worldly" or "advanced" enough. Melquíades's perspective, unlike theirs, is "global"; he has circled the world many times; he seems to know "what there was on the other side of things" (15). Perhaps he even believes he is being honest when he tries to comfort them by promising that such a perspective will soon be available to everyone, through the wonders of science, with no disruption of domestic tranquility, without the inconvenience of travel: "In a short time, man will be able to see what is happening in any place of the world without leaving his own house" (12).

But Melquíades's "theoretical" approach to science, just like José Arcadio's "practical" approach, suffers from a fatal blindness. Both of them are willing to assume that science is essentially democratizing. They do not understand that José Arcadio's misdirected discovery of the rusted armor, and its "calcified skeleton," has already brought to Macondo a vision of "progress" that is both mystifying and applied—but not democratizing. Years later, after the prolonged senility and death of José Arcadio, after the innumerable deaths of Melquíades, Macondo will eventually see the outside world—which José Arcadio tried so hard to discover, which Melquíades leads them to believe he knows completely—and science will be responsible. But, by then, the chicanery of the gypsies will only be displaced by more sophisticated and more determined exploitation.

For the moment, however, José Arcadio is simply inspired by the magnifying glass, so he allows his fantasies to transport him, once again, closer to an "outside" reality that he badly misunderstands. After watching another of the gypsies' demonstrations, in which the magnifying glass is used to set a pile of hay on fire, he immediately decides that this invention has even greater potential than the magnet because it can prove useful as an "instrument of war." Ignoring the protests of Melquíades, and ignoring the legitimate fears of his wife, José Arcadio is compelled, once again, to invest in an invention. This time, he uses a more progressive currency, the two magnetized ingots and three "colonial coins." His enthusiasm prevents him from noticing that his currency is being debased. Many years later, gold, and even colonial coins, will be superseded by the banana company's scrip, which is "good only to buy Virginia ham in the company commissaries" (278); but José Arcadio will never be able to understand how the debasement of the currency helps support the domination of his people.[3] He is happy to dream of progress, to experiment, to burn himself, to almost set the house on fire, and to finally complete "a manual of startling instructional clarity and an irresistible power of conviction" (13)—thus linking, for the first time in the history of Macondo, and without noticing, scientific discovery and political rhetoric.

Then, in his zeal to improve his village, José Arcadio makes the greatest of his many misjudgments: he sends his manual to "the military authorities" (13). With it, he sends all the scientific evidence he considers appropriate, "numerous descriptions of his experiments and several pages of explanatory sketches" (13). He is determined to leave no doubt that he is ready to do his part for the perfection of military technology: if called upon, he will even "train them himself in the complicated art of solar war" (13). Nothing happens. At least, nothing happens in Macondo. But it is clearly not José Arcadio's fault that the government fails to respond. He has even anticipated Star Wars.

José Arcadio never quite recovers from his disappointment at having been denied the excitement of futuristic wars. Melquíades tries to console him with more "new" discoveries: an astrolabe, a compass, a sextant, and the alchemical equipment that Colonel Aureliano Buendía will later use to make the little gold fishes that will ultimately, and ironically, become the symbol of failed subversion.[4] José Arcadio does revive his spirits just long enough to prove that "The earth is round like an orange" (14). By this time, however, his dedication to science only convinces Úrsula, and most everyone else, that he has lost what little was left of his mind. Later, when confronted with the marvel of ice, he will imagine an entire city constructed entirely of the fantastic substance; he will create a memory machine in an attempt to combat Macondo's plague of somnambulistic insomnia; he will spend sleepless nights trying to apply the principle of the pendulum to oxcarts, to harrows, "to everything that was useful when put into motion"; he will even try to execute a daguerreotype of God—but he will continue to lose faith in the reality of his fantasies. So his family must fight a losing battle, struggling to keep him from "being dragged by his imagination into a delirium from which he would not recover" (80). Finally, they all have to be content with his strange senility, interrupted only by prophecies in Latin.

The tragedy of José Arcadio Buendía is that his infatuation with science allows the government to exploit a passion that was, initially, a "spirit of social initiative." His first creations were the traps and cages he used to fill all the houses in the village with birds. He made sure that the houses were placed "in such a way that from all of them one could reach the river and draw water with the same effort" (18); he saw that no house received more sun than another. He was, from the start, a type of "model citizen," useful to his people. It is the appearance of "advanced" science in Macondo that makes him, virtually overnight, useful to authority: "That spirit of social initiative disappeared in a short time, pulled away by the fever of magnets, the astronomical calculations, the dreams of transmutation, and the urge to discover the wonders of the world" (18). That is how his faith in progress, and the faith of his people, is betrayed.

But more important than José Arcadio's tragic disappointment, more important than his invested doubloons—which Melquíades returns in any case—even more important than his final senility, is the fact that he resolves his debate with the gypsy. Throughout the rest of the novel, scientific discoveries will continue to serve two purposes: science will mystify the citizens of Macondo and will lead to their exploitation. The novel's arresting first sentence suggests that these two purposes have always been inseparable: "Many years later, as he faced the firing squad, Colonel Aureliano Buendía was to remember that distant afternoon when his father took him to discover ice" (11). But, perhaps, if his father had avoided such discoveries, Aureliano Buendía might never have wound up before a firing squad of his own government.

The equally arresting ending of the novel is a full-scale denial of José Arcadio's ill-begotten dream. The novel's "apocalyptic closure" is a denial of progress, as conceived by either the scientist or the politician, and a momentary glimpse of the world that might have been, if the great patriarch had not been so carried away with his idea of the future—if he had tried, instead, to understand history. Only Amaranta Úrsula and Aureliano, the last adults in the line of the Buendías, see "the uncertainty of the future" with enough demystified clarity to forsake progress, "to turn their hearts toward the past"; only they are not exploited (375). Their child, Aureliano, is "the only one in a century who had been engendered with love"—but by then it is too late (378). They cannot enjoy their primal, "dominant obsessions" for long; they cannot remain "floating in an empty universe where the only everyday and eternal reality was love" (374).[5] They are confronted, instead, with an end that is as ridiculous as their family's beginning: "The first of the line is tied to a tree and the last is being eaten by the ants" (381). The world has not progressed one bit. In fact, the key to understanding the present, and all of history, is not in the science so valued by José Arcadio but in Melquíades's ancient manuscripts, written in Sanskrit. Macondo is finally devoured by the "prehistoric hunger" of the ants, then obliterated by "the wrath of the biblical hurricane" (383).

Because he is the man of technology, the man of science-as-progress, who brings together, more than anyone else, mystification and exploitation,

José Arcadio is never able to foresee this end, just as he is never able to turn his obsessive nature toward love, just as he is never able to admit the kind of association that occurs to Colonel Aureliano Buendía when he faces the firing squad. He never understands, as Úrsula does, that time is circular. He never really pays any attention to the suit of armor from the past, so he never learns that the rusted coat of armor anticipates the soldiers and machine guns that will support the banana company, that the imperialism of the past prefigures the imperialism of the future. In this sense, Úrsula is capable of learning; José Arcadio is not. Úrsula learns, at least, that her schemes for prosperity have set her up to be betrayed. Ultimately, José Arcadio cannot understand any of these things because his view of the world shares too much with the oppressors who will take over his village in the delirium of banana fever; in other words, whether he realizes it or not, his horizon is determined by the interests he serves. As John Incledon has written, José Arcadio's fascination with scientific inventions—as sources of wealth, power, control—"reveals a frantic desire to grasp and manage his world" (53).

The difference between José Arcadio and the other residents of Macondo—who think he is crazy, when they are not following him—is merely that he is a useful citizen of the active type, whereas they are useful citizens of the passive type. The only exceptions are Colonel Aureliano Buendía and his men, but their revolutions always take place outside of Macondo. José Arcadio is doomed because he has convinced himself that "Right across the river there are all kinds of magical instruments while we keep on living like donkeys" (17). His greatest fear is that he might die "without receiving the benefits of science" (21). The village is doomed by the same belief that magic—in particular, advanced technology—is valuable in itself, uplifting, and the privileged possession of the outside world. Once the people believe that science, like all uplifting things, must come from elsewhere, that the outside world is better because it is more "advanced," then imperialism becomes much easier to justify. The gypsies' "discoveries" are always excessively foreign. Later, the residents of Macondo easily convince themselves of the innate superiority of Italian music and French sexual techniques. The Crespi brothers' business in mechanical toys, aided by their foreign looks and foreign manners, develops into a "hothouse of fantasy" (108).

If the government had only understood this inclination when they received José Arcadio's manual on solar war, it could have saved itself a lot of time. But José Arcadio's plans did not convince it that Macondo was a regular hothouse of applied fantasy; in this sense, it did not fully appreciate its "natural resources" until it learned from Mr. Brown and the banana company.

For their part, the villagers never understand what all these foreign wonders do to them. Like José Arcadio when he bumps into the suit of armor, they let their infatuation with the promises of the future render them incapable of uncovering their past: "Dazzled by so many and such marvelous inventions, the people of Macondo did not know where their amazement began" (211). They merely enjoy, with more moderation than José Arcadio, the excitement of closing the "technical gap" that has separated them from the "outside world."[6] The bearers of science are always exoticized. At the same time, the villagers' "primitive" past is rendered so insignificant that it is not worth remembering. To them, the important things have always happened somewhere else—and their future will be determined by somebody else.

Many years later, when the government massacres thousands of civilians in order to crush a union strike, no one except José Arcadio Segundo, great-grandson of the first José Arcadio, will even be capable of remembering "the insatiable and methodical shears of the machine guns" (284). As for the rest, they will remember only what they have been taught to remember by the technocrats and by the government that supports them: "Nothing has happened in Macondo, nothing has ever happened, and nothing ever will happen. This is a happy town" (287). In this "modern" world, things always happen somewhere else. The banana company, with the help of the government, is raising the village's standard of living, so it must be benevolent. It cannot be responsible for a massacre. The irony that José Arcadio Segundo has the name of his great-grandfather is just one of the novel's, and history's countless circles, one more indication that, despite their "progress"—or, in fact, because of their "progress"—the oppressed have been unable to learn what is really important.

The first José Arcadio has a quality of many characters in García Márquez' fiction: he is so strange, so absurd, that it seems he must be real. José Arcadio Segundo is, in this sense, his precise opposite. He sees the events of the government massacre with a clarity that suggests he is unreal. So when government troops enter the room where he has given up hiding, they cannot see him, even though they are looking right at the place where he believes he is sitting. Opposition, to such a government, must be invisible. It makes no difference that they did not actually kill him, that he jumped off the train on which the corpses had been "piled up in the same way in which they transported bunches of bananas" (284). He is merely left alone, once again, to decipher Melquíades's ancient manuscripts.

In the end, however, José Arcadio Segundo shares something important with the first José Arcadio. "The events that would deal Macondo its fatal blow"—the strike, the public unrest, the massacre, and its aftermath—take shape at the precise moment that the train begins to control the events of the novel (272). Transportation, in Colombia, has inescapable links to the desire for "progress." Aureliano Triste's initial sketch of Macondo's railroad "was a direct descendent of the plans with which José Arcadio Buendía had illustrated his project for solar warfare." Aureliano Triste believed that the railroad was necessary "not only for the modernization of his business but to link the town with the rest of the world" (209). Only Úrsula, who had seen so much of the suffering that results from such schemes, understood that "time was going in a circle"; only she knew enough to fear modernization that came from "the rest of the world" (209).

The train also allows Fernanda to travel back to the dismal, distant city of her birth. She has never stopped thinking of the villagers of Macondo as barbarians; and she is so intent on her desire to sequester her daughter in a convent, away from the "savagery" of the Caribbean zone, that she does not even see "the shady, endless banana groves on both sides of the tracks," or "the oxcarts on the dusty roads loaded down with bunches of bananas," or "the skeleton of the Spanish galleon" (273). At this point it is clear that she has failed in her attempt to colonize Macondo with the manners and rituals of the inland cities; but her "internal colonialism" has been superseded, without her noticing it, by the brutal imperialism of the banana company. When Fernanda returns to Macondo, the train is protected by policemen with guns. Macondo's "fatal blow" is under way. José Arcadio Segundo has already organized the workers in a strike against the banana company, and he has already been "pointed out as the agent of an international conspiracy against public order" (276). Fernanda's two rides on the train are opposite in direction, but tell of a single effect: "civilization," modernization, and progress are finally assured, even in Macondo—if not with "proper" manners and gold chamberpots, then with guns.

The train is, if anything, even more symbolic of this "progress" in Colombia than it is in Macondo. Under the dictatorship of General Rafael Reyes (1904–1909), "British capital was, for the first time, invested in Colombian railways in substantial amounts" (Safford 232). Not surprisingly, this period saw the completion of the railway between Bogota and the Magdalena River; "Macondo" was irreversibly linked to the "outside world." But, of course, that was only the start: "As the transportation improvements of 1904 to 1940 began to knit together a national market, significant innovations occurred in other economic sectors," and it was the nationalization of Colombia's railways that made many such "innovations" possible (Safford 232–234). In the period of the strikes against the United Fruit Company, in particular, reorganization of the railroads was a central issue of American diplomacy in Colombia. The National City Bank and the First National Bank of Boston refused to extend short-term credits until a railroad bill was passed. By 1931, they demanded, in their negotiations with the Colombian government, an even greater control: "that the railroad system be taken out of the hands of the government and placed under the direction of professional management" (Randall 64). In his description of the banana strike, García Márquez makes the implications obvious: the same trains that send bananas and profits toward America transport the murdered bodies to the sea. There—both the government and the "professional management" hope—they will disappear, even from history.

The repeated follies of José Arcadio—like the name and hereditary stubbornness of his great-grandson, like Úrsula's pronouncements, like the end of the novel—are attempts on the part of García Márquez to assert that history is, in some sense, circular. The "primitive" past of Latin America, like that of Macondo, might have provided countless omens of Colombia's future, if anyone had paid attention—that is, if anyone had avoided the delirium of progress. From the first half of the nineteenth century, the combination of foreigners and trains was devastating, in Argentina, in Chile, in Guatemala, in Mexico, and in Uruguay. With their public services, especially the railroads, controlled by foreigners, or by governments serving foreigners—first from Paraguay, then principally from Britain, then principally from the United States—these countries faced extraordinary military expenditures, "a frenzied increase in imports," and growing debts, subject to inflationary manipulation. In Galeano's words, they mortgaged their futures in advance, moving away from economic freedom and political sovereignty" (216–219). Later, in Colombia, the tendency to see railroads as "forerunners of progress" would be just one more failure to remember. For García Márquez, such an assertion of history's circularity is not merely a matter of philosophical speculation; it is a calculated attempt to make the outrages of oppression, ancient and recent, visible again; it is an attempt to make Colombian history credible.

After the massacre, when the train from which he has escaped slips off into the night, "with its nocturnal and stealthy velocity," on its way to dump more than three thousand murdered bodies into the ocean, José Arcadio Segundo cannot see it in the darkness; the last things he sees are "the dark shapes of the soldiers with their emplaced machine guns" (285).[7] Perhaps José Arcadio Segundo came to understand such progress as his great-grandfather could not, and perhaps that is why the government's search squad could not see him. For men indoctrinated by such a government, opposition must not exist.

For such men, the past must disappear. That is why they seem so improbable, and so real. That is why a "resource" like "magical realism" is needed to depict them. And that is why the novel's famous "apocalyptic closure" is not only credible but also anticlimactic. Apocalypse is merely the darkest side of "magical realism," in which the "magic" and the "realism" are most completely fused, in which the most unimaginable event is the most inevitable. The "biblical hurricane" that "exiles" Macondo "from the memory of men" is "full of voices from the past, the murmurs of ancient geraniums, sighs of disenchantment that preceded the most tenacious nostalgia" (383). The ceaseless repetitions of the novel lead to this final conviction that apocalypse is only one more "scientific possibility," which the "primitive world" understands only after it is too late. Apocalypse is only the logical consequence of imperialist oppression, supported by science. The "events" that bring about the end of Macondo were actually determined much earlier, even before the trains came. The end began the first time the gypsies appeared with their foreign discoveries.

Notes

1. Gabriel García Márquez, in "The Solitude of Latin America: Nobel Address, 1982," describes Latin American history as such a fount (208). Gerald Martin provides a detailed and critical summary of this criticism in his essay.

2. I have borrowed this idea from Ariel Dorfman's *The Empire's Old Clothes*: "having a 'brilliant idea' is not only what allows a contestant to win in the game of life. It is also a sign that such a victory is well deserved" (35). In the United States, the belief in such radical insight is one component of our mystification of ideas, in particular our mystification of science. We want to believe that certain people have privileged access to the truth and that they have, therefore, a "natural" authority over those people who lack such insight. Dorfman explains how the government of the United States has tried to cultivate this ideology in Latin America—even through such apparently innocuous vehicles as Donald Duck, the Lone Ranger, and Babar the Elephant—as part of our effort at domination. In *How to Read Donald Duck*, referring to the United States's assistance in the overthrow of the Allende government, Dorfman and Armand Mattelart write: "There were, however, two items which were not blocked: planes, tanks, ships, and technical assistance for the Chilean armed forces; and magazines, TV serials, advertising, and public opinion polls for the Chilean mass media" (9).

3. In his study of nineteenth-century European colonialism, Ralph Schnerb writes of Latin America: "These republics' histories may be said to be that of the economic obligations they incur to the all-absorbing world of European finance," obligations that were quickly exacerbated by "inflation, which produces depreciation of the currency," Eduardo Galeano adds, "The use of debt as an instrument of blackmail is not, as we can see, a recent American invention" (217–218).

4. Perhaps it is no coincidence that Colonel Aureliano Buendía is both the revolutionary and the alchemist—that he is, like José Arcadio Segundo, the heir of both Úrsula's indominability and Melquíades's manuscripts. For the Latin American who would resist domination, a knowledge of transformation, even alchemy, might be much more practical than it would at first appear. Galeano suggests such a connection, at least metaphorically, in his *Open Veins of Latin America*, a book that would be immensely popular in Colombia a few years after its initial publication in 1971: "Our defeat was always implicit in the victory of others; our wealth has always generated our poverty by nourishing the prosperity of others—the empires and their native overseers. In the colonial and neocolonial alchemy, gold changes into scrap metal and food into poison" (12).

5. The final situation of Amaranta Úrsula and Aureliano will become increasingly important as criticism begins to address García Márquez's recent novel, *Love*

in the Time of Cholera. As Thomas Pynchon suggests, with some trepidation, in his review of that novel, critics will inevitably ask "how far" that novel, so dominated by love, has departed from the more "political" concerns of *One Hundred Years of Solitude* and *The Autumn of the Patriarch*: "we have come a meaningful distance from Macondo, the magical village in *One Hundred Years of Solitude*. . . . It would be presumptuous to speak of moving 'beyond' *One Hundred Years of Solitude*, but clearly García Márquez has moved somewhere else, not least into deeper awareness of the ways in which, as Florentino comes to learn, "nobody teaches life anything" (49).

6. I have borrowed the phrase "technical gap," as well as the basic idea of this passage, from Dorfman's reading of Babar the Elephant in *The Empire's Old Clothes*. Of course, there are systems—of ownership, of trade, of education—that keep the gap from actually closing, despite the useful illusion of progress. In this regard see Galeano, especially the section appropriately entitled "The Goddess Technology Doesn't Speak Spanish" (265–268). Dorfman's explanation of the capitalist's equation of childhood and underdevelopment is also worth noting, especially in reference to José Arcadio's later senility. Once he abandons his hope of reaching the "outside world's" level of civilization, José Arcadio destroys his scientific equipment and allows himself to lapse into his "second childhood," to be spoonfed by Úrsula.

7. Later, José Arcadio Segundo would tell little Aureliano his "personal interpretation of what the banana company had meant to Macondo" (322). But no one would want to believe Aureliano, either: "one would have thought that he was telling a hallucinated version, because it was radically opposed to the false one that historians had created and consecrated in the schoolbooks" (322). In *Gabriel García Márquez: Writer of Colombia*, Stephen Minta provides a brief, useful summary of the surviving accounts of the 1928 strike against the United Fruit Company in Ciénaga. Accounts differ, of course, in their estimates of the number murdered. Cortes Vargas, who signed the decree that "declared the strikers to be a bunch of hoodlums" and "authorized the army to shoot to kill," and whose name appears unchanged in *One Hundred Years of Solitude*, wrote his own account, in which he claims that only nine were killed. Officially sanctioned accounts typically mention "the menace of Bolshevism." But perhaps the most telling document is a telegram from the Head of the U.S. Legation in Colombia to the U.S. Secretary of State: "I have the honor to report that the Bogota representative of the United Fruit Company told me yesterday that the total number of strikers killed by the Colombian military exceed one thousand" (171).

WORKS CITED

Dorfman, Ariel. *The Empire's Old Clothes*. Trans. Clark Hansen. New York: Pantheon, 1983.

Dorfman, Ariel, and Armand Mattelart. *How to Read Donald Duck*. Trans. David Kunzle. New York: International General, 1975.

Galeano, Eduardo. *Open Veins of Latin America*. Trans. Cedric Belfrage. New York: Monthly Review, 1973.

García Márquez, Gabriel. *Autumn of the Patriarch*. Trans. Gregory Rabassa. New York: Harper, 1976.

———. *Love in the Time of Cholera*. Trans. Edith Grossman. New York: Knopf, 1988.

———. *One Hundred Years of Solitude*. Trans. Gregory Rabassa. New York: Avon, 1970.

———. "The Solitude of Latin America: Nobel Address 1982." McGuirk and Cardwell. 207–211.

Incladon, John. "Writing and Incest in *One Hundred Years of Solitude*." *Critical Perspectives on Gabriel García Márquez*. Ed. Bradley A. Shaw and Nora Vera-Godwin. Lincoln: Society of Spanish and Spanish-American Studies, 1986. 51–64.

Martin, Gerald. "On 'Magical' and Social Realism in García Márquez." McGuirk and Cardwell. 95–116.

McGuirk, Bernard, and Richard Cardwell, eds. *Gabriel García Márquez: New Readings*. Cambridge: Cambridge University Press, 1987.

Minta, Stephen. *Gabriel García Márquez: Writer of Colombia*. London: Cape, 1987.

Pynchon, Thomas. "The Heart's Eternal Vow." Review of *Love in the Time of Cholera*, by Gabriel García Márquez. *New York Times Book Review*. 10 April 1988: 1, 47–49.

Randall, Stephen J. *The Diplomacy of Modernization: Colombian–American Relations, 1920–1940*. Toronto: University of Toronto Press, 1976.

Safford, Frank. *The Ideal of the Practical: Colombia's Struggle to Form a Technical Elite*. Austin: University of Texas Press, 1976.

Schnerb, Robert. *Le XIXe siècle: l'apogée de l'expansion européenne, 1815–1914*. Paris: Gallimard, 1968.

GENE H. BELL-VILLADA

The History of Macondo

To approach *One Hundred Years of Solitude* is not just to read a novel but to stumble onto a vast cultural territory and glimpse a dizzying array of people and patterns, horizons and meanings. Its chronology actually spans from the beginnings of European settlement in America to the dislocations of our time—later sixteenth century to approximately mid-twentieth. Its characters and their actions represent an awesome range of personality types and happenings. Its world comprises the commonplace and everyday along with the extraordinary and the impossible. Its literary heritage includes ancient scripture, exploratory and family chronicle, Rabelaisian spoofery, and colonial romance. And its appeal is to all ideologies: leftists like its dealing with social struggles and its portrait of imperialism; conservatives are heartened by the corruption and/or failure of those struggles and with the sustaining role of the family; nihilists and quietists find their pessimism reconfirmed; and apolitical hedonists find solace in all the sex and swashbuckling. This is a book that in a very real sense has "something for everyone."[1]

Though the wealth of incident in *One Hundred Years* makes summarizing it all but impossible, here are the bare bones of the plot: The Buendías and followers journey south and found Macondo. Patriarch José Arcadio Buendía starts out enterprising but a mania for science drives him mad; wife Úrsula will provide the practical backbone for the clan. Gypsies

From *García Márquez: The Man and His Work*, pp. 93–118, 215–216. © 1990 by the University of North Carolina Press.

39

regularly visit Macondo, bringing new gadgets; Melquíades, their wisest, writes some strange manuscripts before his death, Macondo's first. The Buendías' two sons, José Arcadio and Aureliano, engender respectively the illegitimate Arcadio and Aureliano José with a free-spirited Pilar Ternera; José Arcadio, afeared, runs off with the gypsies. Dance teacher Pietro Crespi courts the adopted Rebeca, and Buendía daughter Amaranta reacts with a poisonous sibling rivalry. At some point a priest founds a church, and Conservative magistrate Apolinar Moscote settles quietly in town to impose central authority, but an uprising led by the founding Buendía at first curbs Moscote. Liberal agitation and Conservative fraud spark a war in which Aureliano will become a famous colonel and Arcadio, briefly, a local despot. With the wars come the deaths of both illegitimate Buendías, Liberal sellout, an unglorious peace, and an embittered Aureliano. Around this time son José Arcadio, home from his travels, marries sister Rebeca; Pietro Crespi now turns to Amaranta, whose rejection drives him to suicide. José Arcadio soon dies mysteriously, as will the mad founder under a chestnut tree. Before his being executed, Arcadio and his common-law wife Santa Sofía de la Piedad will have the Segundo twins (whose identities are switched) and also engender Remedios the Beauty (apparently retarded). End of part one.

Aureliano Segundo, dissolute, will drink, eat, squander, and fornicate full-time with his mistress Petra Cotes, but also enter into misalliance with the beautiful, rich, stuffy Fernanda del Carpio. Their union begets José Arcadio, sent to seminary in Rome to become pope; Renata Remedios, "Meme," fun-loving and girlish, whose affair with auto mechanic Mauricio Babilonia will engender bastard son Aureliano; and Amaranta Úrsula, sent for her schooling to Brussels. Meanwhile, Remedios the Beauty drives many men to love-madness and death until the bright afternoon when she rises bodily to heaven. At some point Colonel Buendía's seventeen bastard sons show up with their mothers; one of them will bring a train, which brings in a foreign banana company, which in turn brings exploitation, corruption, and the murder of the seventeen sons. (The colonel himself dies soon of natural causes.) A workers' strike ensues; José Arcadio Segundo becomes a labor leader, and will be the sole surviving witness of an army massacre of three thousand demonstrators (a slaughter denied by officialdom and everyone else); a five-year rainstorm brings ruin to Macondo. Thereafter Úrsula, the twins, and Fernanda all die severally; Santa Sofía, exhausted, packs off. The bastard Aureliano grows up a bookish recluse, poring over Melquíades's manuscripts; a languid, hedonistic José Arcadio returns from his nonexistent "studies," turns the old house into a den of high pleasure, and is killed by young delinquents. The arrival of Amaranta Úrsula with husband Gastón will result in a passionate aunt–nephew incest with Aureliano, the affair facilitated by Gastón's business travels. Her baby is born with the tail of a pig; she dies soon; Aureliano suddenly understands the manuscripts, which contain the entire history of Macondo up through the winds of its destruction and his own death, both to occur the moment he finishes deciphering. The End!

The almost bewilderingly high rate of incident in *One Hundred Years* is paralleled by its enormous cast of characters, many of which share names—four José Arcadios, three Aurelianos, an Arcadio, an Aureliano José, the seventeen bastard Aurelianos from the colonel's seventeen different women, and three females named Remedios. All this can be extremely confusing to first-time readers, who are at a loss as to which José Arcadio or Aureliano is it that does what with whom. These assorted name-groups nonetheless present a clearcut system of personality types that is to remain consistent throughout the narrative.

The pattern is established in chapter 1, where we read of José Arcadio with his square head, thick hair, bodily strength, and lack of imagination, and of Aureliano with his eyes open at birth, taciturn temperament, and occasional flashes of clairvoyance. From the start these juxtaposed descriptions set off the physical and sensualist type, José Arcadio, from the sober, rational, slightly cold yet inspired thinking type, Aureliano. The differences will endure; in the course of Buendía history the extroverted José Arcadios will exist in the immediate realm of the senses and for the satisfaction thereof, indeed will live for sex and become its prisoners; more, owing to a lack either of "imagination" or of any need to exercise their minds, they will steer clear of long-range projects requiring thought or planning. The introverted Aurelianos by contrast are born thinkers who drift naturally into their roles as leaders, craftsmen, entrepreneurs, or scholars, and for whom the erotic and affective will remain largely subordinate to their broader schemes. In chapter 10 Úrsula herself notes that "While the Aurelianos were withdrawn but with lucid minds, the José Arcadios were impulsive and enterprising, but were marked with a tragic sign" (*CAS*, 228; *OYS*, 174). And their ways of death are as telling as their paths of life: whereas the José Arcadios all die suffering as victims of murder or disease (their "tragic sign"), all three Aurelianos die with their eyes open and their mental powers fully intact.

There are exceptions to the pattern. José Arcadio Buendía, as originator of the line, will manifest both tendencies, though not necessarily in equilibrium; Arcadio and Aureliano José, as their variant names suggest, are freaks that stand outside the workings of the system; and while the twins do actually conform to the binary-opposition model, José Arcadio Segundo is the Aureliano of the pair and vice-versa, the result of their mischievous exchange of identifying shirts and bracelets as little boys.

For the women characters there is a similar if less elaborate formal architecture. The elegant cosmopolite Amaranta Úrsula inherits the boundless energy and initiative of her namesakes, of Úrsula in particular. In describing Amaranta Úrsula's return in chapter 19, the text compares her directly to the great mother-figure and even employs the same adjectives ("active," "small") that had been applied to Úrsula in chapter 1. There is also a less visible line with the women named Remedios, all three of whom remain immature and either die young or disappear from the scene before they are able fully to develop. Girlish Meme, incidentally, is the only character in the entire book who bears a nickname, the symbol of her arrested youth. In addition there is Rebeca, who shows infantile characteristics such as prolonged thumb-sucking, and the initial syllable in her own name suggests her belonging in part to the Remedios camp.

Outside of the Buendía household are Pilar Ternera and Petra Cotes, both of whose first names evoke the firmness of stone.[2] Less than reputable individuals, with questionable occupations (fortune-telling; raffles), their free sexuality is also disruptive to a Buendía propriety solemnly embodied in Úrsula (and parodically so in Fernanda). They are the reigning erotic figures in the narrative. Pilar deflowers both José Arcadio and Aureliano, and will serve as matchmaker to *all* other Buendías who seek union with the opposite sex. (As Pilar remarks, "I'm happy knowing that people are happy in bed" [*CAS*, 201; *OYS*, 148].) The exceptions to Pilar Ternera's sexual "school" are the Segundo twins, who in turn are initiated by Petra Cotes, a latter-day avatar of Pilar. The two females present a pattern concretely representing our erotic side, and it is not accidental that the last of the original Macondoites to die just before the final whirlwind is Pilar, who outlives her enemy Úrsula, and whose last act was to advise Aureliano to go and seduce his aunt. Her burial at the start of the chapter is capped with the terse reflection, "It was the end."[3]

When questioned publicly about all these names-in-repetition, García Márquez quipped, "Is there anybody here who wasn't named after his dad?"[4] In real life, of course, families, prominent ones in particular, do tend to repeat certain names ("John Paul Doe IV"), continuities obviously being implied. The author of a family chronicle is hence under some obligation to represent these repetitions, and more, to depict "family resemblances" (or their obverse side, "family differences") at work. Mann's *Buddenbrooks*, to pick an earlier classic of the genre, has a "Johann" among each of its four generations. The genius of García Márquez is his having exaggerated so typical a household practice to a point of absurd consistency and comic newness.

Given so many repetitions, the temptation is to see in the one hundred years of Macondo a century without change. It is essential, however, to take note of the differing circumstances that attend those seeming recurrences. While Colonel Aureliano Buendía has done battle against the national Conservatives, his grandnephew (and secret namesake) José Arcadio Segundo is to agitate against a multinational firm that represents a later, imperial phase in the story of Macondo and the world. Similarly, Amaranta Úrsula may carry on her great matriarchal ancestor's name and traditions, but she is at the same time a thoroughly modern young cosmopolite, Europeanized, emancipated, something of a swinger, as is her brother José Arcadio, both of them growing up as products of their family's latter-day preeminence.

Repetition versus change of course is what human history is about, and Macondo fans will tend toward the former or the latter according to their own respective ideological preferences. One key moment that dramatically illustrates García Márquez's subtle interweaving of the two is the opening sentence in chapter 10 (roughly the halfway mark in the book): "Years later on his deathbed Aureliano Segundo would remember the rainy afternoon in June when he went into the bedroom to meet his first son" (*CAS*, 228; *OYS*, 174). Its linguistic shape closely replicates that of the famous opening lines of the novel itself: "Many years later, as he faced the firing squad, Colonel Aureliano Buendía was to remember that distant afternoon when his father took him to discover ice" (*CAS*, 59, *OYS*, 11).

The later sentence distinctly echoes the syntax, verb tenses, and lexicon of the first: the adverbial clause of time ("Years later") and then of place, the subject "Aureliano," the predicate "remember" in a quasi-conditional form ("había de recordar" in both originals), and the closure with an infinitive clause (again, "conocer" in both) followed by direct object. The actual *content* of the chapter 10 sentence, by stark contrast, gives us not the heroic Colonel Aureliano Buendía defiantly facing a firing squad (which he will miraculously survive) but the dissolute Aureliano *Segundo* (literally "the Second") on his deathbed, perishing of a throat ailment; what he remembers, moreover, is not the original wonders of ice but the sight of his firstborn José Arcadio, "languid and weepy," who will himself grow up dissipated and irresponsible, possibly pederastic.

At this point certain caveats and distinctions are in order concerning the way time is represented in *One Hundred Years of Solitude*. First, and most obvious, the effect of García Márquez's decision not to number his chapters is to make readers think of the book as a single entity whose twenty unmarked subdivisions exist not as discrete segments but interlinked members within a unitary whole: one text. This larger design is further stressed by the book's immediately visible format of lengthy, fluid, event-filled paragraphs interspersed with minimal (if carefully chosen) dialogue. From sentence to paragraph, and from episode to chapter to the full text of García Márquez's seamless narrative, things never stop happening, and time ceases only after the final line. The long-term changes and passing time in Macondo can be more or less periodized into a quartet of "stages" that cluster into chapters as follows: utopian innocence/social harmony (1–5), military heroism/struggle for autonomy (6–9), economic prosperity/spiritual decline (10–15), and final decadence/physical destruction (16–20).

On the other hand, it should be borne in mind that *One Hundred Years of Solitude*, while basically chronological and "linear" enough in its broad outlines, also shows abundant zigzags in time, both flashbacks of matters past and long leaps toward events future—as seen in the structure of the very first two chapters (discussed above, chapter 5). Those mortal scenes of the firing squad and deathbed with which the two key sentences from chapters 1 and 10 start out are not actually to occur until—in each case—over a hundred pages hence. In a similar instance, the youthful amour between Meme Buendía and Mauricio Babilonia is already in full swing before we are informed, later on in the same chapter, about the origins of the affair. Time in the novel is as subject to large-scale narrative shifts as it was in Faulkner's now-classic works; García Márquez's temporal dislocations, by contrast, are unobtrusive, and call as little attention to themselves as do his own more celebrated violations of laws physical and spatial.

One Hundred Years of Solitude is unique even among Latin American novels for the degree to which it successfully integrates private and public concerns. The former comprise such things as family life, sexual desire, and romantic love; the latter include the series of migrations, rebellions, wars, ceremonies, strikes, and repressions. Women figure more prominently in the first than in the second.

For all its fantastical exaggerations, and its natural or political catastrophes (those stereotypical Latin experiences), the narrative center of *One Hundred Years* is its faithful and convincing account of the domestic routines and vicissitudes of the Buendía clan. We read of such expected matters as daily housekeeping, matrimonial tensions, the raising of offspring, children at play, and sibling differences, all scrupulously reported by a wise, omniscient narrator. When Úrsula refuses to move from Macondo and peremptorily reminds her husband to tend to his two sons, when Aureliano Segundo marries a woman whom no one else in the family fold likes, when the same Aureliano Segundo is thrown into a quandary over his teenaged daughter's incommunicativeness, or when the elderly kinfolk withdraw into their silent selves, we see some typically intimate household dramas, familiar and familial both. In addition, at different points García Márquez will take note of the current source of Buendía income, be it Úrsula's candies, José Arcadio's landgrabs, Petra's raffles, or the last José Arcadio's pawned heirlooms and hidden treasure. Even in a "magical" Macondo, the everyday meals come from somewhere.

Romantic love and sexual desire provide the means for close ties outside of the family, and of this there is an abundance. It is nothing short of astounding how wide a range of erotic experience (in the largest sense of the word) is to be found in *One Hundred Years*: for instance, conjugal love (José Arcadio Buendía/Úrsula), adolescent crushes (Aureliano/Remedios Moscote), casual affairs (Pilar Ternera/José Arcadio, later Aureliano), traditional, proper, gracious courtship (Pietro Crespi/Rebeca, later Amaranta), marriage by accident (Arcadio/Santa Sofía de la Piedad), ménage à trois (Aureliano Segundo/Fernanda del Carpio/Petra Cotes), misalliance (Aureliano/Remedios, Aureliano Segundo/Fernanda), torrid adolescent passion (Meme/Mauricio Babilonia), possible pederasty (José Arcadio the seminarian/the four boys), modern "emancipated" marriage (Amaranta Úrsula/Gastón), and impassioned true love leading to *Liebestod* (Aureliano Babilonia/Amaranta Úrsula).

There are of course the inevitable brothels, one of them Pilar's establishment, frequented by some men. And there are the assorted erotic (or antierotic) types: José Arcadio the impetuous stud; Rebeca the insatiable wife; Remedios the Beauty, a femme most fatale; Fernanda the haughty and beautiful prude; Petra the eternal mistress; and Amaranta the anguished virgin and the tease, destructive and sad, whose name, ironically, contains the Spanish verb *amar*, but who is herself incapable of love, wanting only those men whom she cannot have while summarily rejecting those whom she can.

One erotic complex persisting like a leitmotif throughout Buendía history is the instinctive impulse toward incest and the corresponding prohibition. The original couple are in fact first cousins (though cousin marriages do admittedly occupy "a special place in the rules of kinship").[5] Thereafter most of the males in the book will either actively seek sexual union with consanguineous females—mothers or aunts—or at the least desire them. Images of Úrsula flash into José Arcadio's mind when he first sleeps with Pilar Ternera; and José Arcadio the seminarian will have his great-grandaunt Amaranta on his mind even when his lifeless body floats in the pool. The earlier José Arcadio actually goes so far as to marry his (albeit adoptive) sister Rebeca.

Of course there is also the concern about babies being born with pig's tails, and it is only because of women's fears of this disquieting eventuality that ordinary incest prohibitions are obeyed by anyone at all. Though Amaranta does lead on Aureliano José for years with her teasing games, she will in time put an abrupt and brutal end to their charade. The single exception to the pattern is Amaranta Úrsula, whose ardent and loving incestuous amour with Aureliano takes place only when the general decay in Macondo has gone so far as to make all social rules irrelevant. By making the dialectic of incest attraction/repression so crucial a force in the Buendías' existence, their Colombian creator succeeds in touching upon the very foundations of human society, for, as anthropologist A. L. Kroeber noted, the incest taboo is "the only universal institution." Or in Lévi-Strauss's words, incest prohibitions are "on the threshold of culture, in culture, and in one sense . . . [are] culture itself."[6]

It is the women of Macondo, moreover, who restrain the larger-scale antisocial impulses of the men and who furnish them basic stability, continuity, and essential order. As Luis Harss long ago remarked:

> In García Márquez men are flighty creatures, governed by whim, fanciful dreamers given to impossible delusions, capable of moments of haughty grandeur, but basically weak and unstable. Women, on the other hand, are solid, sensible, unvarying and down to earth, paragons of order and stability. They seem to be more at home in the world, more deeply rooted in their nature, closer to the center of gravity, therefore better equipped to face up to circumstances. García Márquez puts it another way: "My women are masculine."[7]

Hence while José Arcadio Buendía is vainly pursuing his scientific and technological will-o'-the-wisps, it becomes Úrsula's lot to expand the family home and to bring in income by launching and supervising the animal-candies business; and for all her visionary husband's grand attempts at exploration, it is she who brings back with her from her travels the retinue of new and more "modern" settlers who possess the latest gadgetry and receive regular mail service. In the same way, Aureliano Segundo's monumental dissipation would be impossible without the divers enterprises of his mistress Petra; and once Santa Sofía de la Piedad, the last of the old reliable Buendía women, simply leaves, the house falls rapidly into disrepair. Amaranta Úrsula on her return from Belgium brings temporary renovations and renewed vigor, but the ensuing affair with her nephew leads the two down the path of total irresponsibility, and they all but yield the old mansion to the vegetation and the ants.

Amid Macondo's populous cast about the only personage who comes across as more than two-dimensional, who demonstrates more than a few comical traits and performs a multiplicity of legitimate, necessary roles, whose actions go beyond a kind of caricaturesque extremism and whose emotions show a textured depth and empathetic, complex qualities, indeed the only character in García Márquez's book who is treated without a smiling irony, happens to be the greatest of all the women in *One Hundred Years of Solitude*. In the eloquent words of Cuban novelist Reinaldo Arenas, Úrsula Iguarán de Buendía is "the bride filled with prejudices on her wedding night; she is the loving mother, concerned, at times intolerable, at times heroic; she is the inconsolable widow who weeps under the almond trees in the afternoons . . . ; she is the centenarian who conceals her blindness so as to avoid pity; she is the almost delirious and withered great-grandmother who knows that preparing a dessert in the kitchen is one of the indispensable rituals for maintaining the equilibrium of the home."[8]

Above all Úrsula is the classic figure of the mother, for Latin Americans especially but for others as well. A woman with no use for gratuitous amusements and who "at no moment in her life had been heard to sing" (*CAS*, 66; *OYS*, 18), she is redeemed from joyless drudgery by her moral strength and her sheer energy, activism, and "unbreakable nerves." An unarrogant matriarch who wields considerable authority, it is she who restrains the hotheaded martinet Arcadio, beats him to submission when he is about to shoot Don Apolinar Moscote, and annuls his stupid decrees; she who, when Colonel Buendía is in jail, pushes her way through the prison guards in order to visit her son and sneak him a pistol (but also, being a mother, reminds him to take good care of his sores); she who (in a brief scene of tragic, solemn grandeur) saves Gerineldo Márquez from arbitrary execution at the hands of her same power-intoxicated son the colonel; and she who, in her old age, keeps Melquíades's room in livable condition when a fugitive José Arcadio Segundo ends up hiding there for his remaining days. While many of the more forceful and positive figures in García Márquez's writings are female, amid them Úrsula Buendía stands out as an instance of the potential for simple human greatness. The public sphere in *One Hundred Years of Solitude* includes the social movements, the government actions, the technological changes (railroads, movies, telephones), and the ecological developments, and also those organized rituals such as wakes and group mourning, festive orgies and carnival, all of which affect Macondo life at every possible level and give the book its outer boundaries and broad shape. For this purpose García Márquez builds his narrative around the larger blocks of Colombian (and by extension Latin American) history: the early process of Spanish colonization and inland settlement, the bloody wars of the nineteenth century, the repeated instances of illusory prosperity based on a single product, and the hegemonic power of the U.S. economy in our time.

During each of these historical sections García Márquez evokes appropriate sorts of period detail. In the opening chapters we read about the spear of José Arcadio Buendía that, years ago, had been used for hunting jaguars, or the suit of armor and the landlocked galleon inexplicably discovered in the jungle wilderness, or the "three colonial coins" with which José Arcadio Buendía pays Melquíades for a magnifying glass. The raid by British imperialist Francis Drake on Riohacha really did happen, in 1596; here it functions as prime mover in the chain of events starting with the southward flight of Úrsula's great-great-grandmother. Her indulgent spouse is described as "an Aragonese merchant," in other words a Spanish colonist, who will succeed in settling quietly among some peaceful indigenes—the most benevolent of possible fates for either party (and not the only such instance in history). On the other hand, the fact that the Guajiro Indians, Visitación and Cataure, come of princely stock but now serve the Buendías is an example, however benign, of the submission of the native peoples to the Hispanics. (The plague of insomnia/amnesia, brought by Rebeca from the Guajiros, can be seen as symbolic of the Indians' loss both of bodily peace and spiritual history.) The subsequent roamings of the Buendías and the founder's quest for the sea represent typical early Spanish explorers' enterprises.

With the episodes concerning magistrate Don Apolinar Moscote and the ensuing civil wars, García Márquez telescopes two epochs: the bloody struggles for independence from the Spanish Crown (1810–25), and the endless strife between Liberals and Conservatives that characterized the entire nineteenth century in virtually all of the newly founded Latin American republics. Don Apolinar typifies the centralist tradition of old Spain; he is the only character in *One Hundred Years* with the honorific "Don"; and his very style is that of the straitlaced Spanish bureaucrat. His title, in the original "corregidor"—literally "co-ruler" or "co-reigner"—signifies "a magistrate who exercised royal jurisdiction in his community or district" of the Spanish Empire.[9] His sealed, certified rule is opposed by the organically based authority of the founder Buendía, who informs the stolid official that "in this town we do not give orders with pieces of paper" (*CAS*, 111; *OYS*, 61). (Owing to a false etymology, the word *corregidor* looks like "corrector" in Spanish, which prompts José Arcadio Buendía's untranslatable pun, "no necesitamos ningún corregidor porque aquí no hay nada que corregir" [*CAS*, 111].) We also find out in chapter 4 that the meddlesome priest Father Nicanor Reyna had actually been brought to Macondo by Don Apolinar, the two thus reenacting the notorious Spanish alliance between church and state.

At the same time there is on Don Apolinar's office wall "a shield of the republic," and he issues a decree to have all houses painted blue—the official color of the Conservative party of Colombia. His being the appointee of a remote and shadowy government reflects the fact that, until 1987, town mayors in Colombia were not elected locally but assigned by Bogotá.

The chaotic warfare of chapters 5–9 is, by admission of the author, based concretely on Colombia's nineteenth-century conflicts. The character of Colonel Buendía is closely modeled after General Rafael Uribe Uribe, a legendary figure of Liberal politics and of the Thousand Days' War under whose command the novelist's grandfather Márquez fought. Like Aureliano Buendía, Uribe Uribe was born on a rainy day, won no military victories throughout his long career, spearheaded revolts even when the official party line was antiwar, sparked rebellions on the Atlantic coast when hostilities had all but ceased, was repudiated as "irresponsible" by the Liberal directorate, traveled to Central America in search of support from Liberal governments there, served more than one jail sentence, was publicly paraded on the city streets during one of his arrests, enjoyed good personal relations with a Conservative general, and officially capitulated at the Treaty of Neerlandia (named for a banana plantation then owned by a Dutchman).[10]

The Liberal forces in Macondo fail miserably as a result of dwindling support from Liberal landowners, opportunistic proposals from the six lawyers in frock coats (who essentially call for scrapping and selling out the Liberal platform), and the sheer exhaustion brought about by war. Similarly, throughout the history of Latin America, liberalism has few real success stories to offer—for like reasons of opportunism as well as the lack of a broad enough economic base or of deeply rooted liberal traditions. The brief spells of arbitrary power enjoyed by young zealot Arcadio and by the *caudillo* Aureliano are suggestive of, say, the long illiberal tyranny of the Somoza clan, who nonetheless were of the Liberal party of Nicaragua. Subsequent to the publication of *One Hundred Years of Solitude* we have witnessed the spectacle of bloody military juntas in Argentina and Chile promoting *economic* liberalism while savagely suppressing the more attractive social and cultural aspects of the liberal ideal.

The economic and political takeover of Macondo by the banana firm, the strike by field workers, and the military repression and massacre are all closely based on actual events and specific details of the 1900–1928 period. From modest Colombian holdings the United Fruit Company of Boston would soon grow into a virtual state-within-a-state in a zone stretching from coastal Santa Marta down to Aracataca. As in Macondo, the firm had its separate American-style residential compounds, company stores for foodstuffs, and its own irrigation system and water policy. Hiring its field hands only through subcontractors (so as to avoid Colombian labor legislation), its consistent claim was that United Fruit had no employees on its payroll. Similarly, the six lawyers in *One Hundred Years* argue that "the banana company did not have, never had had, and never would have any workers in its service," and the court establishes "in solemn decrees that the workers did not exist" (*CAS*, 339; *OYS*, 280).[11]

Both in history and in García Márquez's novel the basic demands of the workers were/are for decent health facilities, hygienic dwelling places, one day off in seven, and payment in cash rather than paper scrip valid only in the company's stores. During the agitation for these demands, company executive Thomas Bradshaw was to absent himself in order not to negotiate with labor leaders; García Márquez's Jack Brown pursues this same tactic.[12] And when the thirty-two thousand workers walked out en masse on 7 October 1928, the Conservative government in Bogotá promptly responded with military occupation of the entire area and assignment of strikebreaking troops to cut and ship banana bunches. This sequence is closely retained by

García Márquez, as is the state of siege that was officially declared by the government on 5 December.

That evening a few hundred workers and their families were to gather for a demonstration in the central plaza at Ciénaga (a town located some thirty miles north of Aracataca), and an army detachment was then sent there by General Carlos Cortés Vargas—the name of the author of Decree no. 4 in *One Hundred Years of Solitude*. The state of siege announcement was read to the tense crowd, who were given five minutes to disperse, and another extra (as happens in Macondo). Gunfire broke out; from a nearby hotel someone heard cries of "¡AY MI MADRE!" (a common Spanish exclamation, roughly equivalent to "Oh my God!"); the phrase is reproduced in García Márquez and rendered as "Aaaagh, Mother" in Rabassa's translation. Witnesses would later report having seen the bodies thrown into trucks which then headed toward the sea—the basis for the novelist's two-hundred-car train piled high with workers' corpses. Following the slaughter the authorities arrested hundreds of labor leaders (a railroad foreman recalled having been on a train filled to the brim with detained workers); in *One Hundred Years*, save for a lucky José Arcadio Segundo, the leaders are wiped out.

Concerning casualties for the entire strike, General Cortés Vargas would cite a figure of 40 dead and 100 wounded. By contrast a prominent union leader, Alberto Castrillón, would calculate the dead at Ciénaga alone at 400; for the larger strike he estimated a total of 1,500 dead and 3,000 wounded—García Márquez thus took for his climactic scene the highest of all reported casualty figures.[13] The human damage was minimized by the Conservative press, the government, and the company's supporters; in Macondo it is simply exorcised out of existence. (On my own visit to Aracataca in 1982, I actually met a retired United Fruit timekeeper who passionately assured me that the massacre had never taken place—"it's all just a story," he said.)[14] The five-year rain in the book is initiated by the company in order to evade negotiations; in their respective Indochina wars, the French and later the Americans regularly seeded clouds in order to cause rainstorms for military ends (the former instance being the subject of a 1954 article by García Márquez—*OP*, 3:873–74).

While the decay of Macondo in chapters 16–20 owes more to Faulkner than to "history," the matter of Aureliano Babilonia is most notable for its autobiographical elements. García Márquez likes to recall how, when he was taking on the writing of the final chapters of his novel, he felt so sure of what he was doing that he decided to really enjoy himself and bring his own favorite people into Macondo. Hence the wise Catalonian who gives old books to Aureliano and leaves behind a roomful of manuscripts on his departure is the now-legendary Ramon Vinyes, the erudite Catalan bookseller who introduced young Gabo to the European moderns and left dozens of unpublished works in Catalan at his death. Aureliano Babilonia's four pals have the first names of Gabo's three drinking buddies in Barranquilla ("Gabriel" being the fourth), his best friends for life. At the pharmacy in Macondo there lives "Mercedes, Gabriel's stealthy girl friend"—a loving reference to the novelist's wife, in her youth a pharmacist. "Gabriel" travels to Paris and relives Gabo's hard times there. (In addition, Julio Cortázar's part-Parisian novel *Hopscotch* is alluded to in Gabriel's sad hotel room where one day the baby "Rocamadour was to die.") Amaranta Úrsula wants two children christened Rodrigo and Gonzalo—the names of Gabo's own sons. This most public of novels is thus also well supplied with private jokes. (The reference to German pilots with whom Gastón is competing in chapter 20 is an oblique allusion to the Avianca airline, first started by German entrepreneurs.)

The public and private spheres in García Márquez's book are by no means separate but rather mingle with and interpenetrate one another. Acts that are seemingly private have social consequences—particularly in the case of marriage, whereby families make a mutual "exchange" of members. Young Aureliano nurtures an adolescent love of Remedios Moscote, who it so happens is a daughter of the Buendías' ideological foe, and the ensuing marriage will in fact help Conservative officialdom solidify its hold on the town. In the same way, the love-at-first-sight that seizes Aureliano Segundo for Fernanda del Carpio is emotion directed at a prime specimen of those very reactionaries against whom Colonel Buendía had once fought, a carnival queen whose "royal guard" in Moorish robes is suspected of having gunned down forty townspeople.

Public developments, conversely, can influence private life in *One Hundred Years*. The banana firm is a case in point. The hapless stranger who, from ogling Remedios the Beauty in the shower, slips and cracks his skull, is one of the many out-of-towners who have converged upon Macondo in search of company largesse. In the same way, it is through Meme's adolescent friendship with some American corporate "brats" that she meets her lover-to-be Mauricio Babilonia, himself a mechanic's apprentice for the banana company. Nevertheless, García Márquez's narrator doesn't insist upon these links—in contrast with the flawed United Fruit trilogy of Guatemalan novelist Miguel Ángel Asturias, where everything from sex to baseball occurs in the shadow of Tropical Banana Inc. While the arrival of the nameless fruit company in Macondo sets the stage for a variety of escapades, erotic and otherwise, these in turn have artistic self-sufficiency and a narrative density and vitality all their own.

In addition to the more conflictual aspects of Macondo public life already discussed, there are the organized rituals—such as the different wakes and public mourning for Melquíades, Pietro Crespi, and Amaranta. And there is the mass merriment of the carnival at the end of chapter 10,

evocative of the renowned yearly carnival at Barranquilla, with the crown-
ing of its queen-elect and its conga lines of dancers in bright, colorful cos-
tumes—roles here instanced respectively by Remedios the Beauty (whose
family name will tragically politicize the event) and by a carefree Aureliano
Segundo fulfilling his lifelong dream of dressing up in tiger's garb.[15]

Behind García Márquez's scrupulousness in rendering the history and
folklore of his region is a larger fidelity to reality itself. He never lets even the
humblest of particulars escape him, be it the clothes a character is wearing
on his or her first appearance in the book or the contents of a meal someone
might be eating (often fried bananas, a typical Caribbean snack). Because he
is telling the story of a family, he does not neglect to mention how each successive brood of children is raised, and by whom. This utter care in the use
of detail is beautifully exemplified in an unusually frank recollection made
by the author in an early interview, held in the first heat of the book's best-
sellerdom. The author talked of his consulting books on alchemy, navigation,
poisons, disease, cookery, home medicines, and Colombia's civil wars, as well
as "the 24 volumes of the *Encyclopedia Britannica*," and also having to find out
"how you can tell the sex of a shrimp, how a man is executed by firing squad,
and how you determine quality in bananas. I had to drop a character because
I wasn't able to find anybody who could translate seven Papiamento phrases
for me; I had to look up a great deal about Sanskrit; I had to figure out the
weight of 7,214 doubloons so as to be certain that they could be carried by
four kids. . . ."[16] Needless to say, once he became the subject of thousands
more such interviews, García Márquez would be much less forthcoming
about the secrets of his trade.

The political objectivity of the novelist is also worth mention. Though
García Márquez may personally sympathize with his Liberals, he shuns any
depiction of them as virtuous and of their adversaries as merely villainous.
While his Conservatives are mostly dishonest and practice electoral fraud
(as indeed they have done in history), the Liberals in turn are initially egged
on by agitator-terrorist Alirio Noguera, a fraudulent doctor and professional
adventurer who is possessed by a mystique of violence and sees assassination
as his patriotic duty. Later, during the armed conflict, the Liberal side has
as its local leader a resentful, immature, and impulsive Arcadio, the lonely
bastard Buendía and "the cruelest ruler that Macondo had ever known," who
loves strutting about in his uniform and whose eleven months in power are
characterized by interminable decrees, gratuitous executions, and a general
ambience of fear. Don Apolinar Moscote is thus not completely off the mark
with his off-the-cuff, I-told-you-so sarcasm, "This is the Liberal Paradise."

On the other hand, in General Raquel Moncada, who serves as mayor
of Macondo at war's end, we have the genuinely good Conservative, an anti-
militarist military man who wears civilian garb, disarms the police, gives aid

to Liberals who have lost relatives in the war, and sets up a humane regime in the town. Tragically, in the name of "the Revolution," Moncada is executed by order of Colonel Buendía himself, who most disturbingly embodies the process of political corruption: an intelligent man, idealistic in his youth, later a *caudillo* celebrated by the masses, and eventually driven to harsh and arbitrary rule by "the intoxication of power," who burns down Moncada's widow's house when she dares to defy him, has rival General Teófilo Vargas murdered and then liquidates a young officer precisely for having suggested such an action, and indeed attains such absolute sway that his orders are obeyed even before they are issued! By avoiding any simplistic, Manichaean vision of ideological conflict, García Márquez gives narrative shape to a profound and tragic truth: namely, that retrograde forces can have decent and fair-minded individuals in their ranks, while worthy causes can fall into the hands of infantile zealots, self-seeking opportunists, or hardened cynics.

* * *

Of course *One Hundred Years of Solitude* is best known not for its scrupulous realism (a trait in some ways homely, "unglamorous") but for its imaginative flights of fantasy, its unreal sorts of actions such as a levitating priest, a young woman who rises to heaven, and an apparently conscious trickle of blood. It is not that material of this kind is new in literature—like events are commonly depicted in folk myth, classical epic, medieval romance, fairy tale, gothic novel, and science fiction. What is special about García Márquez's book is its perfect integration of these unusual incidents into the everyday life represented in a text largely realistic. Among critics as well as readers there is well-nigh universal agreement that the fantastical element in *One Hundred Years* is neither obtrusive nor gratuitous but rather succeeds in enriching, supporting, and enhancing the narrative and its array of themes.

The fantasy matter in García Márquez's novel forms a broad and diverse spectrum ranging from the literally extraordinary though nonetheless possible, to the farthest extremes of the physically fabulous and unlikely. As an example of the former, the remotely possible, when Colonel Aureliano Buendía shoots himself in the chest, the bullet comes out through his back without having injured a single vital organ. This has been known to occur; when a despondent young Joseph Conrad attempted suicide in Marseilles, it is precisely (and fortunately for literature) what happened. In another instance, Úrsula secretly figures out the exact trajectory of the sun and the configuration of shadows it will cast within the house, day by day, in the course of the year. In fact many an earlier, "primitive" civilization, without technology, has achieved that level of knowledge of astronomy and given it concrete application in its architecture. Similarly, the account of the thousands of dead birds that fall to the ground in the wake of Úrsula's own death is an incident that has been specifically recorded in South America: in 1925 the north–south El Niño current in the eastern Pacific "caused the death of millions of birds, which were hurled upon the shores of Ecuador and Colombia."[17]

The next level of unreality is the systematic use of hyperbole, exaggerated entities represented with a precision that gives them a distinct, palpable, and cogent profile. García Márquez himself has remarked on more than one occasion that if you say you have seen a pink elephant, you will not be believed, but say that you saw seventeen pink elephants flying about that afternoon, and your story gains in verisimilitude. The exaggeration in *One Hundred Years of Solitude*, accordingly, is almost always numerically specific: Colonel Buendía's thirty-two defeated uprisings; Fernanda's minutely crisscrossed calendar of sex (with its exactly forty-two available days); the ten, fourteen, and then twenty men required to overpower the founder in his climactic fit of madness; the rainstorm that lasts four years, eleven months, and two days; and the overnight erasure from public memory of the massacre of banana workers (a reverse exaggeration of the lengthy process whereby all societies cover up their darker pasts).

Flying carpets and human levitation, in contrast, are events truly magical, and their author's conjuring craft deserves a closely detailed look. As has often been noted, what makes these unrealities convincing and credible is the entire narrative and physical scaffold that surrounds them. In the classic instance, Father Nicanor Reyna gulps down a cup of hot chocolate each time he is about to rise from the ground. The impression created thereby is that the humble beverage has something to do with the priest's powers (though of course it could be merely ritualistic). The fact that Father Reyna performs this feat with a view to raising money for a church—suggestive of a street-juggling act or perhaps of those eclipses used by Western explorers to impress the natives—serves to demystify its significance somewhat. Father Reyna's divine miracle is moreover put into question by the soberly scientific explanation proffered by a mad but still knowledgeable José Arcadio Buendía. (Their exchange in Latin is as follows. The founder: "This is very simple. This man here has entered the fourth state of matter." The priest: "No, this fact proves beyond doubt the existence of God.")

In like fashion the dead bodies of the love-victims of Remedios the Beauty emanate a sweet, secret perfume, the suggestion being that her mortal effects on the men have obscure biochemical origins. (Norman Mailer in his book on Marilyn Monroe observes that one of the blonde actress's attractions was her distinct fragrance, and dress-shop clerks would remark, "She has a *smell*!") García Márquez's beautiful young innocent is also his literal version of the old femme fatale stereotype, who in this case brings about the *immediate* death of her loving admirers, sans the usual intervening rituals of courtship. Her rise to heaven is in turn a parody of the Catholic folk-legend (and official church dogma since 1950) of the Assumption of the Virgin Mary, the colorful image of which adorns millions of Hispanic homes. (Assumption Day—15 August—is a national holiday in many a Hispanic country, and the capital of Paraguay is Asunción.) Remedios the Beauty waves good-bye as her body rises, her other hand clutching Fernanda's sheets (which the women of the family had been in the process of folding), all of it lending solidity and humor to the event, while Fernanda's petty rage over the loss of her precious old linen distracts from the unreality but also makes it funny. The latter sort of flimflam can be seen in the episode of the flying carpet in chapter 3, presented as merely incidental to the sexual encounter transpiring, back on the ground, between José Arcadio and the gypsy girl; and José Arcadio Buendía's telling the ghost of Prudencio Aguilar to "go to hell" is to treat the phantom more as a common nuisance than as a supernatural terror.

The wilder incidents in *One Hundred Years of Solitude* make perfect sense for their respective characters and situations. The subject matter is often death, an event so typically charged with ultimate emotions and concerns that it calls out for meaningful legend (whether religious or literary) from the imagination. The trickle of blood that travels across town from José Arcadio to his mother Úrsula has obvious Oedipal and umbilical implications (the Spanish word in the original is "thread"); its well-grounded trajectory is described in geometric, almost pedantic detail—and is then rerun in reverse for Úrsula! The rain of yellow flowers at the founder's death represents all of Nature in mourning for a great man ("the king," as the Indian Cataure calls him), a theme common enough in world myths, while the perils of pretension are dissipated by the final mention of the rakes and shovels needed to clear the thick carpet of flowers from the street. Fernanda del Carpio's beautiful nondecomposing corpse perfectly befits a woman for whom appearances and propriety are what have most mattered. The utter finality and shock of human death provide the basis for these eschatological fables and little apocalypses from García Márquez's pen.

In another vein Mauricio Babilonia's swarm of yellow butterflies can be seen as representing a soft, "poetic" side to his sensuality, making the apprentice auto mechanic more than just an aggressive stud, and thus more plausibly attractive to a girlish Meme Buendía. The invisibility of José Arcadio Segundo before the government troops, and the physical rise of the parchments beyond the reach of rampant teenagers, both take place in Melquíades's room, a consecrated space where the gypsy's ghost puts in an occasional appearance, where the secrets of Macondo are to be found, and where everything is therefore possible. The expected wonder of all such happenings is nonetheless displaced as the townspeople routinely accept these extravagant unrealities while reserving their incredulity and awe for technological artifacts like moving pictures or false teeth. The magnets on the very first page of the text are presented by Melquíades himself as an "eighth wonder" and the Macondoites are correspondingly amazed, something they will never be in the face of truly fantastical events.

In conversation García Márquez likes to bring up the humble and everyday origins of these episodes, such as the electrician who after every repair job would inadvertently leave behind him (as grandmother Márquez always noted) a white butterfly fluttering about the house. For the story of the rise of Remedios the Beauty the novelist took his remembered cue from a real-life account: apparently there was a young lady in Aracataca who ran off with a traveling salesman; her parents, in order to preempt gossip and deny the disgrace, claimed last having seen her ascending toward heaven, and even commented that "If the Virgin Mary could do it, so can our daughter."[18] The masterful stroke of including Fernanda's linen came to the author reportedly by chance; finding himself stumped, unable to make Remedios the Beauty's comical assumption sufficiently credible, he noticed a maid next door hanging up some wash—whence there arrived the inspiration for the sheets, and the narrative problem was solved.[19] What in the end holds together the many strands in *One Hundred Years of Solitude* is the narrative's consistent unity of voice, a voice unflaggingly sustained throughout the novel. Whether the subject be love or phantoms, orgies or uprisings, the narrator conveys it all with the same serene attitude of unperturbability. García Márquez was retrospectively to credit his story-telling grandmother with having furnished him precisely the style and "sound" he needed, and indeed the descriptive and narrative prose in the book, while neither colloquial nor cutely "folksy," is nonetheless oral in its fluid rhythms, its relatively straightforward syntax and simple lexicon, and its dignified and traditionalist (though unacademic) flavor.

It is a special, distinctively wise voice—omniscient about the townspeople yet still *of* rather than *above* the townspeople. In a fundamental example, the narrator will see both the encroaching Conservatives and the aggressive Americans the way the ordinary villagers see them—as oddly exotic but also as remotely powerful. The only *inside* glimpse we are allowed of the Moscotes or of the Yankees will come via the tender adolescent eyes first of Aureliano (through his love of Remedios) and then of Meme (through her friendship with the manager Mr. Brown's daughter, the stereotypical *gringa* Patricia). "Americans" and "Yankees," it should be remarked, are words notably absent from these chapters, and the strange language the foreigners speak remains largely nameless. Again, company abuses are narrated with a tone of voice indistinguishable from that with which we are told of, say, Aureliano Segundo's dissipation or Meme's frivolity. Despite the importance of the gringos' role in their few chapters, *One Hundred Years* is a book not "about" Yankee imperialism (as is in fact the case with Miguel Ángel Asturias's banana trilogy or César Vallejo's *El tungsteno*)—but about Macondo. The seasoned narrator of García Márquez's text knows that the banana-company exploitation (another absent word), strike, and massacre are key moments and factors, though still only moments, and not the sole factors, in Macondo history.

Just as *One Hundred Wears of Solitude* gathers into its prose a vast range of human experiences, it similarly brings between its covers an impressive array of literary genres. Earlier we examined the determining presence of high biblical and tragical elements in this and other García Márquez works. Equally worth a passing glance is his fruitful use of stock conventions from the other end of the generic scale—the popular melodrama. The assassination of Aureliano José in a crowded theater, the violent suicide-for-love of Pietro Crespi, and the obsessive house-by-house search of Aureliano Segundo for the beautiful "princess" he saw once at a carnival—these are shocking or exciting episodes that, from the pen of a less talented and mature artist, could very well have lapsed into cliché sensationalism or pure corn.

Being a family chronicle, *One Hundred Years of Solitude* puts into play a set of patterns known to us from such classics of the genre as Galsworthy's *Forsyte Saga*, Mann's *Buddenbrooks*, and Giuseppe di Lampedusa's *The Leopard*. The Englishman's multivolume work has forty characters, many of whom show similarities of temperament and bear the same name (e.g., Young and Old Jolyon). Particularly worth mention are the founding act of building a country house (seen as a first step toward civilizing the wilderness), the episodes of near-incest, the emergence of artists among the fold just when the Forsyte family is in decline, and the sense of inevitable destruction brooding over the novel's final pages.

Mann in turn dramatizes the differences between sensual and sober character types, the cultural split between north and south Germany, the material progress that accompanies family decline, the consequences of the death of matriarch Elisabeth, the growing physical decay of the ancestral home, and the final loner Hanno, whose musical talents also mark the terminal stages of the old clan. The Sicilian patriarch in Lampedusa's novel actually has an astronomical observatory of his own, and the book tells of such expected matters as sexual rivalries among siblings, shifts brought by marriages with members of contending political forces, and dwindling family fortunes. Of the three works (randomly selected from a host of others) García Márquez may well have read only the German's, but the conventions of the family-chronicle form inevitably emerge out of the subject matter itself.

The larger tale told by *One Hundred Years of Solitude* is quite consciously built around the usages of two interrelated literary traditions: the colonial

romance and the chronicle of exploration. The history of Macondo, let us
recall, contains such staples of the adventure novel as attacks by pirates, treks
through the wilderness, circumnavigations of the globe, buried treasure (discovered by children), and death by killer ants—all typical of the swashbuckling genre. Perhaps the most renowned of colonial romances is Edgar Rice
Burroughs's original *Tarzan of the Apes*, today the basis of an occasional action film but at one time the reading fare of millions of young boys. Among
its current fans is García Márquez, who often cites the book admiringly.

Burroughs's fast-paced narrative tells of the establishment of a European outpost settlement somewhere in "barbarous" Africa and also shows
the development of technology (there are motorcars in the last scene) from
that remote vantage point. Meanwhile the eponymous hero, orphaned as a
baby by shipwrecked whites, will grow up among apes and lead his primate
companions to another area inland; eventually he will discover the importance of writing and become immersed in his studies, and will feel the call
of sexuality without quite understanding what it is. Among the details a
younger García Márquez might especially have noted are some conversations
about an ancient Spanish galleon, an episode involving buried treasure on
the beach, and the arrival of a cultured French adventurer named D'Arnot (a
kind of harbinger of the erudite and enterprising Gastón, with his palm-oil
investments in the Belgian Congo).

Another of García Márquez's favorite references is *Head Hunters of the
Amazon: Seven Years of Exploration and Adventure* (1923), by F. W. Up de
Graff, a New Yorker who ended up in the Southern American bush almost
on a personal whim. His vivid memoir skillfully evokes the sordid ambience
of the whites' settlements, with their new rubber wealth, and the boom-town
atmosphere in Iquitos, Peru, with its proliferation of get-rich-quick schemes.
While understandably shocked at the head-shrinking customs of local Indian tribes, Up de Graff feels some admiration for their ancestral ways, particularly for their remarkably effective folk-medicine techniques. But he is
most awed by the natural wonders of the Amazon forest: the "fire-flies as
big as June-bugs"; a hill where "the slightest noise" makes "rain . . . come
down in sheets" (we are reminded of the yellow plain crossed by Aureliano
Segundo, "where the echo repeated one's thoughts"); the spectacle of a fifty-
foot anaconda "covered with flies, butterflies, and insects"; and the variety
of ants that at times move through the jungle in army columns, destroying
everything in their path.[20]

The Renaissance chronicles of exploration came into existence from
the moment that *homo Europeus* set out on his path of world conquest and
control. The first such narrations are Christopher Columbus's diaries of his
four voyages, wherein he describes a wondrous Caribbean world (thought
of by him as Asian) in terms of the earthly paradise itself, and recalls such

things as a lizard as big as a calf, an ape with the face of a man, and notably, certain reports of Western Cuban peoples who are born with tails![21] His story of an eighty-eight-day sea tempest, however, does seem plausible for the tropics.

On the other hand, Amerigo Vespucci's letters and questionable accounts of his travels stand out as the reason for the very existence of our geographic name "America," inasmuch as it was he who first posited the idea that those lands were not Asia, but "a new world" with "numerous tribes and peoples [and] kinds of wild animals unknown in our country." Among the marvels Vespucci notes are the nonexistence of private property, the free sexual life, and the absence either of jealousy or matrimony among the New World indigenes, who moreover "live for 150 years."[22] Far less known than Vespucci's works is a fascinating book that is among García Márquez's pet references, the *First Journey around the Globe* by Antonio Pigafetta, who traveled with the Magellan expedition and who tells of a wide range of botanical, zoological, and human wonders, such as Brazilians who have 140-year life spans.[23]

Starting as it does at "the creation," at the very dawn of the European presence in these Americas, *One Hundred Years of Solitude* takes this legacy of colonial-exploratory writing and retells it with a difference, stands it on its head. First, the tale is narrated not by distant, literate Europeans but by an engaged voice from within the Macondo "tribe" itself, while the peoples who arrive periodically with their gadgetry to do barter with the Macondoites are not the usual blond navigators but some nonwhite gypsies of Asian origin. And whereas Úrsula's and Pilar Ternera's 130- and 140-year life spans are reported simply as local fact, the successive European technologies are shown to be as wondrous to the provincial townsfolk as they might have appeared to the original native Americans. García Márquez thus skillfully reimagines his New World history, casting the descendants of Spanish settlers in the role of indigenes being encroached upon by royal bureaucrats, proselytizing priests, and Yankee capitalists, all of whom wish to absorb a peaceable Macondo into their vast global schemes.

Hence, though centered on a limited geography—a small town in the Colombian north country—*One Hundred Years of Solitude* tells a story unmistakably continental in its implications. More, going beyond the Hispanic orbit, the book could be read as an instance of yet another legendary tradition, "the great American novel" in the widest possible sense. The spaces evoked have that fabled New World vastness, and one might indeed assimilate Macondo's life course to certain corresponding phases in Anglo-American history—the initial utopian-egalitarian settlements in Massachusetts; the wars, first against a remote Crown and then against Southern conservatives in 1861–65; the rise of giant corporations and their technology both miraculous and destructive; and the hedonism, aimlessness, and confusion of our time.

And we can go still further and—despite García Márquez's own disavowal of such a reading—see his book as a metaphor for the rise and decline of all human civilizations, which from modest and rugged beginnings do grow, ripen, and become wealthy and wise, but also lose sight of their original roots and better traditions, eventually reaching a state of decadence and anomie. The world readership of *One Hundred Years of Solitude* strongly suggests the potential for such global, trans-Macondian applications to the Colombian writer's locally based narrative.

There is yet another aspect of García Márquez's novel that must not go unexamined: the fact that it is one of the funniest books ever written. More than once the author himself has said that *One Hundred Years* is a work "completely lacking in seriousness," and when asked what the novel is "about" he sometimes likes to reply that it is a story of a family that does not want their kids being born with pig's tails. Behind these flippant remarks stands the Colombian's desire to take Macondo away from the academic theorists, to remove all presumptuous obstacles between the book's basic funniness and the common readers whose needs are not purely mental. Chuckles and guffaws may well be more legitimate responses to García Márquez's great novel than are the best and brightest of critical schemes.

The varieties of humor in *One Hundred Years* are simply astonishing. There is the comic incongruity of José Arcadio Buendía's researches, the sadly spurned truth of his declaration that "The earth is round like an orange," and the sheer madness of his desire to daguerreotype God. There is some jesting with names—for example, "Apolinar Moscote," classical Greek followed by a surname suggesting "horsefly," or more subtly, the parodic echo in "Fernanda del Carpio" of Bernardo del Carpio, the second greatest medieval Spanish hero after the Cid. There is comic-strip farce in the seismic return of José Arcadio, his one-word greeting, his enormous and thoroughly tattooed physique, his Indian wrestles with five men at the bar, and his whores who pay *him* for bodily pleasure. (In typical cartoon fashion, the episode is consigned to oblivion once it is over.) On the other hand, there are deeper historical and character implications in the endless fun and fornication of Aureliano Segundo, one of literature's great comical sybarites (who is nonetheless bested by the elephantine yet delicate Camila Sagastume, with her "spiritual" theory of eating).

There is also a marvelous political satire of Yankee technology and its more grotesque gigantisms in the elaborate hardware applied by Mr. Herbert to a harmless banana. There is the occasional spoof of florid Spanish rhetoric in the letter from Rebeca's first parents and in Fernanda's four-page harangue, the latter a verbal onrush worthy of Molly Bloom (had the Irishwoman been a snob and a shrew). The loftiness of the pretensions of Fernanda's ancient family—with their golden emblazoned chamberpots—becomes that much funnier when it encounters Amaranta's sharp tongue and pig-Latin reminders of real shit in a postmedieval world. And of course there are the countless ribald scenes involving urination, evacuation, and sex, each one unique and with no trace of locker-room sexism or vulgarity.

And finally what brings together these multiple strands is the formal mastery of it all, the total organization to which García Márquez subjects so awesome a stock of materials. This formal solidity is to be found not only in the novel's macrostructure but, more importantly, in the simplest of details. Though García Márquez likes to hint self-deprecatingly at some forty-two inconsistencies in the book, *One Hundred Years* is a narrative in which most every little fact means something and possesses some future role and function. The treasure buried by Úrsula will fortuitously sustain José Arcadio the seminarian in his debauches; the seventy-two chamberpots purchased for Meme's week-long party will serve José Arcadio Segundo's necessities during his long confinement in Melquíades's room; and the English encyclopedia casually bought from a traveling salesman by Aureliano Segundo is the textual link, the "Rosetta Stone" leading to Aureliano's ultimate deciphering of Melquíades's manuscripts. Meme will die silent in Krakow, a medieval city that, however remote, is still within the Catholic orbit (key concerns of her mother); and Melquíades's having written his Buendía history in classical Sanskrit befits a man whose language and brethren originate somewhere in medieval India.

The concluding chapter to *One Hundred Years* gives us, successively, passionate love, desolate bereavement, and absolute wisdom, followed by a "total" and multiply reinforced ending—the end of the manuscripts, of the Buendías, of Macondo, and of Aureliano himself, who reads about himself reading about the end in a text where he is reading about himself reading about the end . . . and so on into infinity. The last of the breed dies in a solitude that is the bane of all Buendías and is the name of the book; and though García Márquez claims to have come up with the sonorous title only upon completion of the novel, it does convey the lack of solidarity which, as he often points out, underlies the Buendías' disintegration (*OG*, 109; *FG*, 75). (At the same time one should note that García Márquez came of age in an era when ideas of existential loneliness were common currency among the educated.) On the face of it, to produce the novel took him eighteen months of full-time work—but also a twenty-year apprenticeship of wide reading, false starts, and preliminary shorter versions. The origins of the book, the circumstances of its writing, the status it rapidly assumed as "underground" world classic, and the infinite riches of its art will long remain among the more inspiring legends in human culture.

NOTES

1. Janes, *Gabriel García Márquez*, pp. 61–62.

2. The noun *ternera* means "veal," but here may rather suggest *ternura*, "tenderness." It is worth nothing that, on a visit I made in 1982 to the cemetery in García Márquez's boyhood town of Aracataca, the first two gravestones I saw were for two women with the family name of Ternera!

3. For a fuller discussion see Bell-Villada, "Names and Narrative Pattern in *One Hundred Years of Solitude*."

4. Vargas Llosa and García Márquez, *Diálogo*, p. 30.

5. Lévi-Strauss, *Elementary Structures of Kinship*, pp. 119 ff.

6. Ibid., pp. 9 and 12.

7. Harss and Dohmann, "Gabriel García Márquez, or the Lost Chord," p. 327.

8. Arenas, "En la ciudad de los espejismos," in Martínez, *Sobre García Márquez*, p. 143.

9. Henao and Arrubla, *History of Colombia*, p. 551.

10. Minta, *Gabriel García Márquez*, pp. 14–19.

11. For a detailed account both of the historical events and of García Márquez's treatment of the facts, see Bell-Villada, "Banana Strike and Military Massacre."

12. Castrillón, *120 días bajo el terror militar*, p. 33.

13. Kepner, *The Banana Empire*, p. 320.

14. Bell-Villada, "Journey to Macondo," p. 26.

15. Friedemann, *Carnaval de Barranquilla*, pp. 79–89.

16. Monsalve, "Una entrevista con García Márquez." Quoted in Peel, "Short Stories of Gabriel García Márquez," p. 165.

17. Maturo, *Claves simbólicas de García Márquez*, p. 155.

18. Monsalve, p. 4.

19: "El viaje a la semilla," interview with *El Manifiesto*, in Rentería Mantilla, *García Márquez habla de García Márquez*, p. 164.

20. Up de Graff, *Head-Hunters of the Amazon*, pp. 11, 38, 79, and 304.

21. Columbus, *Four Voyages to the New World*, p. 11.

22. Vespucci, *The Letters*, pp. 8, 42, and 47.

23. Pigafetta, *Primer viaje en torno del globo*, p. 48.

JAMES HIGGINS

Gabriel García Márquez:
Cien Años de Soledad

Born in 1928, Gabriel García Márquez spent the formative years of his childhood in Aracataca, a small town in the tropical Caribbean region on Colombia's north coast. In the early years of the century the North American United Fruit Company had moved into the area to exploit its banana-producing potential and in the 1910s Aracataca became something of a boom town. By the time of the author's birth the boom had passed, but it was still a bustling, prosperous little community. However, following United Fruit's withdrawal from Colombia in 1941, the economy of the region collapsed, and a few years later, when the writer and his mother returned to arrange for the sale of his grandparents' house, they were to find that the once thriving Aracataca had become a dilapidated ghost town.

Because of the unusual circumstances of his upbringing, García Márquez was to experience solitude from an early age. His mother, Luisa, the daughter of one of the region's long-established families, had married a humble telegraphist, Gabriel Eligio García, against her parents' wishes, but to placate them she returned home for the birth of her first child and left the boy behind to be brought up by them. In his grandparents' large, rambling house, shared by three aunts, he grew up as a solitary little boy among elderly adults. Later experiences were to reinforce the deep-rooted sense of solitude that runs through all his writing.

From *Landmarks in Modern Latin American Fiction*, edited by Philip Swanson, pp. 141–160. © 1990 by Routledge and the individual contributors.

Nonetheless, his childhood was a happy one in which he enjoyed a particularly close relationship with his grandfather, and he was raised in a storytelling environment in that the elders were constantly reliving the past and recounting anecdotes about the history of the family and the town. His grandfather Colonel Nicolás Márquez had fought on the Liberal side against the ruling Conservatives in the Thousand Days' War (1899–1902), the last of a succession of civil wars that had rent Colombia, and would often reminisce about those stirring times. For their part, his grandmother and aunts were credulous, superstitious women who believed in the supernatural and recounted all sorts of magical happenings as if they were everyday events, and the author has often claimed that it was from his grandmother that he learned his narrative manner. That childhood world was to come to an end, however, with the death of his grandfather in 1936, and García Márquez has frequently stated that no other period in his life has matched his first eight years for richness of experience.

García Márquez spent most of the next ten years as a boarder at a school in Zipaquirá, near Bogotá, and in 1947 he entered the National University in the capital to study law. Coming as he did from the Caribbean region, he never felt at home in the alien environment of the Andean highlands, whose cold climate and formal, traditionalist atmosphere proved uncongenial to him. He found solace in books, among which he singles out Kafka's *Metamorphosis* as exercising a profound influence on him, and himself began writing short stories. In 1948 he abandoned his studies and returned to the north coast, where he worked as a journalist, first in Cartagena and then, from 1950, in Barranquilla. The latter city was to have a decisive influence on his literary development, for there he took up with a group of bohemian literati, who introduced him to the work of modern Anglo-Saxon writers, especially Joyce, Virginia Woolf, and William Faulkner. Later he was to render homage to this so-called Barranquilla Group by portraying them in the latter pages of *Cien años de soledad*.

It was in Barranquilla that he wrote most of his early short stories and his first novel, *La hojarasca*, writing at night and in his spare time. The novel was eventually published in 1955, but he encountered difficulty in establishing himself as a novelist and was, in fact, achieving greater success as a reporter. In 1954 he had joined the staff of *El Espectador* in Bogotá and soon became one of Colombia's best-known journalists, boosting the paper's circulation with articles such as "Relato de un náufrago," a serialized account of the ordeal of a shipwrecked sailor.

Like his fellow Colombians, García Márquez was deeply affected by the years of political violence unleashed by the assassination in 1948 of the Liberal presidential candidate, Jorge Eliécer Gaitán, violence that claimed 200,000–300,000 lives in the period from 1949 to 1962 and led to the dictatorship of General Gustavo Rojas Pinilla (1953–1957). An indication of his own political leanings is that in 1955 he was briefly a member of the Communist Party. As a child he had come under the influence of his grandfather's radical liberalism, a lasting impression was made on him by accounts of the massacre of striking United Fruit Company workers in Ciénaga in the year of his birth,[1] and at school in Zipaquirá he had been introduced to Marxist thought by leftist teachers. His flirtation with the Communist Party was transitory, and he has always rejected hard-line Marxist dogmatism, but he has consistently championed left-wing causes and has always maintained that the future of the world lies with socialism.

In 1955 García Márquez was sent to Europe by *El Espectador* as a foreign correspondent, only to discover shortly after his arrival in Paris that the paper had been closed down by the government, and for several months he endured the struggles and hardships of the impecunious artist. In 1957 he moved to Caracas, working there as a journalist for almost two years, and in 1959, following the Cuban Revolution, he joined the Cuban news agency Prensa Latina, first in Bogotá and then in Cuba and New York. In 1961 he resigned in protest against the manoeuvers of the Communist Party hardliners and with his wife—he had married in 1958—moved to Mexico City, where he continued his journalistic career, worked for a public relations firm, and wrote film scripts. In the meantime, he had persevered with his writing and achieved modest success with the novella *El coronel no tiene quien le escriba* (1961), the novel *La mala hora* (1962), and a collection of short stories, *Los funerales de la Mamá Grande* (1962), and in 1967 he was to win an international reputation almost overnight with the publication of his masterpiece, *Cien años de soledad*.[2]

While considerable works in their own right, García Márquez's early writings are also stages in the maturation of *Cien años*. *La hojarasca* and several of the short stories introduce us to Macondo, the fictional representation of the world in which the author grew up. The former shows the effects of the short-lived "banana boom" and the subsequent depression on that small rural community, while "Los funerales de la Mamá Grande" portrays the traditional dominance of the land-owning oligarchy through the mythical story of the legendary matriarch who ruled over the region from time immemorial. *El coronel no tiene quien le escriba* and *La mala hora* recreate the climate of political violence that prevailed in the Colombian countryside in the 1950s, the former linking it to a long tradition of such violence and the latter depicting its corrosive effect on the community. Many of the characters of these early narratives are also forerunners of the Buendías of *Cien años de soledad* in that they are lonely, isolated individuals leading a solitary existence With regard to style, "Los funerales de la Mamá Grande" marks a major evolution. In all of his fiction, García Márquez endeavors to achieve a poetic transposition of reality, but in most of his early work he does so in a style that by and large is still essentially realistic. However, in this story he was to hit on the narrative manner best suited to give literary expression to the world he had known as a child. Here the narrator introduces himself as someone who sits down at his front door to tell a tale as a kind of spokesman for the community. The story, in effect, has the character of popular oral narrative, privileging the legendary and depicting the world in larger-than-life terms, but at the same time its "magical realism" is counterbalanced by an ironic, irreverent tone that subverts the very legend it is propagating. In *Cien años* García Márquez was to perfect that narrative manner and to create an all-encompassing fictional world which incorporates the principal themes treated separately in his earlier work.

Following his success with *Cien años*, García Márquez went on to consolidate his reputation with a number of other books, notably *La increíble y triste historia de la cándida Eréndida y de su abuela desalmada* (1972), *El otoño del patriarca* (1975), *Crónica de una muerte anunciada* (1981), and *El amor en los tiempos del cólera* (1985). His status as one of the world's great novelists was recognized by the award of the Nobel Prize for Literature in 1982.

Cien años narrates the history of the town of Macondo and of its founding family, the Buendías. Following his killing of a neighbor who insulted his honor, José Arcadio Buendía, his wife, Úrsula, and a group of friends abandon their native town and set out in search of a new home, settling eventually in an isolated region in the swamplands. For some time Macondo lives in a state of primeval innocence, its only contact with the outside world coming through the occasional visits of a tribe of gypsies, led by Melquíades, who introduce the inhabitants to wondrous inventions such as false teeth, ice, and the magnet and arouse in José Arcadio the thirst for scientific experiment and the ambition to see the town enjoy the benefits of technological progress. In the course of time, progress does come to Macondo as it gradually emerges from its isolation, but, although it brings relative prosperity, it does not turn the town into the Utopia envisaged by its founder. A magistrate is sent by the central government to assume authority over the district, and, as it is drawn into the sphere of national politics, the town becomes embroiled in a series of bloody civil wars. The establishment of a railway link paves the way for the commercial exploitation of the region's natural resources by the North American Banana Company, and overnight Macondo is transformed into a boom town; disgruntled by their low wages and poor working conditions, the workers declare a strike and are shot down by government troops; subsequently, torrential rain destroys the plantations, the Banana Company withdraws, and Macondo declines into a ghost town. The history of the Buendías began with an "original sin" in that José Arcadio and Úrsula were first cousins, and succeeding generations likewise betray a propensity to incest, and throughout the novel the family is haunted by the fear of punishment in the form of the birth of a monstrous child with a pig's tail. That fear is eventually realized when the love affair between the last remaining Buendías, Aureliano Babilonia and his aunt Amaranta Úrsula, produces the dreaded monstrosity. Shortly afterward, when Aureliano finally succeeds in making sense of the puzzling manuscript written by Melquíades decades earlier and which over the generations various members of the family have vainly attempted to decipher, he discovers that it is a prophetic account of the history of Macondo and that the Buendías and their world will come to an end when he reads the last sentence.

Cien años is a novel that maintains a tension or dialectic between different perspectives. It is, first of all, a comic novel, an entertainment, which adopts an irreverent attitude toward literature "the best plaything ever invented for making fun of people" (p. 462)—as something not to be taken seriously.[3] Yet, at the same time, it is a deeply serious and highly ambitious book that sets out to rewrite the history of Latin America and to offer a view of the human condition. Again, it proclaims its fictionality when, on the closing page, Aureliano Babilonia discovers that, in effect, the Buendías are no more than creatures of Melquíades's imagination with no existence outside the pages of his manuscript, an ending which serves, among other things, to warn the reader that the novel is "a fictive construct, a creation, and not a mirror that meticulously reflects reality."[4] Lurking behind the book is the ontological uncertainty of our times, as is revealed by an earlier episode when the same Aureliano, trying to persuade others of the truth of his version of Macondo's history, runs up against the skepticism of the local priest, who, ironically, is conspicuously lacking in the certainties that he is supposed to embody:

> El párroco lo midió con una mirada de lástima.
> —Ay, hijo—suspiró—. A mí me bastaría con estar seguro de que tú
> y yo existimos en este momento. (p. 484)

Unable to share traditional realist fiction's confident assumption of man's ability to understand and describe the world, García Márquez effectively waives any claim to be "telling it the way it is." And yet, despite his awareness of the limitations of literature, he nonetheless endeavors to do what novelists have always sought to do: to depict the world around him. Paradoxically, he attempts to translate reality into words while casting doubt on the feasibility of such an undertaking.

García Márquez has stated that his primary aim in writing *Cien años* was to recreate the lost world of his childhood.[5] He does so through the vehicle of a so-called magical realism that eschews the documentary approach of realist fiction and instead gives expression to the worldview of a rural people living in remote isolation from the modern developed world. It should be stressed that the magical realism of *Cien años* does not imply that Latin American reality is somehow inherently magical, though the novel does highlight the prodigious dimensions of the natural environment and the excesses of political life. Nor does the much-bandied term "fantasy" have much meaning in relation to *Cien años*, since every event described, no matter how fantastic it might appear, has a perfectly logical explanation. What the novel does is to present events, not as they actually occurred but as they were perceived and interpreted by the local people. Thus, for example, the narrative points to the real explanation of Remedios's disappearance by recording that outsiders were of the opinion that she had run off with a man and that the story put about by her family was an invention designed to cover up the scandal, but it is the family's version—that she ascended into heaven—which the text privileges and recounts in full and plausible detail, since it was the one that was widely accepted in the community (pp. 313–314). Likewise, the systematic use of hyperbole—José Arcadio's prodigious virility, Colonel Aureliano's thirty-two armed uprisings, the seventy-two schoolgirls queuing up to empty seventy-two chamberpots, to cite but a few examples—corresponds to the way in which the popular collective memory blows events up to larger-than-life proportions. The narrative, too, has an Old Testament ring to it—there is an original sin, an exodus, the discovery of an (un)promised land, a plague, a deluge, an apocalypse—that is a reflection both of the cultural environment and of the myth-making tendency of popular history. In effect, *Cien años* transmits the history of Macondo as it was recorded and elaborated over the generations by popular oral tradition, and, by so doing, it permits a rural society to give expression to itself in terms of its own cultural experience.

Yet *Cien años* is a written text, and a story that gives the impression of being an oral narrative turns out on the final pages to be recorded in Melquíades's manuscript.[6] Another layer of tension informing the novel, therefore, is that between the oral and the written. By incorporating popular oral history into literature to convey a Third World experience, García Márquez accords it the status and prestige associated with the written word. He also highlights the relativity of all world-views, for events that appear fantastic to the sophisticated reader—Remedios's ascent into heaven, trips on flying carpets, the parish priest's feats of levitation—are accepted as everyday realities in the cultural environment of Macondo, and, by contrast, the modern technology that the sophisticated reader takes for granted—ice cubes, false teeth, the locomotive—is greeted with awe as something wonderful and magical. *Cien años* thus not only challenges conventional assumptions as to what constitutes reality but subverts the novelistic genre's conventional Eurocentrism and, indeed, the whole rationalist cultural tradition of the West. At the same time, though, the narrator writes in an ironic, tongue-in-cheek manner that distances him from the oral history that he is transmitting. Thus, for example, in the episode discussed earlier, the story of Remedios's ascent into heaven is recounted straight-faced but is undermined by insinuation of the real, more prosaic explanation of the facts. In effect, if *Cien años* sets out to subvert Eurocentric attitudes, it also simultaneously subverts Latin Americans' perceptions of their own history.

As has already been implied, García Márquez is writing against the Western novelistic tradition, and *Cien años* demands a reading which, eschewing the kind of narrow Eurocentrism that disguises itself as universalism, approaches the novel in terms of its own specificity. However, at the same time, the novel draws heavily on literary sources, and, if Borges would seem to be the main influence, it should be remembered that behind the latter lies the whole corpus of Western culture.[7] It is significant that in the provincial environment of Macondo a privileged space should be allotted to Melquíades's room, representing the timeless world of literature, and significant, too, that, having had his horizons broadened by the Catalan bibliophile, the younger writer Gabriel should leave Macondo for Paris. For, while challenging the Western novelistic tradition, García Márquez is also writing within it, and in *Cien años* he has set out not only to portray a Latin American reality but also to express the universal through the local.

In giving a literary depiction of the world of his childhood, García Márquez has also created in the fictional community of Macondo a microcosm of a larger world. The story of Macondo, in fact, reflects the general pattern of Latin America's history. It is founded by settlers fleeing a homeland haunted by the spectre of violence and is born of a utopian dream, being built on the spot where José Arcadio has a vision of a luminous city of houses walled with mirrors (p. 97). By the final page, however, the city of mirrors has become a city of mirages. Macondo thus represents the dream of a brave new world that America seemed to promise and that was cruelly proved illusory by the subsequent course of history. *Cien años*, in effect, is a demystifying rewriting of the history of the subcontinent. The ruling establishment's tradition of manipulating history is exposed in the latter part of the novel, when the authorities hush up the massacre of the striking banana workers and the roundup and disappearance of all potential subversives, claiming that Macondo is a peaceful and contented community where social harmony reigns (p. 383). Later, young Aureliano, brought up by his uncle to regard Macondo as the victim of the Banana Company's imperialist exploitation, discovers that the school history books portray the company as a benefactor which brought prosperity and progress (pp. 422–423). *Cien años* sets out to debunk the official myths by offering an alternative history. In part, this is a popular view of a local community subjected to domination by outside forces. At the same time, however, it is the view of a privileged class, since the dominant perspective is that of the Buendías, the local provincial elite, and their version of history is undermined in its turn by the narrator's ironic distancing of himself from it.

While in strictly chronological terms the events of the novel roughly span the century from the years after Independence to around 1930, the early phase of Macondo's history evokes Latin America's colonial period, when communities lived isolated from one another and the viceroyalties themselves had little contact with the distant metropolis. Latin America's isolation from intellectual developments in Europe is hilariously brought out when José Arcadio's researches lead him to the discovery that the earth is round (p. 75), and colonial underdevelopment is reflected in his acute awareness of Macondo's backwardness in relation to the outside world:

> "En el mundo están ocurriendo cosas increíbles," le decía a Úrsula. "Ahí mismo, al otro lado del río, hay toda clase de aparatos mágicos, mientras nosotros seguimos viviendo como los burros." (p. 79)

The novel thus ironically debunks Spain's claim to have bequeathed to America the benefits of European civilization. Indeed, the Conquest itself is parodied, in a passage reminiscent of the chronicles (pp. 82–83),[8] by the expedition in which the men of Macondo re-enact the ordeals of the Spanish explorers and conquistadores in order to make contact with the civilization that Spain allegedly spread to its colonies.

Furthermore, the Spanish colonial heritage is identified as one of the principal factors in Latin America's continuing underdevelopment. Significantly, the Macondo men's expedition fails to make contact with civilization and succeeds only in finding the hulk of an old Spanish galleon, stranded on dry land and overgrown with vegetation (p. 83), symbol of a heritage that is anachronistic, out of context and ill-equipped to tackle the awesome American environment. Above all, that heritage takes the form of a mentality, personified in the novel by Fernanda del Carpio. An incomer from the capital, she embodies the Castilian traditionalism of the *cachacos*, the inhabitants of the cities of the Colombian *altiplano*, and, beyond that, a whole set of values and attitudes that Latin America has inherited from Spain. Nursing aristocratic pretensions that are reflected in her name—an echo of that of Bernardo del Carpio, a legendary Spanish hero of medieval times—she lives the illusion of a grandeur that no longer exists and clings to antiquated customs in a world that no longer has any use for them; and, as Macondo falls into the hands of the Banana Company and is invaded by lower-class upstarts, she comforts herself with the belief that she is spiritually superior to the vulgar tradesmen who have taken over the world, an attitude that echoes the response of Spanish American intellectuals of the Arielist generation to North American expansionism.[9] The heirlooms that she receives from her father as Christmas presents are ironically described by her husband as a family cemetery, and, as though to confirm the truth of his words, the last present turns out to be a box containing the father's corpse (pp. 289–290). What they symbolize, in fact, is an outmoded, traditionalist mentality that prevents Latin America from coming to terms with the modern world.

The advent of the republican era is marked by the arrival of Don Apolinar Moscote to assume authority over the town as representative of the central government. Reversing the conventional wisdom that has traditionally attributed the political instability of the nineteenth century to the "barbaric" countryside, whose backwardness and lawlessness supposedly hindered the "civilized cities" efforts to lead the subcontinent toward order and progress,[10] the novel identifies government intervention in local affairs as the origin of Macondo's troubles. Till then it had always been a well-ordered community, and, far from bringing law and order, the new magistrate immediately stirs up unrest by decreeing that all houses are to be painted blue (pp. 133–134), the color of the ruling Conservative party, an act symptomatic of the autocratic and insensitive impositions of central government. Moreover, if Don Apolinar introduces Macondo to parliamentary democracy, he also introduces it to the cynical manipulation of democratic institutions, the first elections being rigged to ensure the victory of the government party (p. 173). And as Macondo is incorporated into the national political system, it becomes caught up in the civil violence engendered by that tainted system.

For much of the novel, Macondo is afflicted by the civil wars between Liberals and Conservatives that were a feature of the nineteenth century in Colombia and other Latin American countries. The futility of that bloodshed is conveyed by the progressive disillusionment of Colonel Aureliano Buendía, the champion of the Liberal cause. A principal cause of his disenchantment is the ideological fanaticism typified by the agitator Dr. Alirio Noguera, who conceives a plan for liquidating Conservatism by a coordinated nationwide campaign of assassination (p. 175). While such fanaticism leads extremists on both sides to forget their common humanity, Aureliano establishes a friendship with General Moncada across the ideological divide, and at one point the two men consider the possibility of breaking with their respective parties and joining forces to establish a humanitarian regime that would combine the best features of the warring doctrines (p. 223). Yet he later has Moncada executed, for he himself falls prey to the same fanaticism and is ready to sacrifice even his friends to achieve his political objectives, and before his death his old friend warns him that his obsessive hatred of his political enemies has dehumanized him (p. 235). Fortunately, Aureliano is sensitive enough to realize what is happening to him, and his subsequent determination to bring the war to an end is born in part of the wish to save himself as a human being.

The irony is that, despite their ideological differences, both parties are dominated by the same privileged elite, and in practice the distinction between them ultimately becomes blurred, just as the houses in Macondo take on an indeterminate color as a result of being constantly repainted red or blue according to which group is in control (p. 201). In power the Liberals commit the same abuses as the Conservatives. As Governor, Arcadio Buendía behaves like a petty dictator, and the deal that he strikes with the second José Arcadio, whereby he legalizes the latter's right to lands that he has usurped in exchange for the right to levy taxes (pp. 190–191), exemplifies and reinforces the traditional pattern of oligarchic domination and, significantly, is later ratified by the Conservatives. Committed to a program of radical reform, Colonel Aureliano finds himself not only fighting the Conservatives but at odds with his own party. The Liberal landowners react to the threat to their property by entering into secret alliances with the Conservatives, financial backing is withdrawn, and eventually the party strategists drop all radical policies from their program in order to broaden their support (p. 244). At this point, Aureliano comes to realize that they have been fighting not for change but for power, for access to office and the spoils that go with it, and, disillusioned, he brings the war to an end and withdraws from political life. In the end a compromise is reached whereby the two parties share power, a solution that restores peace but that leaves the socioeconomic status quo intact. Liberals and Conservatives are thus exposed as ultimately representing the same class interests.

As peace and stability return to Macondo, the region enters a period of neocolonial domination. Early in the novel José Arcadio articulates the dream of a world transformed by scientific and technological progress:

> Trató de seducirla con … la promesa de un mundo prodigioso donde bastaba con echar unos líquidos mágicos en la tierra para que las plantas dieran frutos a voluntad del hombre, y donde se vendían a precio de baratillo toda clase de aparatos para el dolor. (p. 86)

What he is voicing, in effect, is a constant of Latin American thought since Independence, the aspiration to "modernize" on the model of the advanced industrial nations in order to achieve a similar level of development. In the event, Macondo does come to enjoy a period of economic growth. However, "modernization" does not come about as the result of internal development but is imported from the outside, and hence José Arcadio's original dream of a city of mirrors takes on an ironic significance in that Macondo's role becomes that of reflecting the developed world. And, though Macondo does undoubtedly prosper and progress, it continues to trail behind the rest of the world, and, furthermore, it finds itself the victim of foreign economic and cultural imperialism.

In fact, the story of the later Macondo illustrates Latin America's neocolonial status as an economic dependency of international capital, particularly North American. No sooner had Macondo embarked on a phase of autonomous economic development than it falls under the domination of North American capital and, incorporated into the world economy as a source of primary products, becomes subject to cycles of boom and recession determined by the fluctuations of the international market. Aureliano Segundo accumulates a fantastic fortune quite fortuitously, thanks to the astonishing fertility of his livestock (p. 267), and the whole community enjoys an equally fortuitous prosperity generated by the banana boom. Macondo's experience of prosperity is thus due not to any real economic development but to the amazing richness of the region's natural resources and to international demand for those resources. Hence it is defenseless against sudden slumps in the market. Symbol of such slumps is the great deluge that ruins Aureliano Segundo by killing his stock and that halts banana production and leads to the departure of the company, turning Macondo into a ghost town. The extent to which the Latin American economy is manipulated by foreign capital is indicated by the suggestion that the crisis was deliberately engineered by the company, whose directors were so powerful that they were able to control the weather (p. 422). In the wake of his ruin, Aureliano Segundo is reduced to running a lottery to make ends meet and is nicknamed Don Divina Providencia. He comes, in fact, to personify Latin America, whose economic role in the world is passively to wait for the stroke of good fortune that will bring it another period of prosperity.

Furthermore, such progress and prosperity as are brought to Macondo by foreign capital are achieved at a price. The Banana Company exploits its workforce quite cynically, as is indicated by the list of complaints presented by the workers (p. 372), and Macondo effectively becomes a colony, a company town run by company men backed up by armed thugs dressed as policemen. And such is the power exercised by the company that when the workers take strike action, the authorities send in troops to break the strike by force, massacring the strikers and liquidating the union leaders. The dominant influence exerted by foreign capital in Latin America is thus seen to extend beyond the economic to the political sphere.

The patrician Buendías represent that oligarchy that has traditionally ruled Latin America. Macondo's founding family, they develop into a land-owning class, the process by which the latifundia system was established being encapsulated in the episode in which the second José Arcadio makes use of his enormous physical strength to appropriate the best lands in the district (p. 190), and subsequently they evolve into an entrepreneurial bourgeoisie by branching into business. The solitude that is their dominant family trait is directly related to their egoism: living exclusively for themselves, they are incapable of loving, of sharing, of giving themselves to others. Perhaps the most extreme examples are the introverted Aureliano, who lives in a private world of his own that no one is allowed to enter, and Amaranta, who ruins the lives of four men by arousing their passion without being able to bring herself to satisfy it, but their egocentric attitude is shared by the whole family, for everyone in the Buendía household is too wrapped up in his own affairs to think of anyone else: "nadie se daba cuenta de nada mientras no se gritara en el corredor, porque los afanes de la panadería, los sobresaltos de la guerra, el cuidado de los niños, no dejaban tiempo para pensar en la felicidad ajena" (p. 432).

Relating to that egoism is the family's propensity to incest. The Buendía dynasty originates with an incestuous marriage, and successive generations become involved in more or less incestuous relationships. Their phobia about the monstrous child with a pig's tail ironically highlights their blindness to their failings, for the apparently normal Buendías are, in fact, deformed by their monstrous egoism, as Úrsula glimpses on more than one occasion (pp. 98, 245). García Márquez himself has pointed out that, as the negation of solidarity, solitude has political implications.[11] The solitude of the Buendías, in effect, is a reflection of the egoistic, individualistic values by which they live. And their propensity to incest mirrors the selfish, inward-looking attitude of a privileged oligarchy jealously defending its class interests against other sectors of society.

Yet, contrary to the view of many critics, there is in the novel a notable progression that seems to offer a way out of the vicious circle in which Macondo/Latin America is caught. For, as the Buendías fall on hard times in the wake of Macondo's economic decline, adversity teaches them how to love. The once frivolous Aureliano Segundo and Petra Cores not only discover a sense of mutual solidarity but take pleasure in making sacrifices to help others in need. The same pattern is repeated with Aureliano Babilonia and Amaranta Úrsula, and the latter is convinced that the child born of their love will represent a fresh start for the Buendías (p. 486). In the event, he turns out to be the long-feared monster with the pig's tail whose birth marks the end of the line. For the emergence of love in the novel to displace the traditional egoism of the Buendías reflects the emergence of socialist values as a political force in Latin America, a force that will sweep away the Buendías and the order they represent.

The ending of the novel reflects, at least on the sociopolitical level, the optimism generated throughout Latin America in the 1960s by the triumph of the Cuban Revolution. The sense of the ending is clarified by an early episode where Melquíades comes across a prophecy of Nostradamus which he interprets as predicting a future Macondo that will be the luminous city of José Arcadio's dream but where there will be no trace of the Buendías (p. 130). In effect, what Aureliano Babilonia reads in Melquíades's manuscript is the imminent demise of his own class. The Buendías' attempts to make sense of the manuscripts can be interpreted as a metaphor of Latin Americans' attempts to understand their history, and it is no accident that it should be Aureliano who finally succeeds where all others in the family have failed.[12] Not only is he one of a new breed of Buendías who have learned to love, but also he has been educated by his uncle José Arcadio Segundo, a union activist, who has taught him history from a working-class viewpoint. Aureliano, in other words, has broken out of the narrow perspective of his own privileged class and developed a social awareness. That awareness enables him to arrive at an understanding of Macondo's history and to see that it must culminate in a new socialist ethos that will do away with the old oligarchic and neocolonial order.

First and foremost, then, *Cien años* is a novel that has to be read in its own Latin American context. But it is also a novel about the human condition, and the story of the Buendías is susceptible to being read as a Latin American version of the history of Western man. Despite its humor, the novel presents an essentially pessimistic view of man's condition. The novel's central theme, highlighted by the title, is human isolation. If, as we have seen, the solitude of the Buendías is directly linked to their egoism, it is so only in part, for it is too pervasive to be explained away so easily and appears, in fact, as an existential condition. Disfigured "forever and from the beginning of the world by the pox of solitude" (p. 469) that prevents all communication with others, the Buendías share a common condition that, paradoxically, isolates them from one another: "the unfathomable solitude which separated and united them at the same time" (p. 448). Rather than a family, the Buendías are a group of solitary individuals living together as strangers in the same house. As such, they personify the predicament of the human race.

The story of the Buendías also reveals the limited nature of the individual's control of his own destiny. Experience teaches Pilar Ternera that "the history of the family was a mechanism of irreversible repetitions" (p. 470), while Úrsula observes that "time wasn't passing . . . but going round in circles" (p. 409). These insights are sparked off by the perception that the same character traits are passed on from generation to generation (p. 258) and that each new generation engages in activities that echo those of its predecessors. Thus, Aureliano Triste's sketch of the railroad is "a direct descendant of the diagrams with which José Arcadio Buendía illustrated his scheme for solar warfare" (p. 297), and when José Arcadio Segundo, following the precedent of other members of the family, shuts himself away to study Melquíades's manuscript, his face reflects "the irreparable fate of his great-grandfather" (p. 387). Implied here is not merely that the human personality is largely shaped by heredity and environment, but also that individual life is subject to generic laws in that, since all men live out a limited range of experiences, every human existence corresponds to an archetypal pattern.

The world that the Buendías inhabit is one that fails to come up to the level of man's expectations, and their history is a catalog of "lost dreams" (p. 438) and "numerous frustrated enterprises" (p. 452). Again and again the characters find fulfillment denied them: the only crown that Fernanda gets to wear—that of a Carnival Queen—makes a mockery of her regal pretensions; Pilar Ternera wastes her life away waiting for the lover who never comes; the virginity that Amaranta preserves to her death is an emblem of her sterile life. José Arcadio re-enacts man's perennial striving to surmount the limitations of his condition, first when he attempts to break out of Macondo's narrow confines and reach the utopian land of the great inventions, and later when he endeavors to realize the alchemists' dream of converting base metals into gold, but in the former case he finds himself hemmed in by the sea and in the latter he succeeds only in reducing gold to a molten mess that reminds his son of dog shit (p. 102). Not only are the Buendías' hopes and aspirations thwarted by life, but also misfortunes arbitrarily befall them, as when Colonel Aureliano sees first his wife die and later his sons or when Rebeca and Meme tragically lose the men who brought them happiness, and the unexplained murder of the second José Arcadio stands as a metaphor for the inexplicable mystery of evil and suffering. For many of the characters, indeed, life becomes synonymous with suffering, and a recurring motif is withdrawal from the world in a symbolic retreat to the refuge of the womb. In *Cien años*, peace of mind is achieved only when the Buendías opt out of active emotional involvement in life.

The character with the acutest sense of life's futility is the disillusioned Colonel Aureliano. After undertaking thirty-two armed uprisings, he comes to the conclusion that he has squandered twenty years of his life to no purpose and withdraws to his workshop, where he devotes himself to making the same little golden ornaments over and over again. This routine represents a recognition of the vanity of all human enterprises: it is completely senseless, but for the Colonel it is no more absurd than his previous activities, and it is a means of filling in the time while he waits for death. A few moments before he dies, a circus parades down the street, and in it he sees a tableau of his own life, a showy, ridiculous spectacle that has given way to an emptiness as bleak as the deserted street (p. 342).

If the story of Macondo reflects the general pattern of Latin America's history, it also reflects the evolution of Western civilization and the progressive alienation of Western man. The mythical account of its history depicts Macondo's early years as a Golden Age and the town itself as an earthly paradise where men lived in happy innocence, in harmony with their world. The Fall comes with its incorporation into the modern age, and, as Macondo keeps changing around her, Úrsula feels reality becoming too complicated for her to cope with: "'Los años de ahora ya no vienen como los de antes,' solía decir sintiendo que la realidad cotidiana se le escapaba de las manos" (p. 321). In a local version of a universal myth that attributes man's alienation to his development of reason as a tool for dominating the world, the expulsion from paradise is depicted as a punishment for the sin of acquiring forbidden knowledge. The mysterious gypsy Melquíades appears as a personification of the intellectual curiosity that impels man to pursue knowledge and progress. It is Melquíades's tribe that brings the first scientific advances to Macondo, but the tribe is punished with extinction "for exceeding the limits of human knowledge" (p. 113). However, Melquíades himself survives and, like the serpent in the Christian myth of the Fall, plays the role of the tempter, inviting men to partake of the fruit of knowledge, and at one point Úrsula identifies the odor of his experiments with the Devil (p. 77). Under his influence, José Arcadio is seduced by the fascination of science and feverishly devotes himself to all kinds of experiments, but his passionate pursuit of knowledge distances him more and more from reality and brings him to a state of madness that leaves him completely alienated. Disoriented in a world turned chaotic, he vents his rage by destroying the laboratory and the apparatus that have brought him to this sad condition and, like Prometheus chained to his mountainside, lives out the rest of his days bound to a tree (the tree of knowledge?).

Moreover, when the progress so desired by José Arcadio reaches Macondo, it brings with it a general alienation as the town suffers a plague of insomnia that causes loss of memory. Lapsing into a kind of idiocy in which they cease to know the function of things and the identity of people and are no longer aware even of their own being, the inhabitants of Macondo are cast adrift in a world bereft of order and coherence. To counter the effects of the plague, they identify things with labels, and in the main street they erect a banner proclaiming the existence of God. This represents a desperate attempt to preserve the old values that gave life a meaning, to cling to a coherent vision of an ordered world, but elusive, shifting reality slips away from them as they forget the written word (p. 123). Reality, in other words, refuses to adapt itself to the old molds, no longer conforms to the old concepts or order, and its meaning becomes increasingly inaccessible. And, although the town apparently returns to normality after Melquíades restores its memory, things are never quite the same again, and, indeed, the memory-restoring potion would seem to be a metaphor of the process whereby men become conditioned to change after the first traumatic impact of progress.

Various members of the Buendía family have the image of Melquíades imprinted in their mind as a hereditary memory (p. 77), and several of them devote themselves to the task of deciphering his manuscript. That image would seem to represent the human urge for knowledge, and the study of the manuscript is a metaphor of man's attempts to discover the secret of existence. For most of the novel, the manuscript, like life, remains an incomprehensible enigma, and it is ironically implied that the search for truth is a useless activity when Melquíades's room is converted into a storeroom for chamberpots. When Aureliano Babilonia finally succeeds in decoding the manuscript in a dénouement reminiscent of Unamuno's *Niebla* and Borges's "Las ruinas circulares," the truth he comes face to face with is a disheartening one. For what he discovers is that the Buendías are no more than fictions created by Melquíades's imagination, that life is a dream, an illusion, that ultimately existence has no meaning. It is significant that that truth should be arrived at by the last of the Buendías, for it is, in effect, the worldview of the last representative of a worn-out, declining society whose perception of life becomes more and more disillusioned as its world collapses around it. The novel's ending, therefore, can be seen as an expression of the existential anguish of twentieth-century Western man.

Given the narrator's ironic distancing of himself from the version of Macondo's history that he is transmitting, it would seem that to some extent he is dissociating himself from the worldview conveyed by the novel and identifying bourgeois individualism as one of the root causes of Western man's existential anguish. Nonetheless, the novel also communicates a sense of the ultimately tragic nature of life, one that goes beyond the subjective perceptions of the characters and resists explanation as the consequence of human failings, and the dénouement would appear to express a view of the world held by the author himself. Such a pessimistic worldview does not seem to me to be incompatible with faith in social progress, as Shaw suggests.[13] Other writers, such as the Peruvian poet César Vallejo, have managed to balance both attitudes, and the ambivalence of the dénouement and of Aureliano Babilonia as a character epitomizes the way in which the novel maintains a tension between differing perspectives, playing off against each other a passionate social commitment and a belief that in the long run nothing has any meaning. Furthermore, it has to be stressed that García Márquez's pessimism with regard to life is tempered by a number of factors. The first of these is his conviction that the advent of socialism will create a healthier and more harmonious world. Then again, the image of humanity projected in the novel is far from being entirely negative, for, despite their many failings, the Buendías come across as sympathetic characters and possess optimism-inspiring virtues: José Arcadio's heroic striving to triumph over circumstances; the tireless tenacity with which Úrsula struggles to keep the family going; Colonel Aureliano's stubborn refusal to be beaten, exemplified by his dying on his feet after urinating on the tree of life (p. 342). Last but not least, *Cien años*'s exuberant humor conveys a sense that, if life is tragic, it is also a great joke.

NOTES

1. This incident is incorporated into *Cien años de soledad*. See L. I. Mena, "La huelga de la compañía bananera como expresión de lo 'real maravilloso' americano en *Cien años de soledad*," *Bulletin Hispanique*, vol. 74 (1972), pp. 379–405.

2. See G. García Márquez, *Cien años de soledad*, ed. Jacques Joset (Cátedra, Madrid, 1984). All references are to this edition. Henceforth the abbreviation *Cien años* will be used. Certain quotations incorporated into the body of this text have been rendered into English.

3. See C. Griffin, "The humour of *One Hundred Years of Solitude*," in B. McGuirk and R. Cardwell (eds.), *Gabriel García Márquez: New Readings* (Cambridge University Press, Cambridge, 1987), pp. 81–94.

4. D. P. Gallagher, *Modern Latin American Literature* (Oxford University Press, Oxford, 1973), p. 88.

5. P. A. Mendoza, *The Fragrance of Guava*, trans. A. Wright (Verso, London, 1983), p. 72.

6. It does not follow, of course, that the novel replicates Melquíades's manuscript. In his above-mentioned edition of the text, J. Joset argues that the narrator is an unknown person who rescued Melquíades's manuscript from oblivion by transcribing the translation, using the key discovered by Aureliano Babilonia (p. 44). He further points out that *Cien años* includes elements that could not possibly have been contained in Melquíades's manuscript (p. 491, n. 42).

7. On the influence of Borges see R. González Echevarría, "With Borges in Macondo," *Diacritics*, vol. 2, no. 1 (1972), pp. 57–60.

8. On García Márquez's use of the chronicles as a source, see I. M. Zavala, "*Cien años de soledad*, crónica de Indias," *Ínsula*, no. 286 (1970), pp. 3, 11.

9. The most influential expression of that response was the Uruguayan José E. Rodo's essay *Ariel* (1900). See J. Franco, *The Modern Culture of Latin America: Society and the Artist* (Pall Mall Press, London, 1967), pp. 49–53.

10. This view, essentially that of the Europeanized urban elites, was given its clearest formulation in Argentina by Domingo F. Sarmiento in *Facundo* (1845) but was widely held throughout Latin America.

11. See E. González Bermejo, "Gabriel García Márquez: ahora doscientos años de soledad," *Casa de las Américas*, vol. 10, no. 63 (1970), p. 164.

12. See G. Martin. "On 'magical' and social realism in García Márquez," in McGuirk and Cardwell (eds.), *Gabriel García Márquez: New Readings*, pp. 95–116.

13. D. L. Shaw, "Concerning the interpretation of *Cien años de soledad*," *Ibero-Amerikanisches Archiv*, vol. 3, no. 1 (1977), p. 321.

Works Cited

Arnau, C. (1971) *El mundo mítico de Gabriel García Márquez*, Península, Barcelona.

Earle, P.G, (ed.) (1981) *Gabriel García Márquez*, Taurus, Madrid.

Giacoman, H.G. (ed.) (1972) *Homenaje a Gabriel García Márquez*, Las Américas, New York.

González Echevarría, R. (1984) "*Cien años de soledad*: the novel as myth and archive", *Modern Language Notes*, vol. 99, no. 2, pp. 358–80.

Levine, S.J. (1975) *El espejo hablado: un estudio de "Cien años de soledad"*, Monte Ávila, Caracas.

Ludmer, J. (1972), *"Cien años de soledad": una interpretación*, Editorial Tiempo Contemporáneo, Buenos Aires.

Maturo, G. (1977) *Claves simbólicas de García Márquez*, 2nd edn, Fernando García Cambeiro, Buenos Aires.

McGuirk, B. and Cardwell, R. (eds) (1987) *Gabriel García Márquez: New Readings*, Cambridge University Press, Cambridge.

McMurray, G.R. (1977) *Gabriel García Márquez*, Ungar, New York.

Mena, L.I. (1979) *La función de la historia en "Cien años de soledad"*, Plaza y Janés, Barcelona.

Mendoza, P.A. and García Márquez, G. (1982) *El olor de la guayaba*, Bruguera, Barcelona; English version (1983) *The Fragrance of Guava*, trans. A. Wright, Verso, London.

Minta, S. (1987) *Gabriel García Márquez*, Cape, London.

Palencia-Roth, M. (1983) *Gabriel García Márquez. La línea, el circulo y las metamorfosis del mito*, Gredos, Madrid.

Shaw, D.L. (1977) "Concerning the interpretation of *Cien años de soledad*", *Ibero-Amerikanisches Archiv*, vol. 3, no. 4, pp. 317–29.

Sims, R.L. (1981) *The Evolution of Myth in García Márquez from "La hojarasca" to "Cien años de soledad"*, Universal, Miami.

Vargas Llosa, M. (1971) *Gabriel García Márquez: historia de un deicidio*, Barral, Barcelona.

Williams, R.L. (1984) *Gabriel García Márquez*, Twayne, Boston.

ARIEL DORFMAN

Someone Writes to the Future:
Meditations on Hope and Violence
in García Márquez

History is full of telling coincidences. So it is with the year 1928. José Eustacio Rivera, until then Colombia's greatest novelist, was dying that year—and across the country, in Aracataca, a woman was giving birth to a man-child who would surpass Rivera's literary achievements—Gabriel García Márquez. Rivera major novel, *The Vortex*, had ended with the famous words: "Y se los devoró la selva"—"and the jungle devoured them," referring to protagonists engulfed by the ferocious, never-forgiving alien land of Latin America. Though nature would certainly be a brooding presence in the future works of García Márquez, his fundamental obsession was extremely different from Rivera's: to find out why history had devoured his people, history, that entity which men and women supposedly make and which should, at least in principle, be the territory where they exercise some command over their lives—hammer out some recognizable image of themselves.

But in that same year, 1928, remotely, perhaps ironically, echoing the cries of labor of little Gabriel's mother, an act was being committed that would express, if not radically symbolize, how far Colombians were from deciding their own destiny. Hundreds, some estimates say thousands, of workers were being massacred by government troops in the town of Ciénaga—an incident which would serve García Márquez as the basis for one of

From *Some Write to the Future: Essays on Contemporary Latin American Fiction*, translated by George Shivers with the author, pp. 201–221. © 1991 by Duke University Press.

81

the most dramatic incidents of his fictitious village of Macondo, an incident which leads to Macondo's irrevocable decline and decadence, as if from that moment onward it would be impossible for its inhabitants to even dream of controlling their own existence. In fact, in the novel, it is only after the massacre that nature begins, Rivera-like, to encroach upon them. What had been a paradisiacal climate turns to horror—almost half a decade of rain followed by ten years more of absolute drought.

That rain, however, is not an objective, neutral force that develops independently of peoples' lives or wills, outside humanity. Not only is the downpour in *One Hundred Years of Solitude* the result of the United Fruit Company's desire to create some phenomenon that covers up the tracks of its villainy, but the author himself has used it, exaggerated its boundaries, in order to press upon his characters some proxy for history, experienced as if it were a deluge or an earthquake or a hurricane, something felt to be beyond the efforts of everyday men and women, somewhat like Rivera's jungle.

The flexible, malleable character of this rain, its openness to the tactics of a literary strategy, can be proven by examining how its author deals with its evolution in his own work. The storm of *One Hundred Years of Solitude* (written in 1967), and which lasts "four years, eleven months and two days," had already appeared in a work by García Márquez twelve years earlier in 1955. In a fragment which was going to be part of *Leafstorm* (*La Hojarasca*), but was then published as a separate story called "Isabel watching the rain fall in Macondo," García Márquez had invented a never-ending shower which swept away rails, opened graves, destroyed the foundations of the town, a tunnel of water in the mind of a woman and her feelings of desolation. Time: one week.

Twelve years later, when the writer transforms that almost commonplace, almost interior, event into an epic and prodigious phenomenon, he is signaling his desire to break out of normal time, to discover ways in which to transcend the limitations of what is conventionally called reality. That ordinary, albeit exceedingly wet, week has not only been metamorphosed into five years, it has become a myth, something unforgettable, that will remain with the generations to come—and as such, it provides a clue to what García Márquez is trying to accomplish in his masterpiece, how far he has come from the world of José Eustacio Rivera into which he was born. And that is precisely what he is attempting: García Márquez will try and tell the story of his country, of his continent, of his century, before his birth, before 1928—in other words, he is going to explore what has transpired without his presence, that which he only knows by hearsay, without having been a real witness. He will recount the one hundred years that preceded him, that led to his conception, the hundred years which have receded from him enough so they are in danger of being forgotten, the hundred years which are still near enough to be grasped and remembered.

The story has been told before, of course. Once by the droning, lying voice of official history which most definitely does not offer any indication of why things have gone wrong, why the people of Colombia have produced so much abundant wealth and are so copiously poor. And it has also been told once, and often, by the mouths, ears, and hands of collective memory. It is time to look back now, before it is too late, and tell the story in such a way that the errors of the past will not be repeated, but also told in such a way that it can be transmitted and understood, the literary act as the form in which readers (and writers) can supposedly break out of the brutal cycle of misery and violence.

In order to do this, García Márquez must be true to two different traditions which have, in general, opposed one another throughout history and particularly Latin American history: one is the literature of an illustrated minority, elaborated with all the forms that belong to so-called "high culture," basically centered in the cities; while the other, nurtured in a popular, oral, folk tradition, finds its roots in the countryside. García Márquez's justly famous "style" is not something artificial imposed upon a distant subject matter, but emerges—with its perfect blend of the colloquial and the cultivated, its ability to address both the most demanding jargon-weary academics as well as men and women who do not care much for literature, its success at home and abroad—from a need to communicate in a new way, attempting to bring together the antagonistic, mutually mistrustful, forms of elite and popular culture that have fractured Latin America so far. *One Hundred Years of Solitude* tries to work out in the space and language of a novel what the people of Latin America themselves have been unable to do thus far in history—combine the separate ways in which they know, in which they understand, in which they inscribe and read (or speak) their reality.

It is a task which has been prepared for by many generations of Latin American writers. This is not the place to examine how, since the beginning of our literature, the challenge from the discourse of excluded majorities in the hinterlands has determined an arduous search for a new language by writers. García Márquez's efforts would not be possible, or even conceivable, without those attempts, particularly in lyrical poetry from the end of the nineteenth century and narrative experiments after the Second World War. But just as important is that those excluded millions, having suffered silence and incessant marginalization, found ways of ferociously keeping their version alive, murmuring it onward to their communities and, beyond them, to children and grandchildren and the unborn. It is only recently that their stubborn dynamic creativity can be recognized by intellectuals and artists as the basis for an alternative cultural (and political) vision. This is as much due to a newfound irrepressible protagonism of those hitherto outcast classes and groups as to parallel developments in twentieth-century vanguard and modernist culture in Europe and the United States. These developments reject the rationalist perspective both in subject matter and in form, coming to see in mythic thinking, in the "primitive mentality" or its equivalent in the unconscious of each of us, the suppressed substratum from which a different story can be told.

When García Márquez narrates the story of the Buendía family from a mythical perspective he is situating his voice at the precise confluence of the popular and the cultivated traditions, satisfying both the cosmopolitan and the local, bringing together the experimentation learned in reading contemporary literature with the demand for a space where collective memory unregistered in books can express itself. This dual heritage of *One Hundred Years of Solitude* is best symbolized, and indeed culminates, in the last image of the book: the text that the final Buendía is reading is his own history, the personal and collective history already written by the gypsy Melquíades but also by every one of the men and women of his family—and simultaneously—the printed literate words in the artifact we are consuming, an artifact that has itself been fabricated, printed, distributed, bought. For an instant, the last instant, we are the Buendías—except that we as readers survive in order to change the way we live, to tell and live, one would hope, our existence in a different manner.

Essential to the structure, themes, and language of *One Hundred Years of Solitude* is the freedom to narrate from within the world of a family historically determined and condemned to extinction and failure, and yet at the same time to find a perspective outside that history so that the telling itself is not so determined or condemned, so the telling does not become entangled in the very forces that destroyed the chances of the Buendías to succeed and prosper.

This freedom explains, to begin with, the capacity of Macondo to be both a place which is tied to specific historical situations it cannot escape (no matter how hard its inhabitants try) and yet simultaneously a metaphor for other human realities. One can trace the evolution of Macondo quite clearly in Colombian history: founded at the beginning of the nineteenth century by José Arcadio Buendía, it is not allowed to live in embryonic isolation but is linked to the larger institutions in the nation when civil and ecclesiastical authorities arrive. It later suffers the sorrows of the prolonged civil wars between liberals and conservatives with one of its citizens, Colonel Aureliano Buendía, serving as commander-general of the revolutionary forces, who, after many battles and years have passed, finally signs a peace Treaty at Neerlandia. The period of prosperity which ensues does not last long. With the first railroad the North Americans arrive—and all too soon the banana company begins to squeeze the town dry. Its reign ends with the aforementioned massacre of the workers who have promoted a strike. This is followed by a torrential rain, the equally devastating drought, and the slow erosion of Macondo until a wind erases the town from the face of the earth. If Macondo's evolution parallels that of Colombia and, beyond it, that of Latin America, its beginning and its end are more metaphoric. The founding act apparently coincides with the start of the nation itself, just after the Wars of Independence, but it also subsumes and represents the previous discovery, conquest, colonization of the continent. José Arcadio, whose son fights the wars of the nineteenth century, is a Renaissance man of the sixteenth and seventeenth centuries, a dreamer of new horizons, fueled by the feverish desire for Eden and Utopia, the search for gold and the opening of new lands which characterized the expeditions of Columbus, Pizarro, Cortés, Pedro de Valdivia. As for the hurricane that sweeps Macondo away, one can sadly read in it the disappearance of these southern lands from the globe, their insignificance and irrelevance in the grand design of history. Perhaps it is a foreshadowing of an apocalypse that awaits our entire species, just as the original days of Macondo, when everything was so new that it hardly had a name, reminds us of the nostalgia every human seems to feel for some form of paradise.

Why does it have to end this way? Why is destruction the final destiny of the Buendías?

One answer is, of course, that the conclusion has already been written when García Márquez begins to tell the story, that he is looking back and seeing that these hundred years have led to disasters and loneliness instead of expansion and joy—in other words, he cannot invent a solution that people in history have not yet found by themselves. Melquíades (whoever he really is) has already written the story of the Buendías—they are trapped in a past that cannot ever be changed. And yet, when we open the novel, though the signs are everywhere, the terrible consummation does not seem that foregone. On the contrary, what has undoubtedly drawn readers to *One Hundred Years of Solitude* is its exuberant vitality, its sense that life was made for laughter and love, each generation renewing its pledge of innocence and youth as if the stagnation and futility awaiting their descendants were mere illusions.

When each new Buendía believes he or she can start anew, unburdened by the past, they are unconsciously imitating the founders of the dynasty, José Arcadio, his wife Úrsula, and their friends, who created Macondo as a place outside time and history and violence, a place with no cemetery. And when their lives end up twisted, crossed by repression and solitude, they are prefiguring the final fate of Macondo, which will be nothing other than a vast burial ground where everyone is finished, past, dead, where the only act allowed to the last Buendía will be to passively read his death in the mirror of the narrator's words.

Two dread events—they might almost be called structures—haunt the family in Macondo, one from the past and the other from the future. The first is a terror that may come to pass—and eventually does. It has been fore-told that if relatives such as José Arcadio and Úrsula marry, their offspring will be born with the tail of a pig. It is Úrsula's refusal to bed her husband which leads to the second terrible event: when his friend Prudencio Aguilar mocks him, José Arcadio's macho instinct, his sense of honor, his need to exercise his virility, explodes. He murders his friend and rapes his wife and then, when the ghost of Prudencio will not leave him alone, sets out to found a new village where sex does not lead to death. Though Macondo originates, therefore, in the twin sins of incest and fratricide, it will ultimately be un-able to avoid them. In each generation, war among brothers devastates and divides the land, and in each generation the Buendías stage approximations and dress rehearsals of incest, sons desiring mothers, a brother marrying his adopted sister, a woman beloved by her nephew first and then her great-nephew, multiple uncles madly in love with their irremediably beautiful niece. The violence will culminate in the great massacre, a Colombian army killing Colombian workers; the sex will culminate in a final violation, that of the last male Buendía, Aureliano, of the last woman Buendía, Amaranta Úrsula, and their child will be born with the tail of a pig and be devoured by the ants.

It is easy to proclaim that this inevitable fate is the consequence of out-side factors which define the Buendías. The fact that the story, even before José Arcadio and Úrsula set out, has been written—quite literally—for them, symbolizes the iron net that awaits them, the boundaries that hold them in. In order to flee from the incest, the endogenous isolation, they are impelled to open up to the external world; but each time they do so—and the novel is full of such escapades—what is brought back from those outer dominions invariably makes things worse. From the political and particularly the eco-nomic point of view, there are already powerful, technologically advanced empires out there that will thwart any effort at independence or self-suffi-ciency. These empires are a given of history: progress will come to Macondo, as in the rest of Latin America, in order to impoverish the people there, taking from them the control over their own existence. No wonder each expansion towards the vast territories beyond Macondo ends up in an almost fetal withdrawal and retreat, the mysterious return to the home as magnet and refuge, a womb which, familiar and repetitive, at least does not seem to pose a threat of extermination. The Buendías have arrived late—and there is nothing they can do about it.

This sense of doom, therefore, arises quite naturally from their depen-dent and secondary status in the world, living on its periphery, left outside modernity, and is expressed, at the literary level, in the feeling that these men and women are poor underdeveloped incarnations of faraway resonanc-es of biblical or Greek classic myths, pale imitations of archetypes created elsewhere. But to see their lives only as a feeble, useless attempt to avoid the encroachment of an external power—be it literary or be it socioeconomic—is to forget that they have come to us because autochthonous versions of those lives did manage to find their way into the future, that they are not merely degraded heirs to a Western literary tradition that is being applied to them from without. The corollary of this idea, its almost inevitable consequence, is that there must be internal factors that have led to that disastrous outcome, choices that the Buendías made or did not make. If these are inscribed in the way they organized their existence, in a history of their own embedded with reasons that did not allow them to break out of their solitude, those reasons and mistakes could be indeed understood by readers in the hope that they will not be repeated.

If incest will destroy the family, if the females attract their relatives with the kiss of death, if most of the Buendía women are associated in one way or another with self-destruction and doom, anticipating the final storm that their sexual relations with their male family members could engender, it is worth our while to examine the problems encountered by these men and women as they try to marry outside and bring in new blood. The Buendía men are constantly fascinated by women from "lower" classes and—though it is not spelled out—of another (black) race. But a permanent, public alliance with these women of the people, Pilar Ternera, Petra Cotes, Nigromanta, is unacceptable, as is the coupling of Meme with the mechanic Mauricio Babilonia. When a marriage is consummated, as with the hard-working, long-suffering Santa Sofía de la Piedad, the woman is totally ignored, treated as a servant. To have crossed and transgressed the invisible, almost unstated, frontiers of their class and race prejudices, indicates a possible direction that the family never allowed itself—made all the clearer by the fact that the one woman who does come from outside and is received with all solemnity is the glacial, repressive, and aristocratic Fernanda. What could signify better the way in which the Buendías are limited by the claustrophobic cultural barriers that they hardly see then the madness of forging an alliance with a faraway figure from the Spanish Inquisitional past rather than with the invigorating sensuous wise lovers carousing in the prodigious backyard?

Something similar could be said about the fratricide which takes over Macondo. The two Buendías who try to change circumstances significantly, who want to be the agents and actors of history instead of its objects, will fail miserably, though for diametrically opposite reasons. Colonel Aureliano Buendía illustrates the danger of recurring to violence, even in the noblest of causes. In a society where there is no democracy, where there is no popular participation, where the military are a law unto themselves, the irrevocable logic of power will isolate even the most decent human beings from reality. Struggling against injustice, the Colonel will end up embracing the violence he supposedly wants to stop, a captive of the macho mentality that decades ago led to the murder of Prudencio Aguilar and many decades later will lead to the murder of the three thousand workers that José Arcadio II witnesses. When they fail, both the Colonel and José Arcadio II retire from the world—a symptom of their initial loneliness, their incapacity to really be part of a movement of innumerable others, a collective where they could have found a meaning, a direction, a superior sense, to their lives. What they found in history is, ultimately, nothing more than a reflection of their basic solitude, their own image mirrored back at them.

The failure of Aureliano Buendía is particularly emblematic because he was the first human being born in Macondo—and as such his life will turn out to anticipate the village's future. And it is all the more heartbreaking because he had in him the possibility of dominating the unknown through other means than violence; born "with his eyes open," looking at everyone with "a curiosity lacking any note of surprise," he is able, through lacerating visions and lightening premonitions, to foretell the future—in other words, to step outside the grinding track of history and see a moment which will come to pass as if it had already happened.

This is an extraordinary faculty in a world that is, of and in itself, quite extraordinary. It is, of course, the most remarked upon feature of Macondo that its inhabitants live innocently immersed in the marvellous. Objects are often magically animated, animals proliferate beyond belief, people levitate, the seventeen sons of the Colonel converge on the village from the most distant corners of the land without prior agreement, not to mention the ghosts, prophetic dreams, fortune-telling cards, precognitions. For the Buendías this incessant presence is treated with matter-of-fact complacency: it is as much a part of their world as breathing, as yellow butterflies fluttering around a poor mechanic. What seems strange and impossible to the people of Macondo are the inventions that come in from abroad, the capacity to transform nature through the use of technology; whereas the readers, watching from the end of this supposedly rational and scientific century, taking those achievements for granted, are amazed at the wonders of everyday life in the remote premodern Colombian village.

This presence of the marvellous is—like the language of the novel itself—not an artificial addition or injection into reality—which is why I object so much to the term "magical realism." That term attempts to explain what happens in novels such as these as a merely literary strategy rather than a cultural experience that comes from the way people in Latin America cope with their existence. Things are marvellous in Macondo because along with living their hard, incontestable, fact-ridden intractability, the villagers are simultaneously living the instantaneous retelling of those events, their conversion into legends, that which will be ledgered—read, registered. The immediate exaggeration of what is happening to us forces those circumstances into memory, ensures that they will not be forgotten, that a "plague of insomnia" will not attack our descendants and allow them to sidestep the relationship between things and their names. People in mis-developed, twisted lands may not be able to dominate what really happens to them; but they can at least control the stories they tell about how they want what happened to them remembered. This does not quite make them masters of themselves. For that, they would have to go beyond mere flashes of clairvoyance, they would have to find a way of grasping permanently the knowledge which comes from seeing the entire sweep of their lives—a quality which only Melquíades, the narrator, and the last Buendía have attained, one at the beginning of the story, the other at its end. The final Aureliano achieves the totality the others—mad explorers of the possibility of omniscience—have been searching for during the whole novel. Catching glimpses of the future from time to time, that final Aureliano becomes the "spoken mirror" where reader and narrator are identical; what he enters is an absolute and useless freedom. On the other side of total knowledge is, of course, death, that point where everything is known because everything is already finished, a nothingness that contemplates what has been used up and can never happen again.

The last Buendía manages to do that which his forefathers (more than his foremothers) always desired: to go beyond a state of blind clairvoyance to a state of absolute cognitive dominion; but the price that must be paid is to die, to have all one's acts fixed and immutable and readable forever.

While they are alive, therefore, the characters have been able to com-municate with the future, with Melquíades's version, with their own version told by their distant descendants, with a complete image of themselves, by means of the imagination, that faculty which is not yet omniscience because it embraces only the possible and reveals only one of many unnamed futures. The narrator knows all, and certainly more than his characters; and he knows it from the realm of aesthetic intemporality. The Buendías have managed, once in a while, to leap over the barriers of time, to see themselves beyond their immediate circumstance, to turn the walls into transitory openings. They can live for a moment what has already happened in the future, but they cannot persist in that magical order, because it would mean becoming static and immobile. If they were only able to see themselves completely while they live, if they were only able to write *One Hundred Years of Solitude* during the hundred years that Colombians suffered those forms of solitude, they would be saved. If they could only know without having to die—without having to fatalistically live all the steps and mistakes that lead to final extinction.

That is what Colonel Aureliano Buendía should have been able to do, was in some way specially equipped to do. He squanders his "pacts with death"—that is, the capacity for seeing things as if they were already past, had already been told, and were finished—by imposing death in the thirty-two wars he participates in. He cannot stand the uncertainty of life and so, instead of exploring it with his imagination, he turns it into something certain and death-like. His answer to his loneliness is to expand his ego, until nothing exists except his desires, until reality itself disappears and becomes a prolongation of his power, anticipating the machos of García Márquez's later novels, the tyrant of *The Autumn of the Patriarch* and, in a bizarre way, the Bolívar of *The General in His Labyrinth*. As for the Colonel, the revenge that reality inflicts upon him is devastating, one of the most moving descriptions of the effects of tyranny to have been written: reality begins to anticipate what he wants, becomes independent, interprets, and carries out his thoughts "before he conceived them." He wanted to control history so much, to make it identical to his thoughts and inner world, that it has acceded to his request, although perversely stripping him of his freedom. There is no longer any clash between his personality and the world. He is made of ice, the very ice that so fascinated him at the dawn of the novel—dead in life instead of running like the Edenic springs and waters of early Macondo. When he realizes he is trapped in a remote mirror he has just enough energy left to put an end to the fratricidal struggle and withdraw. He has tried so hard to determine the future through violence that he has, in fact, lost it, lost the reason why people want to know the future, lost the humanity they should be serving.

That is why the death of this character, the one who was touched most deeply by the marvellous, by the possibility of foretelling the future, is the only one that is narrated indirectly and does not include even the slightest hint of magic. All the other members of his family die in a special way, each of them marked by a miracle, a fantasy of words and events which are woven around the body in order to eternalize it in a characteristic pose, fix it in the popular imagination with an unmistakable funeral identity. Each Buendía freezes in death a surprising summary of his or her life, a categorical essentialization that can thereafter reverberate imaginatively in the memory of others. One dies as one has lived, and in the very act of being extinguished, the people of Macondo try to prolong their being into the outer limits of who they really were. Thus, in order to draw José Arcadio, who is full of dreams and projects, toward death, he must be trapped by illusion, forced to dream his death, led to believe that the unreal room of death is the real room of life. And the supernatural participates in his burial, objectifying the idea that the founder of the dynasty deserves a snowfall of yellow flowers, a live prefiguration of the yellow scrolls that will tell the story ultimately. The gigantism of his son José Arcadio is expressed in the prodigious thread of blood that explodes from his body when he is killed and which goes off in search of mother Úrsula—who herself dies in such a prolonged and centenary way that it almost seems more like a resurrection than a disappearance. One could go on and on—Amaranta's announcement that she would carry letters to the next world, the ethereal flight of Remedios la Bella merging with nature, the twins dying at the same moment in separate rooms, and so on and so forth, all of them personifying in one last act the purified version of what they really were.

Colonel Aureliano Buendía's death is not narrated at all, but merely implied in absentia. If he tries to erase all signs that he passed through this world, it is because he has given up the hope of narrating himself at all; he considers it all futile. His frozen emptiness, his passive and involuntary death in life, his desire to be forgotten is the foreshadowing of the final destiny of the family, that cosmic frozen nothingness, without even the myth that could give a meaning to their destiny. Like the other military figures in the novel, he cannot see the immaculate purity of the room where Melquíades's manuscripts are lodged: he can only see the implacable ruin, the way that room will be when the hurricane blows into Macondo, the destruction that will descend upon Latin America precisely because the many Colonels severed their link with the imagination.

This may be the reason why the Colonel is the only existential character in the novel. All the others may be suffocated by some form of sadness, but they are tragic only inasmuch as they are part of a collective that is doomed. In the case of the Colonel, one feels that it is his own personality—which could have somehow chosen differently—that contains the naked seeds of ambivalence and tragedy, his involvement in an ethical dilemma that will fatally lead him to annihilation. The difference becomes visible if we contrast him with the other characters: his life never produces a smile; his errors are not laughable; and his solitude ends up being a terrifying and compassionate lesson.

Despite this difference, the Colonel shares with the other characters, as one would expect in a novel that is such an example of flowing unity, certain basic laws. Everyone in *One Hundred Years of Solitude* is endowed with a stubborn loyalty to his or her own inner self. Their actions are outlined sharply, unambiguously, unfolding in a uniform, constant, clear line. Their journey inward is brief and savage: they quickly discover in their inner limits a sense of who they are and spend the rest of their life expanding those traits. "Úrsula always tried to go farther"—words that could be applied to the steps all of them take, each more intense and more complete than the one before.

Adolescence is the critical moment, the period when sex—copulation that tends to be, although not always, brutal, fleeting, tangential—makes them confront another human being and, at the same time, reveals the impossibility of escaping from their impregnable egocentrism. Rather than lose themselves in the other, they will hasten to shape in the outer world the stubborn, definitive, absolute being they have glimpsed inside. The way to make that inner being visible to other eyes is to project it onto the world with decisive gestures and attitudes. And what is meant for those who surround and survive us, will eventually reach, of course, the narrator, will force their way into the text that we are reading. In a world which threatens to forget everything, where all traces will be erased, human beings exaggerate the power of their own extreme egos as a means of establishing some permanence, incorporating themselves into the secret structure of what is marvellous and also real at the same time. The basis for Melquíades's ability to tell their story is that they found a way to tell it obsessively. The irrevocable actions which they repeated as a way of possessing their potential unity also created a thread of echoes and cycles in their existence that makes it tangible and imaginable.

If this struggle against death gives the family its dignity, guarantees it a space in memory, it also seals the family's fate. Because it is precisely this enclosure in implacable activity, this refusal to see everyday reality in order to forge the epic adventure of a destiny apart from others, which assures the clan's destruction, their excess of self-suffocation, their lack of self-knowledge. They can unconsciously, through their actions and their words, narrate themselves but they cannot narrate others.

This conflict between the self and the surrounding world had already been developed in García Márquez's earlier works, where men, rotting alive in a hot, impoverished, fatigued reality, only can defy death and differentiate themselves from their environs by making some lonely, brave gesture. This happens principally to persons of the male sex—those who try to dream up some heroism in a degraded world. The male character, faced with a history that would subjugate or devour him, first takes refuge in the whimsical bubble of his personality but will later try to impose his very individual dream upon the overwhelming external reality. In that attempt, he may be destroyed, it is true; but he may also have succeeded in breathing a hint of fresh air, a sense that he will not let the lethargy around him win the battle. The Colonel, for instance, in *No One Writes to the Colonel*, seems pathetic in his blindness, his inability to measure what is real; but to the extent to which he manages to draw from that illusion the energy to overcome his demonically trivial waiting for a letter that never arrives, his figure may touch upon a certain majesty. That inner world, hidden from others, which can make him do ridiculous or foolish things, can also be the source of his pride in himself, the only basis for moral affirmation in a society that has betrayed him. Just like the characters in *One Hundred Years of Solitude*, he needs to find at least one gesture or word—which he pronounces, at the end of the novel—where his inner and external self will be reconciled, where he can be "pure, explicit, invincible." Something similar happens in *Leafstorm* and many of the stories by García Márquez: a final defiant gesture as the result of years of premeditated, but also unexpressed, rebellion. What was subjective, concealed, unable to reach others, finally becomes objective, proves itself in the social reality where it can be seen by all, where the intuition of what we were can be verified publicly. Their imagination has always secretly murmured to them what they should do. The challenge for them is to go beyond conjecture and anticipation, to mold their pre-visions of themselves into inspired and inspiring actions.

These characters do not, nevertheless, reach a mythic state. Their lives are too inconclusive. As readers, we are not given the knowledge of what, finally, happens to them. Volkening has drawn attention to the fragmentary condition of this early world of García Márquez: the story ends at the moment before the victory or the defeat of the characters, when they are about to combat the established norms of society, when they confront the supreme test of their own reality. But for a myth to be born, it is necessary that the figures not be subject to doubt and inadequacy, that they be well-rounded, perfect, memorable—as they are in *One Hundred Years of Solitude*.

In these earlier works the imagination exists only in each human being, sucked out from an enclosed interior life in order to confront adversity, but it still does not have a parallel world at its disposal, the existence of the marvellous text of Melquíades's that accompanies the Buendías, the sign that there is indeed some collective narration that, if we could only gain access to it (read it and live it at the same time), would give us an intimation of a totality.

Before that vision of *One Hundred Years of Solitude* could be fully expressed, García Márquez needed, in the novel *In Evil Hour*, to explore the possibility that a collective could, in fact, establish a parallel sphere of the imagination where words could take on a mysterious semiautonomy. In a town dominated by fear and corrupted by political oppression, where church and government, mayor and priest, insist on affirming that no problems exist, everybody has retreated into the intimate life of their own. But just as the mayor's jaw begins to rot from a dead tooth, and the town's atmosphere is polluted by the smell of a dead cow decomposing beneath the river, posters filled with words will begin to appear on the walls, belying and undermining the false official peace and truth. In these anonymous sheets of paper the private life of each citizen is commented upon, what they gossip about or dare not declare are revealed in the full light of day. These words emanate from the entire town and from no one in the particular: they are the sublimation of its strangled political energy, the collective folklore that each one would like to objectify and cannot. The posters confront the private world of each one with the objective world of the others. These clandestine thoughts go, therefore, beyond the individual acts of the colonels and characters in the earlier works. Those words will end up being more real than the paper on which they are printed or the wall upon which they are nailed. This annihilation of the official truth through linguistic subversion anticipates *One Hundred Years of Solitude*.

This excursus may have helped us to realize that incest and fratricide are structures that shut the Buendías—the Colombians, the Latin Americans—off from the imaginary that is their real heritage, the text that they have been writing but cannot read. Incest which shuts the men inside the boundaries of their own women-mothers-daughters, unable to love anyone else; fratricide which is the way in which men finally end up contacting other men, under the guise of death and violence. Blessed though they may be with creativity, vitality, exuberance, tenderness, humor, none of it will manage to save them from ultimate destruction.

Why not?

Because the Buendía men are unable to grow up—which means to learn from their experience, to assume responsibility for the world as they found it. Like children, their imagination can run rampant but cannot be applied to the community, can give them a glimmer of themselves but cannot serve as a way to contact the others with whom they must build the story of their lives. The incest shuts them in and the violence excludes by killing the objective look from the other, from outside—and so they find themselves caught in a never-ending, ever-repeating cycle, generation after generation, unable to decipher the manuscripts of their own lives, to write reality as they live it.

One Hundred Years of Solitude situates itself in the impossible middle between what is inside and outside, between life and death, between history and imagination. This means that the reader, ultimately, gets to choose. He or she can stay inside the text, like the last Aureliano for whom it is already too late. He must die as the closing act of a tale of love and extinction because his whole contradictory reality, like Remedios la Bella herself, "stagnated in a magnificent adolescence." Or the reader can leap outside that ambiguous relationship with death and, deciphering the repression, reading its causes and its loneliness, manage to take the fiction back into reality, make it historical, try to make sure that the next hundred years will not end in the same way.

The second path is not meant to turn away from the past but to surpass it by looking it in the face. If the readers—as well as the author and his characters—are urged to take this path, it does not require an epic commitment on their part but rather the need to relive the sources of their present circumstances.

García Márquez has, in fact, provided a model for how this might possibly be accomplished in the everyday existence of us all in another of his masterpieces, *Chronicle of a Death Foretold*. If it took at least a century to create the conditions for *One Hundred Years of Solitude* to exist, *Chronicle*, which I interpret as its complement, is the product of a more modest thirty-year period. A symbolic return perhaps to that smaller, less grandiose, dimension of Isabel merely watching the rain go down during a week in Macondo instead of the long years of deluge.

Early one morning in 1951 one of García Márquez's best friends, Cayetano Gentile, was hacked to death by two men in front of his house in Sucre. They were the brothers of a woman married the day before who, having been returned by the bridegroom on their wedding night because she was not a virgin, had falsely named Gentile as her secret lover. The brothers had washed their family's honor with his blood.

Behind the superficial sensationalism of the crime, the sort that drip from the pages of yellow journalism the world over, the Colombian novelist sensed a deeper drama, where the forces of history and myth that have incessantly obsessed him were apparently again at work. How could such savagery erupt, almost unpredictably, in the midst of a peaceful celebration? Where had it come from? And how was it possible that the whole town, which knew that the crime was about to happen, had been unable to prevent it? In a sense, the question he was asking was similar to the one central to all his previous work: Is Latin America doomed to this sort of everyday civil war on its streets and in its bedrooms, does violence narrate us over and over again, whether in our relations with one another or with our rulers?

As if he were one of his own characters, so near to the events and their overwhelming madness, García Márquez could not find right away the form, or the formula if you will, for answering those questions—which is like saying that it took him many years to figure out how a place so familiar could abruptly be transformed into Hell. And at the same time he had to discover how to turn the facts into a fiction that would reveal the concealed and more profound structure of truth.

We have seen that *One Hundred Years of Solitude* depends, for its narrative, on the author's acting as a channel for the oral tradition that is the foundation of that world, presenting without any gnawing doubts the version of people who have re-elaborated their experience, who assume themselves to be the final authority, believing that history and legend are one, and that memory and fact are inseparable. In order to construct the *Chronicle* García Márquez had to, for the first time, submit that popular oral tradition to a test, questioning his own voice. The narrator himself—a journalist—will appear before us researching the event, attempting its reconstruction, from the dozens of fragmented and contradictory accounts, where time, place, weather, and motives shift and lose their anchorage. By blending journalism, so dependent on immediate evidence, with the imaginary, which expands freely according to its own creative laws, the Colombian writer grounds the incredible murder in everyday detail.

As I have argued insistently in these pages, these two forms of communication are not incompatible and, in Latin America in fact, would seem to be almost inevitably symbiotic. I remember the almost childlike joy of García Márquez when he told me—he had just completed the manuscript and we were spending a week together as members of a literary jury in Mexico in 1980—that the coroner's autopsy of the real victim's wounds confirmed his imagined version. "The only [wound] he had in the back, at the level of the third lumbar vertebra, had perforated the right kidney," García Márquez said. That synthesis of what can be seen and what can be envisioned seemed to be proving his *Chronicles* to be a prolongation of the original *Crónicas de Indias*—those wild, eyewitness testimonios with which the first conquistadors recounted the real—and simultaneously fabulous— story of the New World.

In this case, García Márquez invented a narrator who acts as a newspaper reporter would, interrogating during twenty-seven years everyone connected with the crime, trying to make sense out of the chaos in the witnesses' throats, trying to pinpoint how each person who could have avoided that death ended up contributing to it. Those spectators, however, are not allowed to take over the proceedings. Their testimony is rigidly organized within a time frame that lasts exactly one hour and a half. The first sentence tells of the awakening of Santiago Nasar (the name given to Gentile) at 5:30 in the morning of the day he is to die; the book closes, a scant 120 pages later, at 7 o'clock, when he collapses and breathes no more.

Till the very end, we have certainty that the murder could have been prevented. The two killers did everything to force someone to stop them. They bragged of their intentions in the hope that they would be dissuaded or jailed. In fact, they waited in front of the one door that their victim was sure not to approach the whole day. But that day, Nasar disrupted his habitual itinerary and went through that door. And his mother, on the other side, was putting up the bar to shut it, believing that he had already entered the house. This confusion is typical of all the events that accumulate like foul rising water and slowly drown Nasar.

It is as if all the people in town were doors that might lead to life and instead lead to death. Those who rushed after the victim to warn him were unable to find him. Those who could have warned him did not do so for a variety of reasons. We watch the community do the wrong thing and then we watch the swamp of their justifications, their excuses, their pretexts.

The readers, confronted by the double clockwork of the novel—the wizardry of the author and the chain of coincidences and blunders whereby the right doors were being closed while the wrong ones were being opened—

could end up bedazzled, succumbing to the illusion that what we are submerged in is the working out of a destiny that no man can control.

And yet I would suggest that this is not what the novel is really telling us. It is, on the contrary, a political parable that hints at the ways in which the cyclical wheels of copulation and violence that have determined Latin American history up till now can, in fact, be escaped.

When I first reviewed the novel in English (in *The Philadelphia Inquirer*), while praising Gregory Rabassa's precise and hallucinatory translation, I disagreed with its title. Rather than "foretold," which admittedly does sound better, but that smacks of a fatal, delphic, solemn irrefutability, the original *anunciada* (announced) would more reliably indicate that the *Crónica* (the story as it materialized in *chronos*, time) was on everybody's mind, near everybody's tongue, but never was uttered to save the victim.

If Santiago Nasar is doomed, it is not because his life is a circle that an oracle has pronounced complete, finished. He will die because of the sum total of rituals, habits, misconceptions, and prejudices that crisscross and corrupt society like shadows. As García Márquez has pointed out in an interview, most people back in 1951 did not intervene because they felt that this was a social rite—the taking back of honor spilled, the death of the violator—with which they agreed.

The concatenation of misunderstandings and hesitations that spun Nasar's death are only apparently expressions of a culture that needs, expects and creates that death, and that stands by passively while it is enacted. The real cause of the murder is the unproclaimed law of war between men, of machismo. Nasar is foretold only by his own code. Though he is innocent of having despoiled the bride, he is guilty of sharing the same preconceptions that his murderers will use to justify their act.

It is a network of minds that has set the trap for the victim. The closed blind alley minds, marooned in their solitude and unable to imagine a different interpretation of what they see and should do, sentence Nasar to his extinction and themselves to their guilt.

Just one door opening, just one person standing up and shouting what had been announced in murmurs by all, would have been enough to turn tragedy into peace. *Chronicle* is the story, as is *One Hundred Years of Solitude*, of a collective failure and it is, at the same time, a challenge to create a collective difference, a story that asks us to open the doors behind which we hide.

If we dare, we may just have the time—and it is García Márquez himself who said so in his Nobel prize acceptance speech—to give the races condemned to one hundred years of solitude a second opportunity on this earth.

It is a matter of discovering the real story inside each falsehood we have been told.

In this sense, one might almost accuse the prodigious García Márquez of not exaggerating enough.

Two hundred wagons, after all, hardly seem sufficient to transport the bodies of all the workers who have been murdered in Latin America—and in the world—to the funeral humanity is preparing for them in the future that must be written by us right now in order to exist.

MICHAEL BELL

The Cervantean Turn:
One Hundred Years of Solitude

W hile seeking to make a living in the Mexican film industry, Márquez suddenly found himself creatively possessed by the theme which he had been contemplating since his earliest days as a writer. His old idea for a novel called *La Casa* (*The House*) now developed into the historical and family saga *One Hundred Years of Solitude*. The sub-textual concerns of his early fiction go some way to explaining this sudden inspiration.

The novel gives a synoptic account of Colombian and more generally Latin American historical experience through the story of the Buendía family. The original couple, José Arcadio Buendía and his cousin Úrsula Iguarán, delay the consummation of their marriage because of her fear of incest. When their neighbour, Prudencio Aguilar, imprudently remarks on this situation, José Arcadio kills him and the couple go off with a group of young neighbours to found the town of Macondo. Following an initial 'arcadian' period of seclusion from historical experience under the governorship of their young founder, the people of Macondo suffer an increasing decadence and are obliged to participate in the archetypal events and disillusions of Latin American history from colonial to neo-colonial times.

The opening complex of violence and incest, an emotional frustration arising from the deep-seated emotional solipsism of the Buendías, continues to work out its consequences. Only at the very end, as the town is being

From *Gabriel García Márquez: Solitude and Solidarity*, pp. 40–69, 149–151. © 1993 by Michael Bell.

destroyed by a great wind, one of several biblical plagues in the narrative, does the last of the Buendías realise that the whole cycle of the town's rise and fall has been foretold in the parchments of the Gipsy, Melquíades.

The revelation of Melquíades' prophetic chronicle raises, or focuses, the crucial questions of interpretation. It reaffirms, what has been evident throughout, that the novel has achieved its synoptic range by a departure from historical realism for the more symbolic mode that has come to be known as 'magical realism'. This makes it difficult to judge how far the whole experience is to be understood as an historical analysis or through the apparent determinism of Melquíades' foretelling. Like the Buendías themselves, the novel is hermetically closed in on itself albeit in a self-conscious and crafted way. Within the world of the novel, further enclosed by the dead-pan humour of the narrative voice, all the basic elements of violence, sexuality, incest and solitude are highly ambivalent. It has proved hard to distinguish tragedy and farce, critique and affection, idealism and illusion in the overall impact of the Buendías' story. To some extent, Márquez' mode of magical realism is a Latin American equivalent of the North American tall tale. We are never quite sure how seriously to take it.

The book has already been the subject of many excellent close readings, most of which attempt to give it a specific interpretation. I think it is most helpful now to stand back and see it more contextually within Márquez' *oeuvre* and in relation to other works of modern fiction. In this larger context it becomes clearer why it is a work, like Kafka's novels, specifically designed both to invite and to resist interpretation.

Critics writing while still relatively close to the publication of *Hundred Years* found it natural to stress the partly unconscious teleology by which this work grew from the earlier fiction. But with the retrospect of several later and substantial novels of a different kind it is apparent that *Hundred Years* is at once deeply representative and highly untypical. It indeed grew out of the earlier fiction, and provided an important groundwork for the later fiction, but its representativeness is intimately bound up with its *un*typicality; on its having indeed grown *out* of the *oeuvre*. In some ways it is even a reaction against it.

It is important to stress this since the enormous popularity of *Hundred Years* has strongly governed the image of Márquez' fiction at large. That in turn may partly explain his own slightly deprecating attitude towards the novel and his stated preference for other works such as *No One Writes* and *Chronicle of a Death Foretold*. Furthermore, *Hundred Years* is fatally imitable, or rather gives a fatally misleading impression of being so. The mode known as 'magical realism' has aroused, along with its immense popularity, a reaction against what some see as its too-easy recipe book of devices.

This response has been memorably encapsulated by the uptight narrator, and Flaubert fan, of Julian Barnes' *Flaubert's Parrot*, and there seems some danger of Edward Braithwaite's words providing a label to be hung permanently around Márquez' neck:

> Ah, the propinquity of cheap life and expensive principles, of religion and banditry, of surprising honour and random cruelty. Ah, the daiquiri bird which incubates its eggs on the wing; ah, the fredonna tree whose roots grow at the tips of its branches, and whose fibres assist the hunchback to impregnate by telepathy the haughty wife of the hacienda owner; ah, the opera house now overgrown by jungle. Permit me to rap on the table and murmur 'Pass!'[1]

This response is not necessarily Barnes' own, and even his narrator is not strictly thinking of highly original works such as *Hundred Years* so much as the subsequent literary fashion. But it undoubtedly expresses a common response which Barnes has usefully identified with the Flaubertian spirit. That is a theme to develop in connection with Márquez' later fiction. In the immediate context of *Hundred Years*, it is worth noting first that this response points to a real danger for Márquez. He has wisely avoided repeating the mode of *Hundred Years* which might well have led to a sterile self-imitation. But more importantly, he only needed to do it once. It represents a necessary moment in his creative evolution.

To appreciate the force of this point, it is useful first to look more closely at the features which have attracted, for better or worse, the term 'magical realism'. It is not the meaning of the term in itself that matters here but the underlying questions it implies. In other words, I want to look not so much *at* the term as *behind* it. Two critics especially, writing in the early 1970s, have brought out the gradual development of the imaginative mode of *Hundred Years* throughout the earlier works.

Robert Sims has concentrated on the various devices, such as Faulknerian flashbacks, by which the experience of time is spatialised and compacted.[2] This provides the narrative structure through which mythic repetition, the constant re-enactment of past experience in the present, can be dramatically 'present'ed. But Sims's careful study of technique is perhaps too ready to assume that any such spatialisation of time is to be associated with the mythic time sense. Such structures can also express forms of emotional obsession and fixation for which myth is a misleading term and this distinction is very relevant to Márquez. In the event, Márquez' use of such narrative structures continues in his later works without their necessarily invoking the mythic configurations of *Hundred Years* and nor do they always have such a significance even in this novel. Some of these questions will be taken up later, but the issue of the special fictional world is put more radically by the second critic.

In Mario Vargas Llosa's *Gabriel García Márquez historia de un deicidio* there is a similar assumption that *Hundred Years* is the viewpoint from which to see Márquez' *oeuvre*.[3] This excellent reading of Márquez by the Peruvian novelist who was at that time also a friend exemplifies the way Latin American authors have frequently been the best commentators on their fellow writers. Yet the study is also partly taken over by its leading idea: that all writers of fiction, and pre-eminently so in Márquez' case, seek to oust God by creating their own substitute worlds. Accordingly, Vargas Llosa traces the gradual foregrounding in the early fiction of what he calls 'lo real sujetivo' (subjective reality) until by the time of the short story 'Big Mama's Funeral' the whole narrative gets to be subsumed into the subjective. From having elements of fantasy within a naturalistic narrative we move to a narrative form in which the very distinction begins to be elided.

This account is very fair but the central phrase 'subjective reality', like its sister expression 'magical realism', constantly lends itself to a sentimental blankness; if not in Vargas Llosa's own hands then as soon as it leaves them. Above all, the very phrase implicitly acquiesces in the Cartesian dualism which Márquez' literary form is seeking to challenge. It is worth pausing on this philosophical question underlying the literary form.

I. Insomnia Precedes Amnesia

The Cuban novelist Alejo Carpentier, who lived in Paris from 1928 to 1939, consciously adapted the Parisian anti-rationalist movement of surrealism to express a specifically Latin American experience. In a famous essay, he argued that whereas surrealism in Europe was a partial and oppositional movement, it was actually the most appropriate form in which to express Latin American landscape and historical experience.[4] This claim is fraught with problems but it undoubtedly points to an important creative intuition for many Latin American writers. In part, the problem was that surrealism as an art movement was less weighty than some of its underlying principles or insights. Jacques Gilard has remarked how surrealism, in being conceived so much as a movement of cultural opposition, was effectively part of the Cartesian rationalist order to which it was notionally opposed.[5] Some kinds of opposition are really a way of supporting the given order.

The truer influence of surrealism for Latin American writers lay in their assimilation of these underlying insights in such a way as to transform realism rather than oppose it. It is a happy accident that the 'sur' of surrealism in French should mean 'above' while the Spanish 'sur' means south. For the highly conceptual, self-conscious European movement became in Latin

America a downward exploration of a psychic frontier as in Borges' favourite story 'El Sur' (The South).[6] Borges' story is a dream within a dream and answers to one of the stronger moments in Andre Breton's surrealist manifesto in which he speaks of the importance of dream experience psychologically and therefore artistically.[7] So too, Márquez' narrative play with conflicting orders of truth and wisdom creates a subtle disturbance which does not discard our modern rationalist culture nor claim access to a superior one. Instead, it gestures forcefully to important limitations and to their largely unwitting consequences. His synoptic invocation of several centuries of modern history suggests the inclusive nature of his critique of the emotional consequences of the Cartesian split of mind and body, or self and world. The critique is not original but, given the emotional and subliminal nature of the problem, it needs constantly to be mounted in fresh ways.

Márquez's special achievement was to find a comic, popular and local mode for this serious critical purpose. His art is to do it imaginatively rather than analytically and as an aspect of a more external historical theme. Márquez' novel conflates into the story of several generations a much longer period of historical experience extending back to a founding myth. The effect is to suggest the continued impact of historical and pre-historical experience in the psyche of the present. Within this compacted psychic structure of *Hundred Years*, the shift from the 'Arcadian' pre-historical era into historical time is figured by the first of the 'biblical' plagues, the memory sickness, which leads in turn to the need to start creating an historical record. The comically Adamic overtones whereby the people of Macondo now have to point at everyday objects since they have forgotten the names of things, leads us to associate the beginning of their history with a re-enactment of the original fall of man. Like some major philosophers, Márquez interprets the mythic Fall from Eden as the cultural fall into dualism; or more precisely the twin dualisms of self versus world and mind versus body. For what has not been sufficiently remarked in the Buendías' shift from Arcadia to history is the fact that the memory loss arises from lack of sleep. They lose the capacity for a recuperative rest from consciousness. In other words, insomnia precedes amnesia and, properly understood, this constitutes a challenge to the well-known philosophical adage of Márquez' own Parisian days, which were the existentialist 1950s rather than the surrealist 1920s, namely the Sartrean formula that 'existence precedes essence'.

Appropriately, the memory sickness, like the pox, is a result of conquest. In the compacted symbolic history of the novel, the disease is rightly caught from the Indian servants since the destruction of someone else's cultural memory usually involves the guilty repression of your own. But the Indians' very form of memory may also have been different from that of their conquerors in being more obviously related to the world of sleep and dream.

When the people of Macondo are first told they have the insomnia plague they are more pleased than appalled since they now expect to have more time for their daily activities. But the loss of the apparently useless hours of sleep eventually impairs their capacity to perform even the most necessary functions of everyday life. The daytime self is unwittingly dependent on the night-time self, not just as a period of rest but as an opening to a different order of time and meaning through which the daytime activity itself ultimately needs to be understood.

In other words, the relation of memory and sleep in the double disease suggests that there may be different kinds of memory. There is a rough analogy here with the distinction Proust drew in the personal realm between conscious intentional memory, which is often fallacious, and the unwitting emotional memory that is triggered by chance events and which wells up as a fresh emotional experience in the present. Indeed, the narrator's way of expressing Fernanda's failure to find her wedding ring, has in itself a Proustian ring: '. . . sin saber que la búsqueda de las cosas perdidas está entorpecida por los hábitos rutinarios . . .'[8] / '. . . not knowing that the search for lost things is hindered by habitual routines . . .'[9]

In the collective domain, this conscious intentional memory may be akin to the professional activity of historians, while affective memory is more like what Walter Benjamin had in mind when he said: 'To articulate the past historically does not mean to recognize it "the way it really was" (Ranke). It means to seize hold of memory as it flashes up at a moment of danger'.[10] Benjamin was thinking here of history not as an academic discipline but as an immediate living resource and one which is not, in its deepest sources, under conscious control. In this respect the distinction fleshes out Nietzsche's insistence that, for healthy and effective action, it is as important to forget as to remember, and forgetting, even more than memory, must be an effect of time rather than will.[11] To put the point in more homely terms, it is commonly recognised that difficult experiences have, as we say, to be 'slept on' for their longer-term impact to be absorbed and thus to be converted into meaning. This cannot be purely a function of the conscious will.

Borges' story of 'Funes the Memorious', which he himself described as a 'gigantic metaphor for insomnia', is an illuminating inverse of the insomnia and memory sickness.[12] Funes is endowed with a total responsiveness to experience and a complete recall of his past. But this causes insomnia and actually incapacitates him for action and even for thinking. The story is, among other things, an ironic reflection on the arbitrariness of realism and it is appropriate that the narrator's own 'inadequate' memory creates an essentially dream figure in Funes for it is indeed only as an 'unrealistic' dream of Borges himself that Funes can exist for us. The story is, therefore, not only a satire on realism but also the implicit vindication of a different mode of fiction. Something comparable can be seen in *Hundred Years*.

It is significant that during the memory sickness, before the people recover their capacity to function, at least apparently, in the world of daily consciousness, the underlying obsessions of the major characters are overtly dominant. José Arcadio thinks remorsefully of Prudencio Aguilar; Aureliano makes a precious object in his workshop, and Rebeca dreams of her parents. All the characters find themselves, at this time, 'todo el día soñando despiertos' (p. 120) / 'in a waking dream all day' (p. 44). They believe they have been rescued from this state when Melquíades' potion restores their daytime memory. But in truth they have now lost their capacity properly to inhabit both worlds so that the dream world of their suppressed obsessions henceforth imposes itself on their daytime lives. And Melquíades, who like the great epic heroes has himself visited the world of the dead, now retires to chronicle the working out of the Buendías' unconscious destiny in a language they cannot understand.

In the subsequent story of the Buendías it becomes evident that they have lost their proper access to this other realm of sleep; a realm which is commonly expressed, within the terms of daytime consciousness, through magical and dream images. But the fundamental narrative trick of the book, as fundamental as Alonso Quijano's imagining himself as the fictional character, Don Quixote, is that Márquez goes on to tell their story at the level of the Buendías' repressed selves. The inseparability of the two realms is embodied in the narrative mode as the magical dimension of the narrative enacts the structures of which they are not aware. As will be seen in more detail, the narrative adopts a humorous convention of treating the characters' emotions as physical elements and events in the world, so that they, and we, actually see the magical events and elements, but their awareness is more that of sleep-walkers. Their actions in the daytime world are governed by deep structures within which their conscious world, and our narrative world, remain enclosed.

Several times a character is actually described as being 'like a sleep-walker'. This has usually a Quixotic and partly comic implication although it is pathetic in the eventual case of Meme, who wishes to break out of the emotional enclosure of the Buendías and is shocked into a state of sleepwalking trauma, the extreme form of fixated dream, by Fernanda. The implication is that the dream self needs expression and, if its unconscious working is in sleep, its more conscious arena is the imagination. The relation of dream and fiction is unwittingly recognised by the townsfolk as they seek to recover the world of dream by telling themselves the circular story of the capon. Unfortunately, they see this in a simply utilitarian light as a means of exhaustion and miss the deeper instinct which suggests that a story may indeed be the royal road to the realm of the unconscious. Fiction deals importantly with reality but through the dream as well as the daytime self. For Márquez, no less than Borges, a fiction which merely imitates the daily world is itself an empty, and potentially damaging, illusion.

It is useful to see the magical dimension of the story in this way as it helps avoid the more sentimental and dualistic readings to which the narrative has proved susceptible and distinguishes the aspect of psychic projection in the characters from the expressive significance of the narrative mode itself. For magic is ultimately, and most importantly, the chosen mode of the author, Márquez. That is to say, a participation in the Buendías' condition becomes the narrative technique of the book.

This double function creates much of the ambivalence of the narrative. For if the method has a critical implication for the characters, what are we to make of the author's own use of magical projection? The crucial point here is that Márquez' own encompassing insights into the unconscious realm occur under the sign of fiction. Nietzsche, who classically presented the modern anti-dualist critique of Western culture, had some relevant remarks on the artistic use of 'miracles':

> Whoever wishes to test rigorously to what extent he himself is related to the true aesthetic listener or belongs to the community of the Socratic-critical persons needs only to examine sincerely the feeling with which he accepts miracles represented on the stage: whether he feels his historical sense, which insists on strict psychological causality, insulted by them, whether he makes a benevolent concession and admits the miracle as a phenomenon intelligible to childhood but alien to him, or whether he experiences anything else. For in this way he will be able to determine to what extent he is capable of understanding *myth* as a concentrated image of the world that, as a condensation of phenomena, cannot dispense with miracles. It is probable, however, that almost everyone, upon close examination, finds that the critical-historical spirit of our culture has so affected him that he can only make the former existence of myth credible to himself by means of scholarship, through intermediary abstractions.[13]

The reader is not called upon literally to believe in miracles but to respond to them, within the fiction, with a proper aesthetic sympathy. Indeed, for Nietzsche they are an indispensable way of defining that proper sympathy. His remarks catch the humorously disarming, yet challenging, implication of the miraculous in Márquez. For Márquez too has a way of significantly dividing his readers.

On each side of this aesthetic sympathy for *Hundred Years* there lie the two complementary responses which, in their different ways, flatten the effect. One commonly expressed, apparently approving, reaction, which arises in a slightly vulgarised way from Alejo Carpentier, is that Latin American 'reality' is itself magical. This rather collapses the literary effect created with such care by a work such as *Hundred Years* and it should be said that many Latin Americans, such as Angel Rama, would in any case wish to distance themselves from the note of literary tourism this response implies.[14] The opposite response is the rationalist which, like Julian Barnes' narrator, finds merely hokum in the magical elements. What is really at stake is a psychological suppleness which is able to inhabit unsentimentally the daytime world while remaining open to the promptings of those domains which modern culture has, by its own inner logic, necessarily marginalised or repressed.

The effective meaning of this is caught in a conversation between Márquez and his old friend Plineo Apuleyo Mendoza.[15] When asked directly, Márquez admits to being superstitious and gives instances of his premonitions of future events. However, as he goes on to discuss the particular case of the military coup in Caracas where he had felt the imminence of some important event while out walking with Mendoza, his subsequent explanation is far from superstitious. He suggests that he may have heard military aircraft in the night in some half-waking, unremembered interval between sleep. What he is really talking about is a holistic responsiveness whereby his consciousness is open to such promptings. Such a capacity to foretell events is, of course, highly developed in Colonel Aureliano Buendía in his younger years.

Within our culture the language of superstition may well be the only language available for speaking of this; or it may be the most appropriate language in so far as it asserts a conscious countercurrent to the main drift of the culture. It resists the experience being rationalised away. And it is worth remarking in passing, with reference to *Hundred Years* and the insomnia sickness, that Márquez sees his moment of responsiveness as having occurred while half asleep. For the important point is that this capacity does not suggest an either/or choice between rationalism and irrationalism. The daytime world is not an alternative to, nor separable from, this more rounded response. So too, in the same conversation, Márquez acknowledges that the critic Ernesto Volkening was right to detect in him a general view of women as being more whole than men.[16] But he expresses regret that Volkening, by saying so, has made this attitude self-conscious. Márquez does not want everything dragged into the light of daytime consciousness where its meaning and function in the whole economy of the psyche will be changed.

That is why the narrative formula 'insomnia precedes amnesia' constitutes a challenge to the philosophical formula 'existence precedes essence'.

Sartrean existentialism privileged the critical function of consciousness and denied the value, and even the existence, of the unconscious domain. Márquez, by contrast, affirms the crucial importance of the unconscious and avoids the dualistic choice. His narrative mode embodies the difficult necessity of relating them without allowing either to dominate.

An important part of Márquez' achievement in *Hundred Years* was to communicate all this with an appropriate, and popularly accessible, implicitness by simply having the reader share the characters' experience. Márquez does not drag experience into inappropriate consciousness in his narrative any more than in his personal life. Furthermore, the magical dimension of his own tale is able to bring out the condition of the Buendías while placing the narrative itself on a human footing with them. He himself has remarked that critics have generally missed his affection for, and solidarity with, his characters. This may be partly because the authorial relationship is not directly embodied in a personalised narrative voice but arises more intrinsically from the nature of the narrative mode. That is to say, even while seeing how his characters are caught within their own dreamlike obsessions, he himself recuperates the realm of dream and magic in telling their story. Hence although the recuperation is of little comfort to them, they after all do not escape or have 'una segunda oportunidad sobre la tierra' (p. 493) / 'a second opportunity on the earth' (p. 336), his story nonetheless salvages a meaning from their experience. Furthermore, their peculiar form of psychic somnambulism gives them an heroic function as the necessary vehicles of our recognitions. In *The Birth of Tragedy*, from which the remarks on miracles were quoted, Nietzsche also comments that incest and killing, the two central taboos in *Hundred Years*, as in *Oedipus*, are associated with the acquiring of prophetic wisdom.[17] In its very different, deliberately unheroic, manner, the humorous narration of *Hundred Years* expresses both the underlying human relationship with the characters and the insight achieved through their delusions and excesses.

This implicit psychic penetration also arises from the way the book's serious historical material is presented through a consciously linguistic lens. Brian McHale has pointed out how its narrative language constantly equivocates between the literal and the metaphorical so that actual incidents seem to be spawned by metaphor.[18] McHale cites, among others, the case of Amaranta Úrsula who returns from Europe to Macondo 'llevando al esposo amarrado por el cuello con un cordel de seda' (p. 450) / 'leading her husband by a silk cord tied round his neck' (p. 305). At first, we respond to this as a common metaphorical idea. But later it emerges that the cord is quite literal. This stylistic trick is more than a trick in that it foregrounds the deep-lying metaphors in common speech. George Lakoff and M. Johnson, in *Metaphors We Live By*, have traced some of the largely unwitting clusters of metaphor through which psychological and emotional experience in particular are commonly expressed.[19]

On this view, metaphor is a kind of linguistic unconscious. Although we normally read through it transparently, this buried structure of metaphor does, in some unaccountable measure, shape our world. Márquez changes the focus of his narrative language so as to enlarge and literalise this metaphorical order. He brings the linguistic unconscious to the surface in a way that is disarmingly humorous as well as rendering it both strange and familiar. It is a comic equivalent of Freud's 'uncanny'. In this respect, the old Negro 'cuya cabeza algodonada le daba el aspecto de un negativo de fotografía' (p. 457) / 'whose cottony head gave him the appearance of a photographic negative' (p. 311) is an image of the whole narrative medium. It is a constant reversal by which the elements of external reality become shadowy while psychological structures become concretised. So, for example, Remedios' emotional unavailability and airiness become a literal floating from the world. Or the dead remain visible presences as long as they persist in the emotional memories of the living.

In this way, the book recognises a subliminal domain in human personality while, just like the earlier fiction, avoiding introspection and bypassing a Freudian conception of the unconscious. The concentration on the linguistic plane has further consequences. If deep-lying metaphors structure our common world this means they are dead metaphors, or clichés, which means in turn that they are completely shared, and to call Márquez' narrative mode 'subjective' or 'magical' risks losing much of the point. Language in particular resists the distinction of inner and outer, of subjective and objective. It is a human construction but necessarily a communal, not a private, one. Wittgenstein remarked that men may disagree in their opinions but have to agree in the language they use.[20] The very fact of language embodies a fundamental human solidarity constantly obscured by the level of conflicting opinion or interest.

On a similar principle, Stanley Cavell has very relevantly pointed out how the treatment of slaves was at once an explicit denial of their humanity and an implicit assumption of it.[21] Understanding language in this way has therefore a potentially political, as well as an anti-Cartesian, implication. If language constructs the world, then how is this being done, by whom, and whose world is it anyway? These questions, too, Márquez addresses implicitly within his own play with language.

II. Whose World?

I have already suggested that Márquez' narrative mode is an evident, if necessarily elusive, challenge to the rationalism most notably embodied in French culture. It is elusive in that we can more easily see the critique than we can define the positive alternative. This posture underlies a comparable elusiveness with respect to cultural norms more generally. Márquez, like other Latin American writers, saw Paris as the effective cultural capital of the old continent and Jacques Gilard has commented on Márquez' peculiarly balanced and confident attitude to European high culture even when he first went to Paris.[22] Neither awed nor rejecting, he had from the outset a strong sense of the value of who he was and where he came from.

Part of the force of *Hundred Years* is that it addresses the question of provincialism and centrality which had been a constant, if often implicit, preoccupation of his journalism. Metropolitan centres enable a special concentration and rapid transmission of thought but such places also have their dangers. Anyone in the world who troubles to read and think the best that is generally available is not likely in any damaging sense to be provincial and may well have a built in sense of the relativity of cultural horizons. By the same token, it is frequently the conscious inhabitant of the accepted cultural centre who is open to the most insidious and damaging provincialism: the complacent incapacity to imagine anything beyond that horizon. In his journalistic progress from the small coastal town of Barranquilla, through the Colombian capital Bogotá, on to Paris and finally to the Latin American regional purview of *Prensa Latina*, Márquez was constantly riding the multiple ironies of this question. His recognition that he should tell this story in a narrative voice approximating that of his small-town grandmother, who told of marvels as everyday events, suggests the creative breakthrough effected by his appreciation of the 'provincial' viewpoint. It is no accident that the creative significance of his grandmother's voice should have come to him after his culturally mobile career in journalism.

Although I have suggested that a principal value of Márquez' journalism was to save him from putting it into his fiction, this was also to affirm their common roots. His journalism always required a constant adjustment of scale between local and world interests. It was even more evidently part of his function as foreign correspondent to explain external events locally and local events externally. This constant dilation and contraction of the reporter's eye, which is foregrounded in the journalism, underlies the fiction as an implicit sense of scale. Once again, *Hundred Years* is unusual in bringing the question to the thematic surface.

In the journalism, this pervasive awareness is focused in Márquez' repeated use of the word 'world', particularly in the formulaic phrase 'the most . . . in the world'. The phrase is especially revealing because his repeated use of it seems in some measure unconscious, like a verbal tic. The very phrase embodies a constant adjustment of vision and tone, as between humorous appreciation of the provincial and serious awareness of a global or universal scale.

As part of his frequent play with cliché and popular expression, he speaks at one point of Ava Gardner, quoting her publicity notices in ironic quotation marks, as 'the most beautiful animal in the world'.[23] The irony here is directed not at the film star but at the expression itself and at his own adoption of it. The common phrase 'most beautiful girl in the world' is as senseless as it is tasteless when taken literally. Yet it is perfectly comprehensible as an item of popular emotional rhetoric and, of course, it is precisely in its literal absurdity that we recognise its metaphorical truth of feeling. In Márquez, such a use of the formula is always in humorous tension with a spectrum of different uses. The other end of the spectrum can be seen in a remark from a film review: 'The Italians are the second greatest consumers of film in the world'.[24] As a weekly reviewer of films from around the world, and as a journalist commenting on geopolitical events for a specific local readership, Márquez makes a perfectly literal reference to a global criterion.

As the same formulaic phrase constantly modifies from the most subjective rhetoric to soberly statistical statement, it puts the two extremes in a constant ironic conjunction. It is a verbal epitome of his constant adjustment of scales. The local and the global, along with the rhetorical and the literal, are, of course, the axes on which the humorous and political viewpoint of *Hundred Years* is built. Márquez' verbal tic reflects the interpenetration of the local and the universal. Any fully human 'world' must surely be both and this may be an important clue to the immense popularity of *Hundred Years* around the world.

Hundred Years tells a highly local story through a universal biblical myth of origins and foundation. Much of the book's charm lies in the interplay of the two aspects. And much of its ambiguous meaning too. Towards the end, the young aspirant writer, Gabriel, escapes the doomed and enclosed world of Macondo to go to Paris. The big interpretative crux of the book is the question of how far its meaning is enclosed in the local text, the foretold history, written in Sanskrit by Melquíades, or is rather to be found in Márquez' Spanish narrative which, through the medium of further translations, passes beyond this local consciousness to a world audience. And, of course, the capacity to foretell the local future was itself a function of Melquíades' universal wisdom put down in a language belonging to a remote history and coming from the other side of the world. As always in *Hundred Years*, each term dissolves into its opposite.

The larger significance of this question can be seen by comparing Márquez' combination of local history and universal myth with some other mythopoeic historical narratives from earlier in the century. In the time of Joyce, Lawrence, Mann, Yeats and Proust the competing nationalisms and imperialisms of Europe came to a point of catastrophic conflict in the Great War. Although all of these writers were strongly imbued with, and sometimes celebrated, the characteristics of their own national cultures, they shared a fundamental critique of nationalism. They also lived in an era when several key formative systems of thought had apparently revealed universal characteristics in human 'nature' and culture. In the inner domain of the psyche, the Freudian revolution stressed the common structures of the unconscious; an implication to be followed even more strongly by Jung. Likewise, the late nineteenth-century anthropology of Frazer and others seemed to have revealed common patterns in the early stages of all human culture. Hence in turning to myth for their narrative structures these authors were, among other things, appealing to universal values transcending national cultures. It is important to remember this critical and liberating impulse in the mythopoeia of the modernist generation *vis-à-vis* European nationalism since, with the passing of their historical moment, their works have frequently acquired, or been accorded, a different meaning. We are now in a position, partly because of the radical achievement of the modernist generation, to see their works as residually Eurocentric in a way that traduces their original spirit and their historical impact.

Since then, new modes of psychological and anthropological thinking have undercut the universalist premises of such mythopoeia. Furthermore, the Fascist co-option of myth as part of its political rhetoric proved largely successful in tainting the very term despite the attempts of Thomas Mann and others to retain it as a humanist value. Hence in the latter half of the century literary use of myth has been predominantly quizzical and deconstructive, or when it is used positively it is only after being carefully bracketed with a sceptical consciousness. The truth value of myth, in other words, is now generally understood to be at best highly relative. Márquez is of this later generation and illuminates the point of tension between the earlier modernist universalism and a later spirit: deconstructive, relativistic and localised. I say a point of tension since Márquez does not merely debunk the universal either. Myths of a universal humanity constantly irradiate his local tale.

Octavio Paz caught something of the same transitional moment in his own way. In using the theme of solitude to define the peculiar historical experience, and resultant psychological configurations, of Latin America, Paz risked indulging the consolatory sentimentalism, that 'charm of the pathetic', which Borges detected in such theories of specialness.[25] But Paz reversed the terms to suggest that the Mexican, in his very peculiarity, had become the potential, or indeed the inevitable, focus of universal interests.

> The old plurality of cultures, postulating various and contrary ideals, and offering various and contrary views of the future, has been replaced by a single civilization and a single future. Until recently,

history was a meditation on the many truths proposed by many cultures, and a verification of the radical heterogeneity of every society and archetype. Now history has recovered its unity and become what it was at the beginning: a meditation on mankind. And mankind too has recovered its unity.... The decisions we make in Mexico now affect all men, and vice versa.... Each man's fate is that of man himself. Therefore, every attempt we make as Mexicans to resolve our conflicts must have universal validity or it will be futile from the outset.[26]

Hundred Years is a striking instance of Paz' general point which it implicitly thematises. For the book constantly superimposes the private world of the Buendías' somnambulistic solipsism, the archetypal structures of myth, and the geopolitical world of modern history which we glimpse through this narrative prism.

Yet Paz' words, written in the middle of the century perhaps, assume too readily the effacement of local culture and consciousness; and such an effacement was often an ideological commitment of politically progressive thinking. The latter decades of the century have revealed cultural and local differences to be more deeply rooted than had often been supposed, or than political institutions had generally allowed for; except, of course, for right-ist regimes which have deliberately exploited the resulting political vacuum. The importance of writers like Márquez, Carlos Fuentes, Salman Rushdie or Mikhail Bulgakov is to send a complexly regionalised consciousness around the world which political institutions may sooner or later have to learn to reflect. It may be that truly living together on the planet will be a matter not of tolerating, but of celebrating, difference. This is not to be achieved by international touristic culture industries such as Fuentes' has satirised as 'pepsicoatl?'.[27] It may rather be reflected in quite different views of what it means to be human as one looks from the vantage point of a different re-gional history.

It is significant that Márquez grasps all this not at the level of institu-tions and politics but of sensibility, and especially of popular sensibility. The cosmopolitan tendency within all societies is inevitable and to some extent desirable. But many do not wish to leave home either physically or mentally and it may well be that the proper relation between local popular conscious-ness and an educated cosmopolitan consciousness is more like that of con-sciousness and unconsciousness, or waking and sleeping, as figured in the insomnia sickness. Both aspects are necessary although it would be hard to say analytically how they co-exist. Márquez' adoption of his grandmother's voice, and his assimilation of so many local or family experiences in *Hundred Years*, is the enactment of such a combined consciousness. The dangerous nostalgias of the Buendías are differently echoed in the benign nostalgia of the writer, who is able to draw genuine sustenance from this local world precisely because he is no longer simply of it. *Hundred Years* has been generally recognised as expressing the Colombian historical experience assimilated to a regional one. It is the quintessential Latin American history. The apparent naturalness with which it achieves this arises from Márquez' readiness to think simultaneously on these different scales with each acting as an implicit critical check on the other.

These remarks suggest that the popular, as well as the regional, note of *Hundred Years* is an important part of its meaning. Another significant political shift in later twentieth-century fiction, along with the reaction against Eurocentrism, is a rejection of the perceived cultural exclusiveness of modernism. This shift of attitude can be seen crudely and symptomatically in the common use of 'élitism' as a term of would-be abuse. In the period of Joyce, much serious literary expression became technically recondite, and removed from the popular, in a way that had not seemed necessary for George Eliot or Dickens. T. S. Eliot made this point explicitly.[28] Yet the ideological intention of modernist writing was frequently to celebrate the popular. So Joyce, for example, placed the ordinary figure of Bloom at the centre, in evaluative as well as narrative terms, of *Ulysses*. This gap between technique and aspiration often produces a nostalgia at the heart of such works; a nostalgia that surfaces at moments such as the 'pleasant whining of the mandolin' in *The Waste Land*.[29] Certainly, later writers can escape this by slumming, or cocking a snook at high culture, but genuinely to encompass serious expression within a popular form remains a remarkable achievement. When successful, it is a politically pregnant act in itself.

In finding a relationship between the popular and the sophisticated, Márquez modifies both of them although, once again, it is hard to say exactly how. It is worth remembering that Borges saw the falseness of a writer's conscious relation to his tradition as lying not in the fact but in the self-consciousness. A national tradition is either an 'inescapable act of fate' or 'a mere affectation'.[30] The relationship of the sophisticated and the popular, just like that between the local and the universal, properly eludes definition.

III. History, Fiction and Myth

Elusiveness is indeed the hallmark of this book. When one attempts to grasp it as history, fiction or myth it proves to be structured like a Moebius strip, in which each interpretative surface modulates constantly into its opposite. Most fundamentally, we are obliged to distinguish, but can never separate, Melquíades' foretold narrative from the retrospective one of Márquez' novel. In fiction, historical consciousness is always crucially modified by the literary structure in which it is embodied, but Márquez gives us competing structures for the same story. Yet this is not, as sometimes in Cortázar for example, just for the sake of the metafictional trick itself. The trick in Márquez is load bearing. The force of this for *Hundred Years* can be seen through a brief comparison with several classic works of twentieth-century fiction which individually parallel some of the most important of this novel's interpretative surfaces.

Joyce's *Ulysses*, although pregnant with historical consciousness, used a spatialised mythic structure. His post-symbolist aesthetic enabled him to create a viewpoint transcending immediate historical questions. The stance of the book is comparable to what Nietzsche called the 'superhistorical'.[31] This modernist possibility, classically embodied in Joyce, had a decisive impact on subsequent fiction but does not by any means represent the only modern possibility. Other writers sought to stay within the form of historical realism although often with difficulty as if this form was increasingly unable to contain their whole vision. Such writers, pushing at the limits of historical realism from the inside, are the most illuminating with respect to Márquez. In particular, *Hundred Years* can be flanked by Conrad's *Nostromo* (1904) on the one hand and Lawrence's *The Rainbow* (1915) on the other.

In *Nostromo*, Conrad shows the inevitable corruption of political idealism by the 'material interests' on which it depends. He sets his tale in an imaginary Latin American country suffering the impact of neocolonial capitalism. He narrates it through a method of flashback which disorients the linear 'progress' of the story and enforces a sense of inevitability as the outcome is known in advance. By contrast, Lawrence, as a younger contemporary of Conrad, saw him as too ready to acquiesce in the deterministic analysis of contemporary history which had been partly enshrined in the literary form of naturalism. Hence, in *The Rainbow*, which was his own first, fully mature attempt to treat synoptically modern social history, Lawrence challenged this enclosure of sensibility as much as the economic and social vision *per se*.

Our fundamental mode of vision, as implying a radical way of existing in the world, was the true crux of the problem for Lawrence. And so, from within the broad mode of realism, Lawrence sought to push back its frontiers. Hence, in *The Rainbow*, he tells the story of several modern generations of an unusual, but representative, family within whose collective life-span a much longer process of history is compressed. It is compressed most essentially within their individual and collective psyches but it is also expressed in an ultimate myth of origin based on a transformation of the Genesis story. It even has a central female character called Úrsula, who embodies the family's positive traits, and in whose name Lawrence recognised a pagan goddess beneath the medieval cult of virginity.[32]

We may usefully think of Conrad and Lawrence as reflecting respectively the 'Melquíades' and the 'Márquez' narratives of *Hundred Years*. Conrad's vision was perhaps too darkly enclosed within its own pessimistic logic while Lawrence's, as he himself came to see, was perhaps too optimistic. The point of invoking them is to see how cunningly, and equivocally, Márquez has interrelated two similar possibilities. The fatalistic historical vision of the chronicle is mediated through a further narrative level, the novel itself, whose humorous tone and mysteriously external provenance constantly belie enclosure within the terms of Melquíades' prophecy.

Both Conrad and Lawrence sought to stay within a broad conception of historical realism. But Márquez' more obvious foregrounding of the fictional form lends significance to the way Lawrence, even by the time of *The Rainbow*, was already straining quite consciously to transcend the terms of realism. At one point he says of his Úrsula:

> It pleased her to know, that in the East one must use hyperbole, or else remain unheard, because the Eastern man must see a thing swelling to fill all heaven, or dwindled to a mere nothing, before he is suitably impressed. She immediately sympathized with this Eastern mind.[33]

Lawrence's emphasis here falls not on hyperbole itself, but on Úrsula's sympathy for it. So, too, his own narrative does not use hyperbole as a figure of speech but rather creates a hyperbolic dimension within the narrative.[34] Márquez' 'magical realism' is likewise, in its own way, a creation of narrative hyperbole. The hyperbole, that is to say, cannot be isolated as an effect of style because it constitutes the substance of the action. The very events are hyperbolic. For Márquez is also attempting not so much to describe a known world as to expand and enrich the sensibility in which any such 'world' is perceived. It is important to both writers that their fiction not be isolable as mere fantasy. Nor should it, of course, be read too literalistically.

It is also relevant that the radical nature of Lawrence's cultural critique, combined with the frustrations of his reception including the banning of *The Rainbow*, placed an increasing strain on his use of the novel form. He went round the world and eventually gravitated to Latin America to find the place that most embodied his 'world'. In his Mexican novel, *The Plumed Serpent* (1926), realist form broke down completely beneath the strain of his political and psychic speculations.[35] Lawrence's encounter with Mexico, like Carpentier's co-option of surrealism, suggests at once the importance of a Latin American or Third World dimension and a radical dissatisfaction within European culture and consciousness. What is at stake, in other words, is not a special Latin American 'reality' but the value of the Third World standpoint in seeing the limitations of a dominant modern mode of sensibility to be found in the world at large.

Márquez seems to have responded both to the naturalistic determinism which I have exemplified in Conrad and to the mythopoeic recourse most notably seen in Lawrence. And in the figure of Melquíades, in his timeless seclusion, we may also see a hint of the aestheticist transcendence typified by Joyce. Yet none of these fictional modes, with their corresponding orders of interpretation, seems definitively to control the meaning of the book. Just as we can now see much late nineteenth-century naturalist fiction to have had an emotional fatalism mixed up in it, so Márquez seems to view all grandly summative attitudes with suspicion. Yet he does not dismiss them either. He rather keeps all these possibilities in mutual, and humorous, suspension. But what is remarkable is that it never feels like a mere fictional game in the mode of Cortázar or Borges. Neither the humour nor the fictional self-reference diminish its condensed historical impact. Rather than undermining each other as mere cleverness, the different possibilities throw each other into relief. It may be that, even apart from Márquez' evident reflection on the history of the region, his capacity to ride the shifting possibilities comes also from one of the deepest of his literary historical tap-roots: Cervantes.

IV. The Cervantean Turn

Hundred Years is an overtly Cervantean book in its fundamental device of the fictitious foreign historian. But the Cervantean parallel has a deeper significance with implications for his *oeuvre* at large. I have suggested that *Hundred Years* is Márquez' most substantial and representative work and yet is also, in important ways, untypical. In this respect, *Hundred Years* stands in the same relation to Márquez' *oeuvre* as *Don Quixote* does to Cervantes' and for essentially similar reasons. If Cervantes had died immediately after completing the second part of *Don Quixote* (1615), or if Márquez had died after *Hundred Years*, their respective *oeuvres* would not just be shorter, they would have, or would appear to have, a significantly different meaning.

Cervantes lived at a cultural and literary crossroads. He inherited several distinct modes of fiction which he was able to practise individually with equal skill. He began his career with the pastoral romance *La Galatea* (1585) and died while still working on the comparably idealistic *Persiles and Sigismunda* (1616). Yet over the middle years of his career he wrote a variety of tales, many of them sharply realistic, which are included in the *Exemplary Novels* (1613). It is not surprising, therefore, to find throughout his career a concern for the possible truth values of fiction. The incommensurate modes of fiction in which he thought and wrote brought this concern to the foreground with a pressing urgency. He could see the incipient anachronism and limitation of the romance form to which he was nonetheless most seriously committed. And he could also see the complementary limitation of a cynical, earthbound realism such as he would have found in Mateo Aleman's immensely popular *Guzmán de Alfarache* (1602). The composition of *Don Quixote*, like that of *Hundred Years*, seems to have crept up on the author almost unawares in mid-career and to have expanded into his unexpected *summa* as he found a fictional arena in which his various fictional modes could interact and test each other. To some extent, *Don Quixote*, like *Hundred Years*, was conceived as a kind of sport and has disarmingly preserved something of that character while actually providing the unique arena in which the author has been able to air a complex of questions implicit in his *oeuvre* at large. And yet even after writing the second part of *Don Quixote*, Cervantes worked on *Persiles* as his intended masterpiece. Although he saw the popularity, and obviously understood the complexity, of his own achievement, even he was hardly in a position to appreciate its full historical significance. This significance, after all, is partly the story of the novel form itself and the Latin American writers of Márquez' generation constitute one more chapter in its unfolding.

Although Márquez came at the end rather than the beginning of the realist tradition, he was faced with a comparable tension between modes of fiction. He also felt under pressure, as has been seen, to satisfy political demands running counter, but not simply counter, to his own fundamental instincts and convictions about the nature of fiction. Hence, like Cervantes, he found himself in mid-career writing a book in which the underlying, off-stage tensions of his *oeuvre* at large had themselves become the thematic centre and the very action of the work. It is not surprising that both authors felt themselves taken over by these central works. One can also see why neither Cervantes nor Márquez felt the need to do it twice and why they might have been inclined in some measure to underestimate the relative achievement. For the work is in each case the tip of an iceberg; it is an impressive eminence sustained by a lifetime's implicit meditation on its themes.

The superimposition of disparate world views as embodied in different fictional genres is the technique that Márquez in his own day shares with Cervantes in his. Their common theme, the projection of psychic obsessions on to the world, provided a sudden transformative significance for the very medium of their fiction. The relation of fiction to life had been the constant, pressing concern behind all of Márquez' previous fiction. When this underlying concern finally found expression as a necessary and explicit part of what he had previously thought of as the historical family saga of *La Casa*, it evidently came as a sudden, transformative charge of creative energy. This central question, so banal when addressed in the abstract, became the most powerful and encompassing theme when it was suddenly instantiated in a concrete and appropriate occasion. That seems to have happened to both

Cervantes and Márquez in mid-career and to have produced in each case a work that is the more profoundly representative in its very atypicality.

So too Márquez, like Cervantes, uses the errors of his characters as a way of teaching us how to read the novel. Or more precisely, perhaps, how *not* to read it, for any positive model seems elusive of definition and is only to be approached through the correction of error. In particular, both authors play, time and again, on the fallacy of literalistic reading. I have said that the curious trick of *Hundred Years* is that its characters live out their obsessions in the real world and allow us to do so with them. In literalising metaphor within his fiction, Márquez is reversing the literalism of the Buendías in their actual lives. With Don Quixote, the problem strictly lies not so much in the unreality or anachronism of the models he tries to follow as in the literalism with which he understands them. Likewise, at the beginning of *Hundred Years*, the alchemical sage Melquíades offers an idealistic source of wisdom comparable to the novels of chivalry in Cervantes. The error lies in the literalism with which these essentially symbolic forms of wisdom are assimilated by José Arcadio and Don Quixote. Alchemy betokens a search for perfection which came to be vulgarly understood as the attempt to produce gold from base metal and was then in turn superseded by chemistry in the modern scientific world view. In a sense, the traducing of alchemy to a utilitarian end could be seen not just as the decline of one tradition but as already the beginning of the new in so far as modern scientific reason can no longer claim the ancient association of knowledge with wisdom.

Márquez conflates all three levels in his opening chapter. He contrasts José Arcadio's absurdly literalistic response to Melquíades' knowledge and places both conceptions within a humorous narrative consciousness of the scientific world view shared by the modern author and reader. This establishes the essential mode of the book. For the modern world view is humorously, but not really, displaced. We merely glimpse, comically and obliquely, what for us has to be an incomprehensible association of knowledge, wisdom and power. As in Yeats' poem 'Leda and the Swan' this conjunction falls outside of historical time and experience. José Arcadio's utilitarian and literalistic response is only a parodically extreme version of our own culture in this respect.[36] The alchemical allusions thus provide an oblique comment on the inadequacy of our own cultural terms without in themselves needing to be a matter of literal 'belief' any more than Nietzsche thought miracles must be.

The original gypsies, who seem still in touch with some tradition of esoteric knowledge and power, are soon replaced by a band of pure tricksters and the folk memory of this ambivalent tradition persists in Macondo as part of the book's running commentary on its own mode of meaning. The daguerreotype, photograph and film are successive modern techniques of imitation in which a lifelike image can be produced mechanically without artistic skill or significance. Hence when the people of Macondo encounter Bruno Crespi's cinema they see it as another trick of the gypsies and reject it as 'una máquina de ilusión' / 'an illusion machine' (p. 300) whereby 'nadie podía saber a ciencia cierta dónde estaban los límites de la realidad' (p. 301) / 'nobody could know for sure where were the limits of reality' (p. 186). They cannot accept that their tears for the death of a personage one week can be followed by the same 'person' returning in different dress a week later. Behind their comically inappropriate response there lies a further irony reminiscent of the episode in which Don Quixote breaks up Master Pedro's puppet show.[37] For the inappropriate literalism of these responses actually reflects an empty and mechanical illusionism in both the film and the puppet show. At a deeper level the response *is* appropriate. By contrast, the source of true wisdom in *Hundred Years* is either Melquíades' chronicle, which requires dedication to decipher, or else Márquez' own magical and involuted fiction, which is a puzzle to read.

Neither Cervantes nor Márquez seem to propose answers so much as an education in living with a complex consciousness. Of course, what pass for 'answers' in this domain are often emptily abstract substitutes for understanding. Thus in the fundamental structure of both books the device of the fictitious historian presents us with an irresolvable logical conundrum; as irresolvable as the alogical relation of art to life on which it encourages us to meditate. But the open-endedness of the structure reacts in a constantly fresh way with its specific content. Above all, this Cervantean structure of concentrated meditation is brought to bear upon Márquez' sense of a modern and a regional history.

The different historical moments of Cervantes and Márquez are reflected in their different uses of the fictitious historian device. Cervantes was writing at a time when the modern senses of history and fiction were still hardly differentiated within their common nexus of moral exemplum such as we may still see in Shakespeare's history plays. Accordingly, he exploits the idea of history to affirm the independent 'truth' of fiction. Márquez, on the other hand, writes fiction to assert an historical memory which had already proved vulnerable to the forces of history itself. The book contains two important complexes of historical reference, each of which qualifies the other. The massacre of the strikers is a real historical event preserved in the memory of Márquez' fiction even as that fiction traces its suppression in official historical memory. The other important body of direct historical reference is the literary group, including 'Gabriel' and the Catalan sage, who befriend the last Aureliano. These provide a growing point which extends beyond both Melquíades' chronicle and Márquez' text. Where Cervantes in his day used the idea of history to justify fiction, Márquez in his time uses fiction to preserve an essential history.

At the same time, Márquez' fiction is a defence against the cruder demands of history. His formative years were still those in which writers of a politically progressive stance felt the pressure to be politically 'committed', in Sartre's rather narrow and literalistic sense. Over the course of the 1960s and after, the period in which vulgar Marxism was superseded by the new left, a more subtle pressure has been put, not just on writing, but also on the perceived significance of literature at large. This is the view espoused most notably in Fredric Jameson's *The Political Unconscious*, whereby all fiction, and all experience, is ultimately political, although often unconsciously so.[38] On this account, it is then the function of critical readers to bring the political unconscious of the fiction to the surface. Jameson, I would say, is taking an important, but familiar, truth and expanding it into a populist falsehood. It is true that all experience, and therefore all fiction, is political. It does not follow, however, that politics provides the ultimate horizon of significance for all human life and actions. There are complex questions here, of course, which is why one can always play to the gallery with fashionable half-truths. Márquez' use of the fictitious historian, the solitary and enigmatic sage, Melquíades, is an emblematic affirmation of the opposite truth. Although everything is indeed political, politics cannot instruct us on the purposes and values of human life. Márquez is far from being anti-political but he resists the half truths which often have to underlie political action, and affirms the importance of self-knowledge, the contact with the dream self, which remains a *sine qua non* of individual and collective life.

Whether or not he was responding to this general pressure that Jameson has more recently embodied, Márquez uses his Cervantean structure to hold the radical question constantly before our eyes: the distinction and yet inseparability of fictive and historical 'truth'. The great early modern writers such as Joyce, Lawrence and Thomas Mann assimilated history and fiction into a Nietzschean understanding of myth. For them, the human horizon is necessarily a cultural construction but one within which human beings can nonetheless only live if they have an enabling faith. Healthy life and action require an existential trust in the world. Hence the high modernist mythopoeia expressed, in its fundamental structure and metaphysic, a consciously constructed world within which the characters nonetheless behaved with an intuitive acceptance of their reality.[39] This is the serious recognition underlying the modernist use of 'simple' figures such as Leopold Bloom and Hans Castorp.

But in many ways this self-conscious mythopoeia enabled a traditional humanist conception to continue on a new metaphysical basis, much as ancient buildings are given a new modern structure from the inside while preserving their character and façade. As this mythopoeic inheritance passed to Márquez' generation, however, and to non-European writers, there was an increasing suspicion of its recuperative and potentially mystifying posture. Márquez' own imagination, after all, seems to have been fired by the bottomless scepticism of Kafka rather than the high modernist syntheses of Joyce or Mann. Yet in his own way he also wishes to effect a positive synthesis. Literature may well be 'el mejor juguete que se había inventado para burlarse de la gente' (p. 462) / ' the best plaything ever invented for making fools of people' (p. 314) but it is also a supreme, and uniquely holistic, form of understanding. Hence in Márquez' synthetic structure the different elements of fiction and history are visible even as they are inseparably interwoven. The threads remain distinct while the cloth is whole.

Márquez' Cervantean structure is crucial to this multiple meaning. It keeps these threads separate; it enforces their unresolvable relation at any abstract or general level; and it nonetheless communicates a positive vision of their combined meaning. Literature can communicate its understanding of life because it is not life. Cervantes justified a literature of entertainment with the apparently modest remark that 'the bow cannot always be bent'. But if one ponders his image one recognises that a bow which *was* always bent would actually lose its spring. The relaxation is integral to its proper functioning. One might say something comparable of the human psyche while, of course, allowing for its being a much more complex affair. In the human case, for example, it might be desirable to distinguish different forms of relaxation.

V. Solitude and Solidarity

All this helps to explain why *Hundred Years* is, in several senses, a hermetic book. It invokes the secret lore of alchemy to suggest an ideal association of knowledge and power with wisdom. But just as this can only be glimpsed in a form incomprehensible to our culture, so the book is hermetically sealed in on itself at the level of its narrative logic. At the same time, the effects of fiction are not fully contained by logic. As in Primo Levi's *The Periodic Table* (1975), we see fiction to be a kind of alchemy whereby experience is turned into meaning. By enclosing his historical material within an overt and jokey fiction, Márquez has actually made that history available to understanding, and particularly to emotional understanding, in a new way and in a form which is at once popular and subliminal.

At one level, he presents a synoptic vision of regional history in the light of deep emotional structures. All readers sense its fatalistic momentum. Yet the fatalism is of the characters as much as in the 'external' events. Fatalism rather than fate is their problem. In this sense we stand outside it and can see the whole hundred-year cycle as a process that is now hermetically sealed into an historical, comic, bitter and nostalgic story. The whole action is being consigned to the past. Where Joyce's autobiographical Stephen Dedalus wished to 'awake' from the 'nightmare' of history, Márquez shows Gabriel actually escaping from the somnambulism of the Buendías.[40]

Virtually all commentators have remarked on Cervantes' ambivalence towards the chivalric romances which he was ostensibly satirising in *Don Quixote*. As Borges notes, it was his nostalgia *for* these tales which actually powered his narrative.[41] Profiting from Cervantes' example, Márquez has built a similar ambivalence into his tale more consciously and thematically. The nostalgia which is the besetting sin of the Buendías is the powerful, but critically self-conscious, emotion of the narrative; the Buendías being, of course, the vehicles both of the nostalgia and of its critique. When Márquez' Nobel prize acceptance speech reversed the ending of *Hundred Years* to affirm that 'the lineal generations of one hundred years of solitude will have at last and forever a second chance on the earth' he was only making explicit the reversibility of terms which constantly characterises the overall structure and the individual themes of *Hundred Years*.[42] Just as Cervantes saw that the cautionary *tale* of the *im*pertinent curiosity was most appropriately listened to out of curiosity, so the nostalgic psychology of the Buendías will be best understood through a nostalgic narrative.[43] What gives the jokey formal circularity of *Hundred Years* its deeper life is its appropriateness to this complex structure of feeling. The jokiness partly disguises the deeper feeling while more subliminally focusing it.

This is also why the apparently conflicting readings of *Hundred Years* have arisen at the more consciously interpretative level as people have tried to make intellectually tidy sense of it or have used it to support their own preferred emphases. But, more subliminally and intuitively, readers seem constantly to respond to the deeper and more complex emotional experience of the book. Gramsci spoke of the pessimism of the intellect needing to be counteracted by optimism of the will. By mediating the pessimistic narrative of Melquíades through the Cervantean humour of his own novel, Márquez suggests something beyond Gramsci's politically conceived alternatives.

What this 'something' might actually be, as defined in the abstract, remains hard to say, but the thrust of the book is to suggest that it should indeed remain elusive. Márquez seems to embody this recognition in the figure of Melquíades. In the double enclosure of the inner room and the incomprehensible parchments, Melquíades focuses the ambivalence of the narrative structure and of the central term 'solitude'. For solitude seems not an entirely bad thing for Márquez; as indeed we might perhaps expect in a culture where the writer's own sister is called Soledad. Melquíades' chronicling of the story, and the subsequent deciphering of it, both depend on a willed seclusion. Writing is a homeopathic form of solitude which serves an ultimate purpose of solidarity. On this reading, the imaginary or vicarious nature of fiction has a positive purpose. Just as Cervantes' 'idle reader' learns of the disastrous effects of reading upon an idle man, so the nostalgia of the Buendías is nostalgically narrated.

And the same applies to solitude, the central motif of Márquez' *oeuvre*. Artistic self-consciousness and the solitude theme are combined in Melquíades. He seems perhaps partly a trickster yet also a reminder of the lonely God of *In Evil Hour*. Whereas the divine Creator was necessarily lonely, Melquíades as a human being adopts his solitude for a creative purpose. On the one hand, he is the image of the writer as one whose meaning is incomprehensible until the reader has actually lived the experience. For there is no short-cut to wisdom through literature. But for anyone who wishes to take the trouble there are patterns and shapings to experience which literature can help us to understand. Most importantly, there are inner and emotional shapings which may be therapeutically re-enacted in the controlled seduction of fiction. That is why the reader needs to be in some measure seduced as well as aesthetically detached. To come to such fiction with a prior, ideological conviction of meaning, which the work can then only instantiate or otherwise, is likely to rob it of its proper working. It is an extraordinary achievement on Márquez' part to have combined this meditation on the enigma of literary meaning with such a weight of historical experience.

Melquíades embodies the deliberately enigmatic structure of the narrative by which it actively frustrates interpretative closure. Márquez' long-standing ambivalence about overtly 'political' writing, and his consequent meditation on the paradoxical relations of art and life, have resulted not just in a formal play with the fictitious historian but in an especially acute awareness of the necessary solitude which, if you can get it right, is really a profound form of solidarity.

Notes

1. *Flaubert's Parrot* (London: Cape, 1984).

2. *The Evolution of Myth in Gabriel García Márquez* (Miami: Universal, 1981).

3. *Gabriel García Márquez: historia de un deicidio* (Barcelona: Barral, 1981).

4. Prologue to *The Kingdom of this World* (1949).

5. See Gilard's 'Prologo' to *Obra Periodistica*, Vol. 2, *Entre Cachacos* I, p. 70.

6. Jorge Luis Borges, *A Personal Anthology*, ed. Anthony Kerrigan (New York: Grove Press, 1987) pp. 16–23.

7. André Breton, 'Manifesto of Surrealism' in *Manifestos of Surrealism*, trans. Richard Seaver and Helen R. Lane (University of Michigan Press, 1972) pp. 10–14.

8. *Cien Años de Soledad*, ed. Jacques Joset (Madrid: Catedra, 1987) p. 323.

9. *One Hundred Years of Solitude* (London: Pan, 1978) p. 202.

10. *Illuminations* (London: Fontana, 1973) p. 257.

11. *On the Uses and Disadvantages of History for Life*, trans. Peter Preuss (Indianapolis: Hackett, 1980) p. 10.

12. Jorge Luis Borges, *Labyrinths*, ed. Donald A. Yates and James E. Irby (Harmondsworth: Penguin, 1970) pp. 87–95.

13. *The Birth of Tragedy*, trans. Walter Kaufmann (New York: Vintage, 1967) p. 134.

14. Rama points out that the 'magical' is not peculiar to Latin America, as Carpentier claimed, but to uneducated folk culture, as his example showed. Angel Rama, *Gabriel García Márquez: edifcación de un arte nacional y popular* (Universidad de la Republica, Uruguay, 1986) pp. 97–8.

15. *Fragrance*, pp. 114–15.

16. *Fragrance*, p. 106.

17. *Birth of Tragedy*, pp. 68–9.

18. Brian McHale, *Postmodernist Fiction* (London: Routledge, 1989) pp. 134–6.

19. *Metaphors We Live By* (Chicago University Press, 1987).

20. 'It is what human beings *say* that is true and false; and they agree in the *language* they use. That is not agreement in opinions but in form of life.' *Philosophical Investigations*, trans. G. E. M. Anscombe. (Oxford: Blackwell, 1958) p. 88.

21. '. . . if a man sees certain human beings as slaves, isn't he . . . rather missing something about himself, or rather something about his connection with these people, his internal relation with them so to speak. When he wants to be served at table by a black hand, he would not be satisfied to be served by a black paw. When he rapes a slave or takes her as a concubine, he does not feel that he has, by that fact itself, embraced sodomy. When he tips a black taxi driver (something he never does with a white driver) it does not occur to him that he might more appropriately have patted the creature fondly on the side of the neck. He does not go to great lengths either to convert his horses to Christianity or to prevent their getting wind of it. Everything in his relation to his slaves shows that he treats them as more or less human—his humiliations of them, his disappointments, his jealousies, his fears, his punishments, his attachments . . .', *The Claim of Reason* (Oxford: Clarendon Press, 1979) p. 376.

22. 'Prologo' to *Obra Periodistica*, 4, *de Europa y America*, pp. 14–15.

23. *Obra Periodistica*, 4, *de Europa y America*, p. 414.

24. Ibid., p. 174.

25. *Labyrinths*, p. 217.

26. *The Labyrinth of Solitude*, p. 161.

27. *Change of Skin*, trans. Sam Hileman (Harmondsworth: Penguin, 1975) p. 263.

28. '. . . it appears likely that poets in our civilization, as it exists at present, must be *difficult*', *Selected Essays* (London: Faber, 1932) p. 289.

29. 'The Waste Land', line 261. *Collected Poems* (London: Faber, 1963) p. 73.

30. *Labyrinths*, p. 219.

31. *On the Uses and Disadvantages of History for Life*, pp. 12–14.

32. *Women in Love*, ed. David Farmer, Lindeth Vasey and John Worthen (Cambridge University Press, 1987) p. 529.

33. *The Rainbow*, ed. Mark Kinkead-Weekes (Cambridge University Press, 1989) p. 258.

34. I discuss Lawrence's narrative hyperbole in *The Rainbow* in *D. H. Lawrence: Language and Being* (Cambridge University Press, 1992) pp. 55–7. The whole

chapter on *The Rainbow* provides a fruitful parallel with the present discussion of *Hundred Years*.

35. See my chapter on *The Plumed Serpent* in *D. H. Lawrence: Language and Being*, op. cit., pp. 165–205.

36. Compare Primo Levi's *The Periodic Table* (1975) for a magnificently positive intermingling of story, alchemy and chemistry.

37. *Don Quixote*, trans. Cohen (Harmondsworth: Penguin, 1950) Part II, chaps 24–7, pp. 624–51.

38. *The Political Unconscious* (London: Methuen, 1981).

39. I have discussed modernist mythopoeia in 'Myth, Art and Belief' in *Context of English Literature: 1900–30*, ed. Michael Bell (London: Methuen, 1980) pp. 19–43.

40. *Ulysses*, ed. Walter Gabler (Harmondsworth: Penguin, 1986) p. 28.

41. *Labyrinths*, p. 229.

42. Reprinted in *Gabriel García Márquez: New Readings*, ed. B. McGuirk and R. Cardwell (Cambridge University Press, 1987) pp. 207–11.

43. I have discussed the relationship of the curiosity in this story to the curiosity in its narrative context. See 'How Primordial is Narrative?' in *Narrative in Culture*, ed. Cris Nash (London: Routledge, 1990) pp. 172–98.

FLORENCE DELAY AND
JACQUELINE DE LABRIOLLE

Is García Márquez the Colombian Faulkner?

The publication of *One Hundred Years of Solitude* in Buenos Aires in 1967 created an explosion on the literary scene. With twenty thousand copies sold in one month, a new edition had to be issued as rapidly as possible. Soon all Latin America had its eyes fixed on the imaginary village of Macondo, the foundations of which Gabriel García Márquez establishes on the first pages of his novel and which an apocalyptic cyclone totally destroys four hundred pages later. Although the author conceals the identity of Macondo in his novel, it oddly resembles Aracataca, the small village in Colombia where he had lived as a child close to unforgettable grandparents who created for him a fabulous childhood from which he drew his inspiration. In later novels, just as Illiers becomes linked by hyphen with Combray, Aracataca assumes the surrealistic name of Macondo.

Once the joy and agitation created by the discovery of a great new Latin-American novelist subsided, critics turned to García Márquez's earlier works to find in them evidence that the roads the author had previously traveled inevitably led him to this masterpiece. Thus they were surprised to discover that Macondo existed not only in his first novel *La hojarasca*[1] but also by reference in his long novella, *El coronel no tiene quien le escriba,*[2] as well as in various other tales and narratives. No doubt the choice of a single place as an abridgment of the world, fixed in time and space by its own laws,

From *The Faulkner Journal* 11, nos. 1 and 2 (Fall 1995/Spring 1996): 119–138. © 1996 by the University of Akron.

and the permanence of this imaginary village whose inhabitants reappear in García Márquez's work inspired the original comparison with Faulkner. Once discovered, the idea was repeated more or less in the same form:

> In transforming Aracataca into Macondo, García Márquez has done something similar to what Faulkner did when he gave the name Jefferson to his town of Oxford. (Vargas)

> He returns as if obsessed to the same village, creates and recreates the same situation, as if he were working in an experimental country forged in his own laboratory. . . . This trait brings him close to Faulkner. (Rama)

> In his short stories and tales, by dint of insisting on and coming back to the same themes, the same characters, and the same countryside, García Márquez has given to Hispanic-American letters what Faulkner gave to North American literature, a fictional world which is convincing and sufficient to itself. (Carballo)

It would be tedious to multiply similar comments. It should be noted, however, that *One Hundred Years of Solitude* was quickly translated into Italian, English, and French—in France it was named the best foreign novel of 1969. Critics took up the same theme, and in *Le Monde*, on March 23, 1968, Claude Fell wrote the following:

> Macondo is an imaginary village of Colombia that Carlos Fuentes compares to the Faulknerian county of Yoknapatawpha.

This critical idea, or rather this comparison agreed upon and repeated by the critics, was frequently evoked in the presence of Gabriel García Márquez. In the beginning, he responded in good humor that it was quite true that he had been inspired by the American writer. In 1966 he told Luis Harss that when he first read Faulkner he thought, "I must become a writer." He said that he had discovered that the "chaotic materials that went into Faulkner's art . . . were much like the raw stuff of life in Colombia (Harss 322–23). Implicitly the interviewer and the author were referring each other to the author's first book, to *Leaf Storm*. After 1967, García Márquez retracts, always with good humor. Interviewed by Armando Durán in Barcelona in 1968, he declares:

> Critics have insisted so much on the influence of Faulkner in my books that, over time, they have succeeded in convincing

me. The truth is that I had already published *Leaf Stories* when I began, purely by chance, to read Faulkner. I wanted to know what constituted the influences that the critics attributed to me. Many years later, during a trip to the American South, I thought that I had encountered the explanation that I had not found in my books. Those dusty roads, those scorchingly hot and miserable towns, and those hopeless people greatly resembled those I evoked in my stories. I believe that the resemblance was not accidental: the village where I was born was constructed in large part by a North American banana company. (23–24)

Just a sally? An upswelling of artistic and Colombian pride intended to confound the critics attempting to track his readings? If it is true that the two climates—the physical and the mental—present undeniably common characteristics, how are we to believe that the economic and social conditions are sufficient to provoke analogous works without the slightest connection to themes and forms? *Leaf Stories* presents an obvious relationship in structure to both *The Sound and the Fury* and *As I Lay Dying*. Would a young writer as strongly conscious as García Márquez not have known, even if it were secondhand, about the Faulknerian revolution belatedly consecrated by the 1950 Nobel Prize? For if he conceived his first novel before his twentieth year, around 1948, it was during the time in which Faulkner's work, having fallen unjustly into discredit, finally acceded to its first level of literary recognition.

* * *

In fact, *Leaf Stories* involves three interior monologues that appear to be much closer to the monologues of Faulkner than to those of Joyce. It is known to what extent the priority allotted by this technique to the subjective life of the characters leads the narrator to dislocate the historical succession of events—i.e., the chronology, with the determinism this chronology supposedly founds—to the advantage of an affective logic which reorganizes the facts—or rather what each one perceives of them—into a totally personal constellation governed by their most secret obsessions. The ensemble of monologues provides the reader all the pieces of the puzzle that he must reconstruct. . . .

Another element connects the reading of *Leaf Stories* to the reading of a Faulkner novel: the enigmatic character of a story in which zones of intended shadow exist. It is not a matter of obscurity linked to the technique of the monologue, nor is it a matter of possible error on the part of an artist caught up in an overwhelming project. It is rather a matter of questions left deliberately without an answer—who was that mysterious doctor? who was the father of Christmas? why? Because reality itself remains ambiguous and no one—except God—ever knows the answer to everything. Hence the pseudo-detective allure of these narratives in which the reader is first shown the corpse before he is transported into the past in order to unmask those responsible. This formula, with some variations and in conjunction with other techniques, is evident in *Light in August* and *Absalom, Absalom!* Certain enigmas will never be resolved. For we are on a tragic plane rather than on a realistic one. In order to create the tragic space in which the news item is transfigured into a symbol of the human condition, the two story-tellers employ cultural references. García Márquez places in exergue a quotation from Sophocles's *Antigone*—the interdiction to bury Polyneices and the penalty of death imposed. The analogy thus operates in an explicit way on the level of the storytelling. In Faulkner—except in some details such as the names of Jason and Clytie or the evocation of a Choëphore—the suggestion remains implicit and global but operates profoundly on the level of vision, to the extent to which Fate . . . governs all plots. . . .

In short, García Márquez worked first in the same manner and in the same direction in which Faulkner worked. The limitations of his attempt—the monotony of the voices, the disorder a little too intentional—seem to prove that he was testing his skills with instruments that were not his own. According to Vargas Llosa, García Márquez then turned to Hemingway as an antidote to Faulkner, quite resolved to find his own voice this time. Does this mean that, doing so, he accomplished in *One Hundred Years of Solitude* an "anti-Faulkner" work, as Durán supposes?

* * *

One who assiduously studies the two novelists remains impressed by the diverse "coincidences": the writer's design, his attitude, and his major themes—themes expressed by a comparable use of proper names, times, and cultural references. We will leave aside similarities based on references to historical facts of the same type—the faking of elections by Southern planters or by Colombian conservatives—or to a common folklore, exemplified by the eating competition in "A Courtship."

García Márquez's design in *One Hundred Years of Solitude* was to regroup all of his favorite themes into an integral story about Macondo—during the course of the century that terminated in his birth in 1928. He confirms having conceived the work as early as age eighteen under the title *La Casa* and having postponed it for lack of inspiration and experience. Hence his joy at having accomplished his design and his willingness to change direction. We know how much this imaginary village owes to the stories told by a grandmother as gifted as Caroline Barr, Faulkner's black mammy, and to the memories of a grandfather, a civil war veteran, who appears episodically in the work. In the same manner, Faulkner drew from the "postage stamp" of his native Mississippi his illustrious county of Yoknapatawpha of which he proclaimed himself "the sole owner and proprietor." Faulkner's chronicle of Yoknapatawpha, enriched by successive properties, extends for a hundred years through different periods: going back in time to trace the punishment of the Sutpens (1909) to the birth of Thomas Sutpen (1808); recapitulating the saga of Jefferson, scattered through the entire work, from the first settlement until the present time;[3] picking the saga up again at the end of the War Between the States for another century (1865–1965), with comparatively little anticipation or transgression. Is it simply a matter of a "rounded tale" or of a destiny fulfilled?

Just as Faulkner expresses the fundamental drama of the ruined and alienated South by means of a local chronicle, García Márquez illuminates the present difficulties of Macondo by creating in his imaginary village "the microcosm of Colombian reality."[4] Both writers are concerned with analyzing the cursed "solitude" that cuts through the men of the region and denounce it as the root of evil, as the condition of all men.[5]

These analogous projects give evidence of similar attitudes regarding the role of the writer. In order to remain himself—"a country boy"—Faulkner abandoned high school, then college. García Márquez finds no pleasure in academic studies. Both practiced various trades but remain turned toward the legendary past with which they were enchanted during their childhood. García Márquez takes pleasure in saying that from the time of his grandfather's death—when García Márquez was eight years old—nothing held any more interest for him. Loyal to their roots, they are passionate writers, hostile to "intellectuals," although they practice an art more consciously than they would like to admit.[6] If García Márquez chose the novel, he did so "in order to liberate himself from his obsessions and his passion," according to Claude Couffon, as Faulkner tried to do—hopelessly, he would insist—to express "what cried within him in order to be set free" (Nathan 11).

What their obsessions have in common is a poignant conviction of a present impasse, of a fatal decadence. It is frequently noted how much the weight of the past alienates Faulkner's characters, depriving them of their future and even of a genuine present. Nor is there any freedom in *One Hundred Years of Solitude*: the parchments of Melquíades prove that everything was ordained. The present-day marasmus inspires in the two writers the same nostalgia for the "heroic" generation, a generation of men of war and action, founders of cities and dynasties. Hence the myth of the Great Ancestor: Colonel Buendía, a somewhat rougher counterpart of the epic figure of Colonel Sartoris, the hero of *The Unvanquished*, a figure itself inspired by

Faulkner's great-grandfather. There is the same ubiquity, the same fabulous unexpected attacks, the same defiance of danger. After defeat, their ruined descendants have lost all energy; they are no more than "intellectuals" like Quentin Compson, that "academic Hamlet" spellbound by the memory of Henry Sutpen, or the last Aureliano, "imprisoned in the written reality," shut in with the gypsy's book of spells. Neither the laborious deciphering of the past—in *Absalom, Absalom!*—nor the belated decoding of what was supposed to be a prophecy—in *One Hundred Years*—saves either from despair or from death. Through them, both Faulkner and García Márquez project their obsessions and their regret for being only writers. But like the great ancestor, who does not appear himself without fault, nostalgia also develops a myth of the golden age. For Faulkner it is the time before the spoliation of the Indians and the destruction of the wilderness, of the primitive forest such as the one glimpsed in *The Bear*; for García Márquez it is the innocent beginnings of Macondo when nobody knew decrepitude or death. It is an illusory compensation. . . .

Does this major theme of fatal decay in One Hundred Years follow the same scheme found in all the Jefferson saga or in the case typified by the House of Sutpen? In García Márquez's work, an initial act of violence—the murder of Aguilar—provokes the departure for a new land, Macondo, where a small community directed by an exemplary family—the Buendías—is founded and prospers.[7] But calamities follow each other—the plague of insomnia, civil war, the banana-tree pestilence, the flood—while the same crimes are repeated from one generation to another until the final cataclysm. Thus the plagues which come from the outside—politics, the "gringos," progress—become the allies of personal failings—cruelty, greed, debauchery—in order to destroy the patriarchal values and ruin the House of Buendía. In Faulkner's work we already had the foundation—of Jefferson or of Sutpen's Hundred—corrupted at the base by an injustice—the spoliation of the Indians or Sutpen's rejection of his first wife and son. The energy of the pioneers led to success—at the cost of another violent act, the enslavement of blacks, but everything has been destroyed by the War Between the States, and the upstarts and newly rich have accelerated the moral ruin of the South. In fact, under the mask of virtue, the country has already been corroded from the inside by the same violence, the same avarice, and the same lust as Macondo. The curve of greatness and fall is revealed thus as analogous, more brutal perhaps in Faulkner, for Macondo experiences several remissions as evinced by the successive "restorations" of Úrsula's lodgings.

The exterior calamities are not unrelated, if not objective, at least in the manner in which they are experienced. The hatred for the Yankee and the Carpetbagger in the works of one corresponds in García Márquez's works to the hostility toward *gringos* responsible for the present-day stagnation. Both also show the ravages of technical progress: for Faulkner, it debases man by cutting him off from nature. Hence the exaltation of the black and the Indian. For García Márquez, "the innocent yellow train" has chiefly brought exploiters, strangers, and French matrons. The cinema has imposed the same illusions on everyone. As for politics, everything is corrupt. Indeed the thirty-nine popular revolts aroused by Colonel Buendía cannot be seen as parallel to the aristocratic war conducted by Southern planters—on the whole, a "guerilla" war as opposed to the War of the "Vendée."[8] But both wars develop the same myth of the "rebel" ensnared by an odious power. They are both suffered as a divine punishment, even though they provoke new injustices, as evidenced by the "reconstruction" of the South and the rapacity of the Snopeses. As for the Buendías, their "just cause" does not prevent them from plundering other people, from reigning by terror, or from doing away with an Indian general who offends them. War is not humanized, as Granny Millard believed it to be, or as Aureliano and his "friend" Moncada dreamed of it. Ferocity is not taken into account. The Colonel will be infected by it as much as the "soldiers" against whom he revolts. Peace restored, in Macondo or in Jefferson, will not prove itself more humane.

Only several female characters react against so much violence and corruption. By turns Úrsula protects the victims: those of Arcadio, then Arcadio himself, his prisoner son, then the friends that the latter repudiates—Moncada, even García Márquez. A heroine if the occasion presents itself but above all a mother, she nourishes, takes in, and takes care of the entire clan, including the bastards. Like a good shopkeeper, she keeps the family alive. Less adventurous but more efficient than Granny in *The Unvanquished*, as petite and as energetic, she will be broken only by time and the madness of others. In a more familiar fashion, she recalls "the unconquerable race of women" celebrated by Faulkner, such as Miss Jenny, a witness of human folly who maintains and waits, or Judith, who does the work of men in the absence of men. Her energetic love connects her especially to Dilsey, the Mammy of the Compsons, a simple soul and an "immovable rock," the only true Christian of the family. Their courage cannot but delay the expiration and ruin of their respective "houses."

The house of the Buendías, enlarged and decorated with love, then three times more devastated, can be seen as the village replica of the proud "house" of Sutpen, turned into a tragic wreck within a half century. Again the same scheme: sin, splendor and destruction. The cyclone that swallows the last Aureliano—along with the little monster—corresponds to the fire from which the poor Negro idiot who carries the last drops of cursed blood escapes howling.

What sins, then, do these calamities punish? The idea of a supreme justice, explicit in the works of Faulkner beginning with *Absalom, Absalom!*

in which the divine "great Creditor" replaces the "Player," is suggested in the works of García Márquez by the Biblical character of these calamities. They are essentially sins of pride, the withdrawal into self, the celebrated Solitude. They provoke, in addition to murders, those incestuous and homosexual tendencies which, along with bastardy, lead to the extinction of the Sutpens and the Buendías.

* * *

Is not the theme of incest, which obsessed Faulkner for more than ten years and which plays a tragi-comic role in the fall of the Buendías, linked also to solitude? For those beings immured within themselves, this is a fallacious issue, since they look for refuge from the exterior world within the enclosed world of family and childhood which renders all catharsis impossible. In Faulkner's work, the scheme becomes more complicated from one novel to another. . . . The mixing of bloods further aggravates the situations created by turbid desires and illegitimacy. The third Carothers McCaslin, for example, in joining with his cousin from the black side of the family, repeats unknowingly the incest by which their common ancestor produced a son by his own illegitimate daughter—a slave—and renders fruitless in the eyes of his Great-Uncle Isaac the atonement that the latter had imposed on himself for the entire clan. One does not escape original sin. In order to prove the return of the same madness, Faulkner chose as the narrator of Henry Sutpen's tragedy the character of Quentin, obsessed with the same incestuous and vaguely homosexual tendencies.

To the contrary, there is nothing cerebral in the incest found in the work of García Márquez. For the reader, the taboo which protects the women of the clan is expressed by a comic terror: the threat of a pig's tail. Consequently, the threat of hell no longer exists, but there is an immediate sanction. Cases are more varied in Faulkner's work, in which a sister often serves as a substitute for a weak mother. On one hand, the *fear* of incest—the distant cousinhood between Úrsula and her husband or the *appearance* of incest between José Arcadio and Rebeca, his adopted sister—and the *risk* of involuntary incest—Pilar diverts her desire for her son Arcadio toward Santa Sofía de la Piedad—can be distinguished from real incest, *drawn in outline* between Amaranta and her nephew Aureliano José,[9] *dreamed of* by José Arcadio upon his return, and joyfully *consummated* without knowing it by Amaranta Úrsula and the last Aureliano. Too late, they are seized with horror upon discovering their kinship, but the evil has been done: Destiny has triumphed. Likewise, the homosexual tendency suggested in *Absalom, Absalom!* is set against the affirmed vice of the ex-future-pope, a vice which costs him his treasure and his life. Another phenomenon reveals perhaps the same tendency: the two brothers José Arcadio and Aureliano keep company with the same woman, Pilar Ternera and, two generations later, the twins—José Arcadio II and Aureliano II—share Petra Cotes. As for the illegitimate offspring, they are received into the home of the Buendías, as at Sutpen's Hundred, and contribute to the decay.

The root of evil is the dissociation of sexual life from family life. In this manner, the conviction is made manifest that there exist two categories of women: the sensual woman of color and the chaste white woman.[10] Opposite the austere Fernanda stand the gentle octoroon rival of the proud Judith and the joyful Petra Cotes—a great-hearted mulatto.[11] In this dichotomy the Puritan tradition and Spanish asceticism join together. The same exaltation of virginity—the same fear of the flesh—nurtures the inexpiable malice Miss Rosa holds against Sutpen and the singular obstinacy of Amaranta, who refuses two suitors—who please her—only to surrender to a "swampy passion" (282). There is no doubt that Faulkner gives preference to the octoroon: Judith will be for Charles only the instrument for his revenge. In his case, García Márquez makes fun of Fernanda and her calendar of abstinence and modest lingerie. He imparts to Petra Cotes all the traits of generosity and magnanimity, which she displays even toward Fernanda, who fills her with contempt. It is Petra who makes of Aureliano II the only sociable, the only *bon vivant* of this taciturn line. But lust remains the instrument of Destiny: Caddy transmits to her daughter Quentin her own condemnation. Christmas will atone for his mother, just as Temples son will atone for his. As for the little monster with the tail of a pig, the offspring of incest and the son of a bastard, García Márquez delivers him to the ants.

* * *

Will one be astonished if he notices the use of comparable methods in order to express analogous themes? The most evident is the recurrence of the same names from one generation to the other in order to signify the recurrence of the same acts of folly. García Márquez exploits it as virtuoso, but Faulkner showed him the way. The reader of *Sartoris* discovers in the course of pages how two brothers from the "heroic" generation, Bayard and John, bequeathed their first names to the two great-grandsons of the Colonel, whose son was also named Bayard and the grandson John. The diagram becomes complicated in *The Sound and the Fury* in which one finds, in addition to two Jasons (father and son), two Quentins of a different sex (uncle and niece)—the risk of confusion being sought after, of course. There would even have been two Maurys, the maternal uncle and the nephew, if Faulkner had not imagined that the latter was renamed Benjamin (Benjy) when he was found to be an idiot. The reprobation of the blacks on this subject proves that the first name was considered to be linked to the person, to be "sacred." Moreover, it is the master's privilege to choose it.[12] In order to place five José Arcadios and four Aurelianos who succeed each other under the same family roof—without forgetting several ancestors of the same name and seventeen Aurelianos sired by the Colonel during twenty years in the fields—one cannot do without a table. García Márquez amuses himself prodigiously in shuffling the cards and inventing variations such as Aureliano José and Amaranta Úrsula. Previously in Faulkner's work surnames—Cass and Roth—distinguished the second and the third Carothers McCaslin from their ancestor. One finds the numbers already in the Compson "dynasty" as Faulkner completed it backwards in time in a later appendix: in opposition to the "lost generation" of Caddy and her brothers, he presents the "brilliant" ancestors Quentin I and II and Jason I and II—a bitter irony which emphasizes the defeat of their princely pretensions.

Although these customs most certainly exist (witness the "dynasty" of the Fords, of the Rockefellers, etc., by reference to the European tradition), it is the intention that interests us. A theory of names is made explicit by both novelists: like blood, the name conveys the same vices; it is a sign of fatality. When Miss Jenny, the defender of a tradition from which she nevertheless suffers, wants to baptize John the last offshoot of the Sartoris family, Narcissa objects in order to break the chain and names him Benbow—her own family name—in order to neutralize the hereditary violence of the family line. Miss Jenny remains skeptical—although she had suggested herself that the Johns were less fierce than the Bayards.[13] "Do you think one can change one of 'em with a name?" she asks (*SAR* 380). She is altogether convinced that "It's in the blood. Savages, every one of 'em. No earthly use to anybody" (*SAR* 298). Name and blood remain linked in *The Sound and the Fury*: young Quentin was destined to share "the blood vice of the Compsons"—the lascivious nature of her mother and the neurasthenia of her uncle whose name Caddy imposes on her. Likewise, it is not by chance if incest, as we have seen, is repeated among the Buendías between couples who carry, with several close variations, the same first names. Like Narcissa, Úrsula tries two times to break the curse: at the birth of Arcadio's daughter—"We won't call her Úrsula because a person suffers too much with the name" (134)—and following the escapades of the twins—"she decided that no one again would be called Aureliano or José Arcadio" (194). But she gives in and the calamities continue, in spite of her efforts to make a future pope of the fourth José Arcadio. Also vain is the effort of Amaranta Úrsula to name her son Rodrigo (417 cf. 386–87): "'No,' her husband countered, 'We'll name him Aureliano and he'll win thirty–two wars.'" Nevertheless, he perishes the next day. Regarding her Arcadios and Aurelianos, Úrsula practices with conviction Miss Jenny's deductions about the Johns and the Bayards: "While the Aurelianos were withdrawn, but with lucid minds, the José Arcadios were impulsive and enterprising, but they were marked with a tragic sign" (186). She therefore suspects the twins of having made a game of exchanging names, for their constitutions and their characters contradict the characteristics signified by their names. But at their death, their coffins are reversed: destiny has restored order. In this manner, the imagination of García Márquez plays on the diagrams outlined by Faulkner.

In contrast to Gowan, Bayard, Charles Bon, and other heroic surnames which reflect the patriarchal pretensions of the respective family, García Márquez recalls the simplicity of the Buendías through the family name. Irony plays a major role in all these processes, especially in the repetition of names—harsher in Faulkner, livelier in García Márquez. But if both writers aspire to mislead the reader, they do so in order to require his increased attention.

Both also demand that the reader make the same effort in order to place events in time. The two storytellers displace chronology, not for the sake of simple "narrative perversity," but in order to prove, by another method, the fatal decay . . . : "'I know all of this by heart,' Úrsula would shout. 'It's as if time had turned around and we were back at the beginning'" (199). In more familiar language, it is the equivalent of the circular images that Faulkner willingly attributes to his characters. For the "street" where Christmas flees for thirty years, far from liberating him, has led him to his fate, to the curse in which Doc Hines imprisoned him at his birth—to be treated like a Negro: The street "had made a circle and he is still inside of it" (*LA* 373). Although her departure had a "direction"—to find again the father of her child, Lena pursues her journey after her defeat, conquered, it seems, by the eternal present that she tasted in a movement that appeared immobile, "in identical and anonymous and deliberate wagons as though through a succession of creak-wheeled and limpeared avatars, like something moving forever and without progress across an urn" (*LA* 7). For worse more often than for better, in both García Márquez and Faulkner, a cyclic conception of time carries the work.

In the works of both storytellers there exists the same contrast between the "objective" time of the narrated stories, which progresses, and the subjective conviction which denies this progression, for the experience lived is that of an obscure fatality. The last Aureliano collapses, "unable to bear in his soul the crushing weight of so much past" (420). García Márquez's formula, which applies to the village as well (390), coincides with the collapse of Quentin—"one is not cured of his past"—and with that of the entire South. In Faulkner, this conviction requires the dislocation of chronology, which becomes illusory, in order to enhance the major scenes around which the narratives are organized. But several reference marks exist for the reader: each of the four parts of *The Sound and the Fury* is dated by way of the title.

The sequences in *Absalom, Absalom!* are also dated—whether with precision: "It was in June of 1838" (*AA* 37), or in a relative manner: "So it was six years now" (*AA* 20), or "on that afternoon thirty years later" (*AA* 198)— and a helpful appendix conveys useful details. In contrast, García Márquez does not provide dates, deliberately so. There are, however, several historical references which serve as time markers: the attack of Riohacha by Francis Drake—three centuries before the espousals of the patriarch; the Treaty of the Netherlands—November 4, 1902; the establishment of the banana company—from 1918 to about 1928. The ironically precise details provided by the narrative—"Two weeks before" (124), "ten days after" (148)—serve no purpose except as coordinates. Amaranta begins to embroider her shroud "the sixth of April," but in what year? The flood lasted "four years, eleven months and two days," but when exactly did it begin?

This supposedly "objective" time constitutes an *elastic milieu* in which a "century" concentrates within itself the entire history of humanity and in which generations coexist almost simultaneously. For example, Úrsula is described as being "between one hundred and fifteen and one hundred and twenty-two" (349) and Pilar Ternera as "one hundred and forty-five years of age" (401). In the same manner, Francisco the Man is reputed to remember Sir Walter Raleigh (52). Is it therefore proper to apply to García Márquez himself the project of Melquíades, who "had not put events in the order of man's conventional time, but had concentrated a century of daily episodes, in such a way that they coexisted in one instant"? (421). It is the old dream of *totum simul*, of a divine and transcendent vision,[14] such as Faulkner acknowledges to Malcolm Cowley: "My ambition . . . is to put everything into one sentence—not only the present but the whole past on which it depends and which keeps overtaking the present, second by second" (112). Therefore, this suspension of time plays less in favor of an eternal present—as it occurs during the course of Lena's journey or in the privileged chamber of Melquíades—than in a display of the past in which the persistence of ghosts in both works provides the same meaning, even though their literary treatment is strongly different.[15]

As already indicated, these discourses on time are no doubt rooted in the experience of the two regions that nurtured Faulkner and García Márquez. It is no less certain that simultaneity is familiar to the Latin American writer and reader, whose continent presents, no less certainly, all historical epochs as juxtaposed rather than as successive. With regard to the Deep South, Faulkner was acquainted with a time when the primitive forest—"the state of nature"—was only a journey of several hours by wagon from town. But literary tradition cannot be excluded, nor can ideas from the contemporary scene—those games on time which are more or less inspired by generalized relativity, or rather by what poets drew from it in order to modernize or rejuvenate the old theme of the "prophecy." The fantastic denouement of *One Hundred Years*—the prediction is fulfilled in the same instant in which it is deciphered—evokes the scene in Act II of Giraudoux's *Electra*, where the narrative of the Beggar—the modern Tiresias—outruns the actual death of Aegisthus by several seconds: "I went too fast. He's just catching up with me" (2:246). García Márquez draws an even more startling effect from an exact coincidence. The concern of this prophecy—the most original element in the structure of *One Hundred Years*—is, as in tragedy, to emphasize the weight of Destiny: even had they known it in time, the Buendías would not have avoided it.

But is it possible to talk about tragedy in connection with García Márquez based on the sole argument that Fate governs the structure and the contents of his narrative? For it is self-evident that pure tragedy is never found there, except in the sequence of the massacre of strikers—which is not imaginary—and in the denouement. More often it is toned down by the comical, by rough obscene details, or by the marvelous. . . .

* * *

García Márquez breaks away from Faulknerian tragedy through fantasy and the marvelous—and he does so with tremendous force. From comparable themes and methods, he creates an entirely different world in which the reader finds himself smiling rather than caught up in "nightmares" (Coindreau 40). In the world created by García Márquez, horror is tamed, and battles are fought with the weapons of irony.

Not that irony is lacking in Faulkner's work, but more often than not it emphasizes the tragedy instead of toning it down: Popeye's punishment—for a crime that he did not commit—does not compensate for the lynching of Goodwin. The ridicule of McEachern adds to the odiousness of his fanaticism. The details that demystify martial heroism are also bitter: Uncle Bayard Sartoris gets himself killed for anchovies, just as Hightower's ancestor was killed for having stolen a chicken. In this derisory universe, humor charged with sympathy is rare—the chase after the architect (*AA* 206) offers a rare privileged example. Still more rare is the liberating smile, exemplified by Shreve's sane reaction to the drama of Sutpen.[16] True, in his maturity Faulkner loosens a little the jaws of the vice of despair, but the "bonhomie" that one takes pleasure in attributing to his later works and to the frontier humor that animates his stories about horses—bartered, painted, runaway—hardly modifies his deep-seated conviction: "Man stinks the same stink no matter where in time," he concluded in 1946 (Cowley 15). If in *Requiem* he caught a glimpse of an issue for those subject to doom in the South and in the universe, it is still by a tragic route: the suffering of the innocents. Even the "comic" escapade of *The Reivers* concludes with the injury inflicted on a child's soul by the discovery of Evil. Even if Faulkner denounced the cruelty and hypocrisy of the Puritans, his vision remains marked by Calvinist anguish and by a certain horror of life, of which his disgust for sexuality offers the most flagrant proof. In this religious perspective, laughter is hardly suitable, for Hell has already begun.

In contrast, García Márquez adopts a free and familiar tone, the very opposite of tragic "grandeur." "*One Hundred Years* represents anti-solemnity," he asserts justly in his interview with Durán. The pinprick of humor deflates rising emotion. In his universe, people hate and they kill as much as they do in Faulkner, and fortune's farces are no less cruel: Rebeca is saved from poison only by the death of the innocent Remedios; Úrsula's treasure is used to pay for the orgiastic feasts—the Saturnalias—of José Arcadio, etc. . . . But the scenes which could be dark are treated with a tone so lively—Aguilar's death—or so detached—Aureliano's abortive suicide—and they are stocked with details so comical—the washing of José Arcadio's tattooed corpse—or so prosaic—the starving Petra Cotes's backbone is like "a row of bobbins of thread"—that horror is averted. The only pure "nightmare" is José Arcadio the Second's awaking in the convoy of three thousand corpses (312–13).[17] Even into this episode García Márquez introduces a note of black humor: the corpses are laid out in rows in the train like the precious bananas that brought misfortune to Macondo. When García Márquez gives free vent to his spirit, with more malice than bitterness, he does so in order to caricature a puerile religion—the famous "miracle" of Father Nicanor (86) or "the watchful and glacial eyes of the tattletale saints" (375)—or the foolish pretension of Fernanda, her gibberish language (216), and her piety, all too ready to fabulate: far from remaining intact, the body of Don Fernando cooked "slowly in frothy stew with bubbles like live pearls" (219)—a macabre detail but less grating than those of Faulkner.[18] More cutting examples include the denunciation of governmental troops, with their "pestilential" odor, brutalized by "the chancre of blind obedience" (308) and the criticism of the liberal lawyers who make a compact with the regime after having "supplied funds for the war from exile" (168). The same species of "crows" who had betrayed Colonel Buendía and his veterans become the accomplices of capital: the "sleight-of-hand lawyers" (307) pilfer Mr. Brown and take away the banana company to the grief of the workers—"So that the fable of the Virginia ham was nonsense, the same as that of the miraculous pills and the Yuletide toilets, and by a decision of the court it was established and set down in solemn decrees that the workers did not exist" (307).

In this passage worthy of Swift and of Montesquieu, García Márquez's characteristic tone brings him as close to Rabelais as much as it sets him in opposition to Faulkner. In the work of this "Latin" writer, the conviction of decadence does not alter the love of life and the pride in all that is natural. For García Márquez, the body is not an object of scandal. In contrast to Christmas and other Faulkner characters, no physical detail—whether it pertains to belching, sweating, or using the chamber pot—is repugnant. García Márquez displays a healthy reflex and denies hypocritical idealism. To say no more, he lays aside morality in order to demystify "heroes": even the Colonel can suffer from boils in the wrong places. Hence the irony in the fables which "protect"—if little—the family honor: the naive fable of the Assumption of Remedios the Beauty or the cruel fable of Mauricio Babilonia, Chicken Thief. It is not that sexuality is always maintained as joyfully as by the previous couple or even by Rebeca, up to her absurd crime. García Márquez conceals neither the agonies of desire nor the evil of prostitution. But he feels only pity for "the streetgirls who make love in order to eat." Whereas Faulkner blackens such characters—at least up until *The Unvanquished*—García Márquez does not crush a single one of his: he has two of his shameless "libertines" show the generosity of their hearts in the face of misery (362–3); he turns the most lecherous couple into a loving household restored to childhood complicity (413–14). Even the arrogant Fernanda becomes sweet (359). Our narrator sketches them without ferocity: Rebeca is "curled up like a shrimp" (350); Aureliano Segundo has a tortoise-like face which became iguana-like during the flood. Faulkner prefers harsher images for Sutpen's eyes, which are like "two pieces of broken plates," or for Popeye's eyes, which are like "two black rubber buttons." There is little need for García Márquez to assert that he does not hate Macondo, even ruined and suffocating from dust and boredom, as Quentin does about the Deep South.[19] With great sympathy he evokes the nostalgia felt by those absent—the second Úrsula in Belgium, the future pope in Rome, the Catalan bookseller back in his own country.

Is this maybe anachronistic love for his village—this amused sympathy for the little people with whom he grew up—the key to the "marvelous" which has caused so much scholarly ink to flow and which has accounted so much for the success of the novel? The marvels such as flying carpets or the raining of flowers, the apparitions, the presentiments—all these elements were the daily bread of naive souls, their way of taming the unknown, the impossible, even death. A rational reader can judge as suspect the feigned candor and the casualness with which García Márquez mixes "objective" reality with the delirious universe of magic and superstition. According to J.M. Duque, the fantastic is that there still exist people who believe in it. The imagination of García Márquez, formed in a "backward" provincial milieu, knew none of the "modesties" that the century of enlightenment and the naturalistic period imposed on the novelists of the intelligentsia. Thus, his great achievement would be to denounce, as he had lived it during his childhood, that "anachronism encysted in modernity" that characterizes Latin-American reality. Still one would have to be sure that García Márquez aspires to denounce rather than to celebrate the richness of the fabulating power of his people, which is its form of intelligence and of heart, as passionate and as highly colored as the realistic vision is flat. When one reads *One Hundred Years*, he recovers a child's spirit, as the author wishes him to do. Perhaps the creole critic complicated the problem by insisting along with the author that in their world it is reality which is hallucinatory; in their world, "everything is possible." For the difference between the incredible proportions of historical or geographical reality—the massacre of three thousand strikers, for example, or the "diluvian" floods—and pure, simple invention such as the raining of flowers is radical. The line of demarcation between the two is not, however, easy to establish, and that is how the author would have it. In this respect, he is linked up with the line of magical realists who, following Miguel Ángel Asturias and his "magical realism," or following Alejo Carpentier and his "real marvelous," laid the foundations for the new Latin-American novel. "The task confronting the South American writer is the task Adam confronted in naming things," Carpentier declared more than ten years ago, and García Márquez responds on the first page of *One Hundred Years*: "The world was so recent that many things lacked names, and in order to indicate them it was necessary to point" (1). Writers have often evoked unbelievable proportions for their continent, its irreducible originality, and its never-before inventoried fauna and flora in order to justify the first of their tasks: to describe their land. Invention in the work of García Márquez is often only the baroque proliferation of a natural truthfulness.

* * *

How does this famous "magical realism" function? In his interview with Durán, García Márquez insists that he acquired his secret from his own grandmother: "She would tell me the most atrocious things without becoming confused, as if she had just seen them. Then I discovered that this imperturbability and this wealth of images were what gave verisimilitude to her stories". One example from among thousands is Úrsula's vision following the murder of Aguilar: "One night when she could not sleep, Úrsula went out into the courtyard to get some water and she saw Prudencio Aguilar by the water jar. He was livid, a sad expression on his face trying to cover the hole in his throat with a plug made of esparto grass" (22). More often, García Márquez employs symbols in the literal sense, as so many concrete realities: the "voice of blood" which warns Úrsula of her son's murder is the trickle of blood which ran from José Arcadio's right ear and which "came out under the door, crossed the living-room, went out into the street, continued on in a straight line . . . and came out in the kitchen" where Úrsula noticed it and followed it in reverse (135). The "cross of ashes," indelible on the foreheads of seventeen Aurelianos, does more than announce their destiny; it also positively identifies them to their executioners (222). From the skull of the third victim flows, instead of blood, the perfume of Remedios the Beauty, "and then they understood that [her smell] kept on torturing men beyond death, right down to the dust of their bones" (239). Whereas in Faulkner's work reality—a scene, a countryside, a silhouette—tends toward the surreal, in *One Hundred Years* hallucination is treated as a fact, with all its practical implications.[20] Nothing is more typical of these two storytellers than their presentation of "ghosts." One is aware of the burden they place on the imagination of Quentin: "listening, having to listen to one of the ghosts"—Miss Rosa—and "having to be one of them for all that" (*AA* 4; 7–8; 289–90) or the imagination of Hightower or of Bayard Sartoris: "As usual, old man Falls had brought John Sartoris into the room with him . . ." (*SAR* 1).[21] After Falls' departure, "John Sartoris seemed to loom still in the room . . . so that as old Bayard sat with his crossed feet propped against the corner of the cold hearth . . . it seemed to him that he could hear his father's breathing. . . . After a while John Sartoris departed also, withdrawn rather to that place where the peaceful dead contemplate their glamorous frustrations . . . (1–2). It is quite evidently a question of a "manner of speaking," as it is for Rosa, for whom the various images of Sutpen include "demon," "ogre," or "Bluebeard." If some "ghost" haunts Sutpen's Hundred, it is a survivor, Clytie (*AA* 172). García Márquez takes a leap beyond: in his work, a specter enjoys an apparent autonomy:

> José Arcadio was still dozing under the shelter of palm fronds that had been rotted by the rain. [Aureliano] did not see him, as he had never seen him, nor did he hear the incomprehensible phrase that the ghost of his father addressed to him as he awakened, startled by the stream of hot urine that splattered his shoes. (269)

In the same way, in Faulkner the ghosts are period figures, who "are the now merely initials or nicknames out of some now incomprehensible affection which sound to us like Sanskrit or Chocktaw" (*AA* 80) or which have the magical power of the letter which—at Harvard, in 1910—gives rise to the drama of the Old South. As the motif of the letter reappears, a succession of metaphors becomes apparent. First of all, the mechanical action acquires a supernatural dimension: "the rectangle of paper folded across the middle and now open, three quarters open, whose bulk had raised half itself by the leverage of the old crease in weightless and paradoxical levitation" (*AA* 176; 192–3). Then the malignant aspect is expressed directly: "the fragile

pandora's box of scrawled paper which had filled with violent and unratio-
cinative djinns and demons this snug monastic coign" (*AA* 208). Finally a
metamorphosis takes place: in Quentin's eyes, the letter radiates with the
pale light of the winter night.[22] In opposition to such "images" as these,
García Márquez places the "records": in *One Hundred Years* the unraveling
of destiny is coined in black-books of magical spells, in preliminary lectures
for which Melquíades furnishes (supernaturally) the references, etc. As for
the levitation of Father Nicanor, according to the grandmother's counsel, it
is as if García Márquez had just seen it: the stimulant containing chocolate
gives him a completely natural appearance. Thus one passes merrily to the
other side of the mirror.

In this alliance of the marvelous and the everyday, García Márquez
found his personal register. He experiences such joy that he concludes his
work in exaltation: "I am on top of the world," he wrote happily to Luis
Harss in November 1965 (339). Henceforth, he abandons himself to his
heroic-comic imagination. The Faulknerian "agony" is finished.[23] "I no
longer suffer when I write," he remarked to Claude Couffon in December
1968. Faulkner will have been for him an exceptional stimulant, a master of
lucidity, of boldness . . . the time to find and to make heard his own Latin-
American voice.

NOTES

1. Published in 1955, but written several years earlier—about 1947, according
to Márquez. Translated into English in the collection *Leaf Storm and Other Stories*
(1979).

2. Published in 1959. English translation published in 1968 as *No One Writes
to the Colonel*.

3. Faulkner does not fix the date of the first settlement, but he speaks several
times (in 1951) of a hundred years in estimating the duration of Jefferson (*Requiem*
Prologue 1).

4. See Claude Couffon.

5. Faulkner denies being a regionalist writer and insists that at all latitudes
man experiences "the same anguishes, the same hopes" (*FU* 87). García Márquez
emphasizes the political aspect of the concept of solitude that he sets in opposition
to the solidarity necessary in strife or struggle.

6. Faulkner willingly presents himself as a literary "craftsman" (*FU* passim).
García Márquez insists that technique is secondary (Durán).

7. Jaime M. Duque attributes to this name an origin already mythical: it
would be a place "from which one does not come back."

8. "Vendée" is the title of a short story by Faulkner.

9. In *One Hundred Years* García Márquez signals ironically that certain liberals
were claiming a person's right to "marry his own mother" (153). All references to *One
Hundred Years of Solitude* in the translated text are to the American edition translated
by Gregory Rabassa (New York: Harper, 1970).

10. Such as one who is called "a lady" in the South and is referred to by Charles Bon as a white sister "of a mushroom yesterday" (*AA* 92).

11. In the same way that José Arcadio flees in order to follow a gypsy, a negress who consoles the last Aureliano. Perhaps Rebeca has some Indian blood.

12. Sutpen in *Absalom, Absalom!* (48). Úrsula, in the absence of Aureliano (134–35).

13. "I believe it was the name. Bayard. We did well to name him Johnny" (*SAR* 371). She does not yet know that his name is Benbow because she was bedridden the day he was named.

14. Accordingly, the novelist survives Sartre's objections.

15. Cf. Part III. With regard to the display of the past, cf. Quentin's formula: "Maybe nothing ever happens once and is finished. Maybe happen is never once but like ripples maybe on water after the pebble sinks, the ripples moving on, spreading . . ." (*AA* 210).

16. See, for instance, when "Judith too began to feel like the other one to a pair of goldfish" (*AA* 257).

17. García Márquez asks if it necessary to be reminded that it is a matter of an historical episode falsified by the official "version."

18. See, for example, the burial of Red, in *Sanctuary* (the bullet hole revealed in the fall of the casket) or that of Sutpen tumbling "*sabre plumes and all, into a ditch*" (*AA* 151).

19. "*I dont. I dont! I dont hate it! I dont hate it!*" (*AA* 303).

20. The problem lies outside the scope of this article, although one can cite as typical examples the crossing of the river in *As I Lay Dying*, the lynching of Goodwin in *Sanctuary*, twilight observed by Hightower in *Light in August*. On the comic side, there is even a shift toward the unreal—the automobile stuck in the mud in *The Reivers*: "something dreamlike about it" (87); the vision of the "spotted horses" from Texas, species of demons and sprites in *The Hamlet*.

21. Cf. 89–93, the deceased Sartorises reunited in the abandoned attic. Cf. the ghost of John Sartoris (his father) between the young Bayard and Narcissa, etc.

22. The handwriting is rather obscured, but it seems that the letter has at the same time become luminous (in a double sense) and impalpable: "Now he (Quentin) could read it, finish it—the sloped whimsical ironic hand out of Mississippi attenuated, into the iron snow" (*AA* 301).

23. ". . . the agony and the sweat of the human spirit" in which Faulkner composed his work ("Nobel Prize Acceptance Speech" Stockholm, 1950).

WORKS CITED

Carballa, Emmanuel. "Un gran novelista latino americano." *Revista de la Universidad de México.* 12.3 (Nov. 1967):10–16.

Coindreau, Maurice Edgar. "Preface to *Light in August.*" *The Time of William Faulkner: A French View of Modern American Fiction.* Ed. and chiefly trans. by George McMillan Reeves. Columbia: U of South Carolina P, 1971. 31–40.

Couffon, Claude. "Entretien: García Márquez, *Cent Ans de solitude.*" *Le Monde* 7 Dec. 1968, 4–5.

Cowley, Malcolm. *The Faulkner-Cowley File: Letters and Memories 1944–1962.* New York: Viking, 1966.

Duque, Jaime M. *Mito y realidad in Gabriel García Márquez*. Bogotá: La Oveja Negra, 1970.

Durán, Armando. "Conversaciones con Gabriel García Márquez." *Revista Nacional de Cultura* 29.185 (July–Sept. 1968): 23–34.

Faulkner, William. *Absalom, Absalom! The Corrected Text*. New York: Random House, 1986.

———. *Faulkner in the University*. Ed. Frederick L. Gwynn and Joseph L. Blotner. New York: Random House, 1959; New York, Vintage,1965.

———. *Light in August. The Corrected Text*. New York: Vintage, 1985.

———. *The Reivers*. New York: Random House, 1962.

———. *Sartoris*. New York: Random House, 1956.

Fell, Claude. Rev. of *Cent Ans de solitude. Le Monde* 23–4 March 1968, supplement: N. pag.

Giradoux, Jean. *Three Plays*. 2 vols. Trans. Phyllis La Farge with Peter H. Judd. New York: Hill and Wang, 1964.

Harss, Luis and Barbara Dorman. *Into the Mainstream: Conversations with Latin-American Writers*. New York: Harper, 1967.

Márquez, Gabriel García. *One Hundred Years of Solitude*. Trans. Gregory Rabassa. New York: Harper, 1970.

Nathan, Monique. *Faulkner par lui-même*. Paris: Editions de Seuil, 1963.

Rama, Angel. "Un novelista da la violencia americana." *Nueve Asedios a Gabriel García Márquez*. Santiago: Editorial Universitaria, 1971. 106–25.

Vargas, Germán. "Un personaje, Aracataca." *Recopilación de textos sobre Gabriel García Márquez*. Havana: Casa de las Américas, 1969. 139–42.

ANDRÉ BRINK

Making and Unmaking.
Gabriel García Márquez:
One Hundred Years of Solitude

1

'I merely wanted to tell the story of a family who for a hundred years did everything they could in order not to have a son with a pig's tail', Gabriel García Márquez explained, no doubt tongue in cheek, about the writing of *One Hundred Years of Solitude*, 'and [. . .] ending up having one' (quoted in Wood 1990:24). That there must be more to it is obvious from a mere glance at the veritable library of scholarly studies which have been accumulating ever since the first publication of *Cien Años de Soledad* in 1967.[1]

There have been illuminating studies on the relationship between the local and the universal in the novel, and on the relationship between Márquez and Cervantes; on the nature of magic realism; on the themes of incest, and genealogy, and taboo, and patriarchy; on characterisation, and tragedy, and comedy, and musicality; on mythology and history, and the mythology of history, and the history of mythology; on the temporal structure of the novel, and on its spatial structure, and on its spatio-temporal structure; there have been Marxist readings, and Feminist readings, and narratological readings, and deconstructive readings; psychoanalytical readings and mythopoeic readings and biographical readings. Yet in spite of all this, in one study after the other, there are admissions about the seeming inexhaustibility of the book, its 'elusive and

From *The Novel: Language and Narrative from Cervantes to Calvino*, pp. 231–252, 350–352. © 1998 by André Brink.

enigmatic' nature (see Williamson 1987:45). It is, clearly, as Bell (1993:41) says, 'a work, like Kafka's novels, specifically designed both to invite and to resist interpretation'.

Within the context of the text's relationship with language one of the most stimulating essays is Aníbal González's study on 'Translation and Genealogy' (González 1987), which has the additional advantage of reading *One Hundred Years of Solitude* against the backdrop of the *Don Quixote*. González argues that not only the South American novel, but the novel as a genre, has its origins in the notion of translation, specifically 'in the transport—through violence or exchange—of meaning from other texts and other languages into the literary text' (González 1987:77; cf. also p. 65, and p. 79 n. 24).

From a close scrutiny of the many references to foreign languages in the text (a feature to which we shall soon return), González discusses the imperative of translation which arises from such confrontations. This concept is read against the background of three theoretical approaches: the first, suggested by Walter Benjamin, posits the existence of an overriding 'sacred text', an 'expressionless and creative Word, that which is meant in all languages' (González 1987:69); the second, derived from Derrida, focuses on 'a transgressive struggle between [. . .] two equally "proper" languages, one of which tries to deny the other's specificity' (p. 70); the third, based on Borges, proposes 'that the notion of translation is intimately linked to the nature of literature, and that translation can serve as an instrument of critical inquiry into the workings of literature' (p. 71).

On these premises González proposes an exciting extension of the notion of 'translation' by reading into the narrative of *One Hundred Years* a Derridean 'dissemination' of meanings from different signifying systems, discovering a parallel between the Buendías' task of translating the gypsy manuscript into 'the language of kinship (with all that it implies in terms of the incest taboo and of the importance of proper names)' (ibid.:72). This reading is motivated by the consideration that 'translation and incest both share a transgressive nature, both are "improper" acts that imply breaching the barriers between members of the same family or between two languages' (p. 75). He concludes this line of argument by asserting that

> translation, like incest, leads back to self-reflexiveness, to a cyclonic turning upon one's self which erases all illusions of solidity, all fantasies of a 'pure language', all mirages of 'propriety', and underscores instead language's dependence on the very notion of 'otherness', of difference, in order to signify 'something', as well as the novel's similar dependence on 'other' discourses (those of science, law and religion, for example) to constitute itself. (p. 76)

It is a seductive reading, even if one may question the parallel González assumes between sexual relations between individuals linked by kinship and intercourse between languages (like Sanskrit and Spanish) which belong to the same Indo-European family.[2] And it may come close to breaking down when the relationship also concerns, as it does in *One Hundred Years*, languages like Spanish and Guajiro (the indigenous tongue Arcadio and Amaranta learn before they can speak their own) or Papiamento (which Aureliano junior speaks, haltingly, to the old West-Indian 'Negro'). Also, not all the languages that feature in the text impose a need for translation: in many episodes the function of those languages—ranging from Latin to English, or from the gypsy language to the one fabricated by Fernanda)—lies precisely in the fact that, at least in their specific context, they *cannot* be translated.

This does not mean that González's reading can be discounted; it remains one of the most stimulating contributions to the growth industry of writings about Márquez in general and *One Hundred Years of Solitude* in particular. But it does mean that reading language as translation does not go far enough towards illuminating the view of language presented by the text, and its relationship with the narrative that unfolds in it.

2

Certainly, the proliferation of references to foreign languages in the text (foreign, that is, to the Spanish spoken in Macondo) provides an important early pointer towards the role of language in this novel. As González (1987:66–8) already shows, an early distinction is made between the language of Macondo and that of the gypsies when the 'tender obscenities' whispered by José Arcadio in the gypsy girl's ear 'came out of her mouth translated into another language' (p. 35); Arcadio and Amaranta are taught Guajiro by the family's royal servant Visitación; when Rebeca arrives it turns out that she, too, can speak Guajiro; in addition to Spanish and the gypsy language, as well as several others, Melquíades speaks 'a complex hodgepodge' (p. 65); after being tied to the chestnut tree in the yard old José Arcadio Buendía speaks a strange tongue which turns out to be Latin (p. 75); José Arcadio's Spanish is 'larded with sailor slang' and his 'unusual masculinity [is] completely covered with tattoos of words in several languages intertwined in blue and red' (p. 80); Pietro Crespi translates the sonnets of Petrarch (p. 94); the manuscripts of Melquíades which provide the ultimate clue to the 'hundred years of solitude' of the Buendía family, are written in Sanskrit; and in his attempts to translate them, the youngest Aureliano has to learn, not only Sanskrit, but 'English and French and a little Latin and Greek' (p. 309), while he also picks up Papiamento (p. 311). In addition to the examples cited by González, languages other than Spanish obsessively intrude in the world of Macondo: Amaranta dreams of a Utopia 'of handsome men and women who spoke a childlike language' (p. 94); Arcadio speaks to the Indians in their own language (p. 97); what marks Mr Herbert as an outsider is that he speaks 'broken Spanish' (p. 186); Fernanda, as we have noted, invents her own language in order to avoid uttering words she regards as improper (p. 175); Mr Brown is marked by his 'strange tongue' (p. 208); Meme learns English from her friends in the enclave of the Banana Company (p. 225); the old Catalonian bookseller speaks his native tongue (p. 297); the labels on the bottles in the pharmacy are in Latin (p. 301); the encyclopedia from which Aureliano Segundo teaches his children is in English (p. 302), and so on.

But there is also what one may call a 'language of things' in many of the mysterious happenings in the Buendía household (like the empty flask which grows too heavy to be moved, or the pan of water which boils without any fire under it, observed by José Arcadio Buendía and Aureliano, 'unable to explain them but interpreting them as predictions of the material': p. 36). In the episode where Meme is taken away from Macondo to the convent, the young woman, having renounced speaking altogether, travels through what appears like a landscape without language, but in fact it is a landscape which has itself turned into a reified language, and on behalf of Meme (who registers nothing herself) the narrator reads it as if it were a book, allowing the reader to rediscover in it the whole history of Macondo (p. 240).

Once the reader has been alerted to the existence of such other signifying systems, the process is expanded. There is a language of the future read by Pilar Ternera from her cards. There is a language of the past which can only be read by deciphering codes like the galleon stranded in the moors or the submerged suit of armour. There is a language spoken by the ghost of José Arcadio Buendía which only his great-great-grandson Aureliano can understand (p. 216). There is a language of sex, markedly different from the language of social intercourse, in the encounters between Pilar Ternera and, first, José Arcadio, then Aureliano, as there is between Aureliano Segundo and Petra Cotes (quite distinct from the articulation of his relationship with his emotionally repressed wife Fernanda); and ultimately a language of 'lyrical voracity' (p. 327) between the youngest Aureliano and his aunt Amaranta Úrsula,[3] which begins, significantly, in an amorous encounter precisely while her husband is writing a letter (p. 302), as if each activity is a mirroring of the other. And, in confirmation of the language of sex, there is a clear hint of a gendered language when it is said of Remedios the Beauty that 'men's words would not penetrate her' (p. 194).[4]

What all these moments cumulatively come to communicate, I would argue, is both the *isolation* of Macondo from the outside world and its distressing *vulnerability* to threats from that outside.[5] Or, in different terms, the sense of *difference* imposed by language on the reader's perception of Macondo and the rest of the world (which in itself, of course, is shown to be multidimensional, or stratified: the world of science and the world of intuition; Europe and the 'Third World'; different experiences and definitions of sociopolitics, commerce, history, culture, and so on).

This awareness of difference permeates, and determines, almost every aspect of the novel, which presents difference in terms of time and space (here-and-now as opposed to other places, other times); in terms of inside and outside; in terms of beginning and ending; in terms of whatever in a given situation is perceived to be real and what as not-real, unreal, supra-real, imaginary, or magical; in terms of the identity, of Self and Other. It quite literally establishes and subverts, creates and undoes, makes and unmakes the narrative world. *Hacer para dehacer* (Márquez 1987:347)—'to make [or to do] in order to unmake [or undo]'—is a key phrase for *One Hundred Years*. It designates specific actions of specific characters: Colonel Aureliano Buendía who makes little gold fishes which he sells for gold to make new fishes to sell for gold to make new fishes, until he stops the selling and confines himself to manufacturing only two fishes a day 'and when he finished twenty-five he would melt them down and start all over again' (p. 216); or Amaranta who weaves her shroud by day only to unweave it, like Penelope in the *Odyssey*, at night (p. 212). But it also informs the overall design of the novel, its patterns of creation and/or evolution (the founding of Macondo, the establishment of the Banana Company, the love relationships, all the enterprises of the imagination) followed by decay, destruction and obliteration. The Banana Company grows into a monster until it is literally washed away by rain; consecutive attempts of José Arcadio Buendía, Colonel Aureliano and others to smash and destroy everything they have established during their lives are followed by the apocalyptic wind that blows Macondo from the face of the earth.

In the final analysis these creations or imaginings are obliterated by *language*. After José Arcadio Segundo's horrifying experience of the worst act of annihilation in the novel prior to its apocalypse (the massacre that ends the workers' strike and his discovery of the train of 'almost two hundred freight cars' transporting the corpses of the dead to be dumped in the sea: p. 250) he returns to Macondo where a woman dresses his wound and offers him some coffee; but when he tries to discuss the event, the woman cuts him short: 'There haven't been any dead here [. . .] Since the time of your uncle, the colonel, nothing has happened in Macondo' (p. 251).

This goes further than the earlier court decision in the dispute between workers and management of the Banana Company, 'that the workers did not exist' (p. 246), or the subsequent official announcement that, 'Nothing has happened in Macondo, nothing has ever happened, and nothing will ever happen' (p. 252), because these pronouncements merely establish the discrepancy between 'reality' or 'history' on the one hand, and its official versions on the other. When the woman addresses José Arcadio Segundo it is the ordinary language of ordinary people which accepts and disseminates as truth the 'fact' that nothing has happened whereas the reader has just been told that something *has* happened. The point is no longer whether something is 'officially' announced or 'popularly' believed, or even that the events witnessed by José Arcadio Segundo may be corroborated by at least some historical versions of the great United Fruit Company strike in Colombia in 1928 (see Martin 1987:107–8 or Wood 1990:vii): the point is that at one moment in the narrative a series of events (the strike and its outcome) is established by and in language, and that at another moment the same series is obliterated, once again in and by language.

Naturally, in such a situation, the reader's first reaction is to read the matter as a 'cover-up', whether imposed by the authorities or induced by shock among the population, and to trust what the narrator has just revealed about the massacre—especially when it concerns a character with whose viewpoint the narrator has persuaded us to sympathise. But what if the narrator's version of what Martin (1987:107) terms 'the central shaping episode of the entire novel', is just as suspect as that of the officials, or of the kindly woman?

Let us look at another episode, near the end of the novel, when the youngest Aureliano leaves the corpse of his beloved Úrsula Amaranta, puts his new-born pig-tailed child in a basket and goes in search of help:

> He knocked at the door of the pharmacy, where he had not visited
> lately, and he found a carpenter shop. The old woman who opened
> the door with a lamp in her hand took pity on his delirium and
> insisted that no, there had never been a pharmacy there, nor had
> she ever known a woman with a thin neck and sleepy eyes named
> Mercedes. (p. 333)

Once again the reader still conditioned by a particular convention of reading might wonder who to believe: the woman of the pharmacy, or the narrator? Unlike the Good Samaritan encountered by José Arcadio Buendía this woman has no 'reason' to cover up. And the narrator does specify that she sympathises with his 'delirium'. Given the state Aureliano is in, he may well be suffering from a form of delusion. Yet the reader has encountered the pharmacy before, and knows about the girl Mercedes who has presumably left Macondo with her fiancé Gabriel Márquez when he went off to Paris 'with two changes of clothing, a pair of shoes, and the complete works of Rabelais' (p. 325). We may even know from a variety of sources, including a number of interviews with Márquez himself, that this Gabriel bears a strong resemblance to the 'real' Latin American author who left Colombia for Paris—the only apparent difference being that the Gabriel in the book carries a Rabelais with him while the Gabriel outside of it took *A Journal of the Plague Year* by Defoe.

'The suggestion', says Wood (1990:55), 'is not that history and fiction are the same, but that the borders take a lot of traffic, and have been known to shift' (p. 55). Certainly much can be made (and has been made) of the two texts which largely coincide in *One Hundred Years* while nevertheless retaining their differences: the manuscripts of Melquíades and 'the book of Gabriel' (Wood 1990:52).[6] But the two episodes I have referred to, and above all the stupendous apocalypse at the end (when it turns out that what the Buendía family has been experiencing over seven generations coincides exactly with what the old gypsy wrote down a century before, each the perfect supplement to the other, each perfectly cancelling the other), amount to more than a choice between two versions. What is really illuminated by them, and by countless other moments in the narrative, is that only by virtue of language do such versions, and such choices, become thinkable. On each occasion when the community of Macondo experiences a form of obliteration—whether in the form of the sleeping sickness, or the imposed amnesia following the massacre of workers, or the near-interminable rain which all but washes away the town, and ultimately the hurricane which obliterates the whole place (and Melquíades's manuscripts with it), *language* enters into the void to recover from silence everything that would otherwise have been lost—that is, everything which has been established by language to begin with. This goes far beyond what Martin (1987:104) and innumerable others have explored as instances of circularity. It demonstrates the awe-inspiring capabilities of language, through which a reality can be established by weaving together a textual world of signifieds, and then can be undone again by severing the link between signifiers and signifieds. It is an act of prestidigitation which outperforms anything the gypsies first brought to Macondo. It is both a celebration and a radical questioning of language. Language giveth and language taketh away. It establishes links in time and space, and cancels them. It does and undoes. *Hacer para dehacer.*

3

But language can only function significantly in this manner if it can be *seen* to be doing so—in other words, if it highlights itself, self-consciously, in the act of making and breaking. One of the ways in which language foregrounds itself, we have seen, is in consciously setting up Macondo (and its language) in distinction to the outside world (and its many languages). But there are other strategies as well, and each of them modifies, and adds different dimensions to, this general perception.

Perhaps the most visible of these strategies to highlight language is the trope of *writing*. It begins early in the first chapter, when not content with witnessing the marvels of Melquíades, José Arcadio Buendía insists on getting a set of *written* instructions from the gypsy, 'in his own handwriting [. . .] so that he would be able to make use of the astrolabe, the compass, and the sextant' (p. 11). At first sight writing appears to confer a sense of authority on the gypsy's language—which would be the exact opposite of Derrida's *écriture*—but this soon turns out to be, like most of the later instances of writing in the narrative, an illusion, because all the gypsy's instructions lead nowhere, or, if they may be said to lead anywhere, it is only into a Borgesian labyrinth of dead-ends and forking paths.

In Macondo, a world 'so recent that many things lacked names' (p. 9), an adamic process of naming is set in motion by the gypsy's instructions—and throughout the novel the activity, first of writing, and later of deciphering, the manuscripts of Melquíades, will form an undercurrent to all the multifarious other activities and incidents in the narrative.

When the sleeping sickness descends on the town, inherited from the Indians who have been silenced by the processes of colonisation, it becomes necessary to attach written name-tags to all objects:

> With an inked brush he marked everything with its name: *table, chair, clock, door, wall, bed, pan* [. . .] Little by little, studying the infinite possibilities of a loss of memory, he realized that the day would come when things would be recognized by their inscriptions but that no one would remember their use. Then he became more explicit: The sign that he hung on the neck of the cow was an exemplary proof of the way in which the inhabitants of Macondo were prepared to fight against loss of memory: *This is the cow. She must be milked every morning so that she will produce milk, and the milk must be boiled in order to be mixed with coffee to make coffee and milk.* Thus they went on living in a reality that was slipping away, momentarily captured by words, but which would escape irremediably when they forgot the values of the written letters. (p. 46)

If the danger appears to be averted when Melquíades arrives with a magic potion to dispel both the insomnia and its corollary, amnesia, we are reminded towards the end that the escape has been illusory too. This happens when the last Aureliano, significantly named Aureliano Babilonia, is revealed to be 'a man [. . .] holed up in written reality' (p. 314). The Spanish phrases it even more strongly: '*encastillado en la realidad escrita*' (Márquez 1987:425). As Minta (1987:177) puts it,

> On the final page he discovers, in the words of Emir Rodríguez Monegal, that he is simply 'a ghost who has been dreamed by another man', just a fictional character, 'trapped in a labyrinth of words', and that his fate, completely conterminous with the Macondo that is dying, is to be annihilated so totally that not even a memory will remain.

Like Tweedledum and Tweedledee in Carroll's *Through the Looking-Glass*, Aureliano turns out to be the product of another man's dream, the prophetic writing of Melquíades—but at the very moment of his reading about his end as he approaches the moment of his end,[7] Aureliano is recovered, together with the whole written history that has just been cancelled by his reading, by *another* text, written by (a persona of) that Gabriel Márquez who earlier escaped from Melquíades's text by leaving Macondo for Paris. Either way, he remains a figment of writing—but in the process both his writers, Melquíades and Gabriel, have also been transformed into *écriture*: Melquíades who is written by Gabriel, and Gabriel, who has first been written by Melquíades.[8]

No wonder that when the first government-appointed magistrate, Apolinar Moscote, arrives in Macondo with a flurry of written orders, José Arcadio Buendía calmly informs him that 'in this town we do not give orders with pieces of papers' (p. 53). The snowballing irony is that as language begins to draw more and more attention to itself in the form of writing, it also increasingly undermines its own validity. This is both the quandary and the triumph of a text which 'establishes the frontiers of reality within a book and the frontiers of a book within reality' (Fuentes 1990:192).

When Colonel Aureliano falls in love with Remedios and is driven to writing poetry it would seem to offer an escape from the developing conundrum:

> The house became full of love. Aureliano expressed it in poetry that had no beginning or end. He would write it on the harsh pieces of parchment that Melquíades gave him, on the bathroom walls, on the skin of his arms. (p. 61)

And poetry remains his most urgent activity throughout the years of his thirty-two armed uprisings, which would seem to lend credence to a view of written language as, at the very least, a search for meaning. But if the first of his love poems held no meaning for others because they were without beginning or end, his later outpourings remain strictly private and no-one is ever allowed a glimpse of them. And a central activity of his preparations for suicide, as he attempts to destroy 'all trace of his passage through the world' (p. 146) is the methodical burning of all his poetry. Far from being a demonstration of language as communication, Aureliano's writing wholly escapes from the public domain to become as much a secret and solitary indulgement as José Arcadio Buendía's habit (copied by several of his descendants) of talking to himself. This incident will, later, reflect new light on a small scene towards the end of the novel, when one of Aureliano Babilonia's intimate friends, Alvaro, leaves Macondo on 'an eternal ticket on a train that never stopped travelling' (p. 325); and as he watches the passing landscape from the window of his coach, and sends his friends postcards about these 'instantaneous images', he is described 'as if he were tearing up and throwing into oblivion some long, evanescent poem' (p. 325). Recalling the destruction of Colonel Aureliano's poetry, this would suggest that the whole world of geography and history through which Alvaro is travelling, is transformed into writing—which voids it of meaning and makes it destructible.

Acquiring the skill of writing appears to be an important concern in the Buendía household: Aureliano teaches it to Rebeca, Amaranta teaches Aureliano José, Fernanda teaches her children, Úrsula teaches Amaranta Úrsula; and sooner or later they all turn into more or less assiduous letter-writers. Yet for all their inveterate writing not one of them ever achieves anything in the process. In her old age, when Rebeca compulsively writes to the Bishop, she never receives any reply; Aureliano's letters to Úrsula during his absence on his many wars communicate either a distorted image of what he is engaged in, or a totally false impression (receiving a note he has written from Santiago, Cuba, Úrsula concludes: 'We've lost him forever': p. 124); and what General Moncada writes to him to remind him 'of their common aim to humanize the war' (p. 132) has so little effect that it might just as well not have been written. The same applies to the several letters written by Colonel Aureliano to the president after the war (pp. 150, 198). It is fitting that the terms for peace between Conservatives and Liberals (like, much later, the ultimatum to the striking workers, p. 248) should also be put in writing, only to be ridiculed and negated by both sides (p. 141). And as for the destructive consequences of writing, it is revealing that the prelude to Arcadio's rise towards eminence as an unscrupulous tyrant is his copying of his military uniform from a design in Melquíades's books (p. 91).

There are innumerable love-letters in the narrative, but they meet with no better fate. Rebeca, having finally won her family's consent to marry Crespi, writes 'a jubilant letter' to her fiancé (p. 64)—but the moment José Arcadio makes his appearance she forgets all about her earlier feelings and intentions. José Arcadio himself presents another form of writing, the tattoos all over his body, including his monstrous penis—to the extent that González (1987:73) speaks of his 'body-become-text', but this writing remains 'cryptic' (p. 80) and cannot be deciphered by anyone in Macondo. Crespi declares his love to Amaranta in 'wild notes' (p. 96), which she returns unopened. Aureliano Babilonia and Úrsula Amaranta correspond during her absence in Brussels, but when she comes back they both discover that their 'real' selves, whatever these may be, have nothing at all in common with the imagined Other each has been writing to. Mauricio Babilonia is practically the only one truthfully to attempt declaring his love in writing when he sends Meme a card, but it is restricted to the merest statement of intent ('We'll get together Saturday after the movies': p. 235), and it is, moreover, characterised as a laborious inscription 'by someone who could barely write' (p. 235). To compound the situation, it is this tryst which leads to their discovery by Fernanda and results in the fatal retribution that puts an end to their love. Even when writing appears to 'mean' something, it has only devastating consequences.

Fernanda and her children dutifully correspond during all the years they spend away from home—but most of their writing amounts to barefaced lying, each communicating to the other a totally false image of their lives and emotions; in due course Fernanda even places her letters in the wrong envelopes (p. 292). This puts into perspective her habit, assumed since a very early stage in her strained relations with Amaranta, never to talk to her sister-in-law again, but to communicate only in writing (p. 175). Ultimately these letters 'mean' no more and no less than Fernanda's compulsive writing to a collection of 'invisible doctors' about her imaginary complaints,[9] a correspondence which, in any case, ends 'in failure' (p. 281).[10]

The whole business of letter-writing, and the function of language demonstrated and disseminated by it, is perhaps best summarised in the wonderful episode of Amaranta's death when she invites all the people of Macondo to bring her letters which she can deliver to the dead on the other side of the grave (p. 229).

These dead-end correspondences (together with others, like the old Catalan's letters to Aureliano and his friends, the last of which remains unopened because they do not want to read what they know it must contain (p. 331), or those exchanged between Amaranta Úrsula and Gastón after he has left (p. 327) lend a particular effect of futility even to small throwaway scenes like the one in which Gabriel Márquez pays a prostitute in a brothel, not 'in money but in letters to a smuggler boyfriend who was in prison on the other side of the Orinoco' (p. 320). In a way *all* these many letters which, as Barthes might say, 'star' the text, are attempts to reach out from the *here* of Macondo to the *there* of the Outside and of Otherness; from the real to the unreal or the magical; from the known to the unknown; from present to past, or future, or timelessness (it is surely meaningful that Fernanda's writing 'made her lose her sense of time': p. 293).

4

All this accumulating mass of writing, within the overarching writing of the narrative itself, culminates in the deciphering of Melquíades's manuscripts. If it is a vast act of translation, as González (1990) has shown, it is above all a testing of the validity, and of the limits, of language as writing.

The first of the family to dedicate himself to this task, after the manuscripts have originally been entrusted to José Arcadio Buendía, is Aureliano Segundo. But he receives no help from Melquíades, who nevertheless visits him regularly for long discussions. 'No one must know of their meaning', the (ghost of) the old gypsy explains, 'until a hundred years have gone by [*Nadie debe conocer su sentido mientras no hayam cumplido cien años*]' (Márquez 1987:208)—which, unfortunately, as several critics have already pointed out, has been erroneously translated by Rabassa as 'No one must know their meaning until he has reached one hundred years of age', demonstrating once again, I suppose, the unreliability of written language. It almost amounts to saying that their meaning cannot be divulged within historical time (a century, broadly speaking, comprises the whole history of Macondo).

Even when, many years later, Aureliano Babilonia succeeds in deciphering the original Sanskrit (with the help of books presumably 'last read [. . . by] Isaac the Blindman': p. 297) they remain incomprehensible as they turn out to be 'predictions in coded lines of poetry' (p. 316)—a dire warning, at the very least, to any reader who has taken note of the fate of Colonel Aureliano Buendía's poetry. Only at the 'prodigious instant' of Amaranta Úrsula's death, following the birth of their pig-tailed son who is consumed by ants,

> Melquíades' final keys were revealed to him and he saw the epigraph of the parchments perfectly placed in the order of man's time and space: *The first of the line is tied to a tree and the last is being eaten by the ants.* (p. 334)

This is 'the history of the family, written by Melquíades, down to the most trivial details, one hundred years ahead of time'—but written, not 'in the order of man's conventional time [. . .] but [. . .] concentrated in such a way that they coexisted in one instant' (p. 335). This is a Postmodernist reprise of Diderot's 'Great Scroll' which also moves from a chronological/causal relationship with Jacques's life towards commensuration and co-existence.

As Aureliano reads, he starts catching up with himself reading; and outside the apocalyptic wind, which also exists in the writing, springs up to obliterate him, and the whole Macondo, in the instant of his reading about that obliteration. Genesis and Revelations coincide in this moment. And everything is subsumed in writing: language has led the reader from the opening page to this last one where the writing consumes itself—only to be decanted from the text of the gypsy into that of Gabriel García Márquez. We are caught, here, in a bind as inescapable as the one between that famous beginning which was no beginning, *riverrun, past Eve and Adam's, from swerve of shore to bend of bay* . . . and that ending which was no ending, *A way a lone a last a loved a long the*

5

The great act in which the narrated world (and the condition of its own narration, the manuscripts of Melquíades) is annihilated at the end of the novel, can be effected only if it has been constructed to begin with. In both processes, as I have begun to argue, language is implicated.

One of the most visible strategies of narrative construction in *One Hundred Years*, on which a host of critics have already commented, is what Wood (1993:18) terms 'almost a signature of the book', that is, its construction of 'loops' (ibid.:67), through which it becomes possible to look both forward and back in the same moment in order to achieve an impression, or at least an illusion, of Melquíades's motto: 'Everything is known' (pp. 302, 309). This strategy has been discussed as a feature of the time structure of the novel, as a marker of the interaction between the real and the imaginary, as a mnemonic device, as an indicator of decisive turns in the plot, as a clue to the philosophy of the epistemology of the novel . . . Our present concern is to look at it as a device of language which marks the textualising process as decisively as the acts of conjuring performed by Melquíades and his band in the streets of Macondo. And, of course, in a very real sense, the language of the novel as a whole *is* a trick performed by the old gypsy himself, in the solitude of the study assigned to him: a trick of prestidigitation which requires a complementary action, the attempts of Aureliano Babilonia, before it can be completed—by obliterating itself. It is a block of ice melting under its own weight, in the heat of deciphering.

In a bleak moment during his many wars, Captain Aureliano Buendía expresses the confusion of his thoughts in the face of death in rhymed verse—poetry which will eventually be destroyed in a marvellous prefiguration of the self-destruction of Melquíades's world: 'Then his thoughts became so clear that he was able to examine them forward and backward' (p. 116).

This is precisely what happens in the syntax of the famous opening line
of the book:

> Many years later, as he faced the firing squad, Colonel Aureliano
> Buendía was to remember that distant afternoon when his father
> took him to discover ice. (p. 9)

—a variation of which will also introduce the second major movement in the
narrative: 'Years later on his deathbed Aureliano Segundo would remember
the rainy afternoon in June when he went into the bedroom to meet his first
son' (p. 152).[11]

Just as Einstein invented, from the old Newtonian categories of time
and space, the new concept of spacetime, Márquez here establishes his own
distinctive *language-time* which will come to define the novel as a whole.
The effect is immediately to dislodge the time of the narrative from ordinary
time, by subverting the possibility of a fixed point of reference: is the episode narrated in a present from which a glimpse of the future is offered, or
is this 'present' *already* viewed from a narrative future, with the advantages
and disadvantages of hindsight? In the opening passage the issue is further
complicated by the consideration that the expectation of Aureliano's death
by firing squad will be frustrated in the discovery, later, that he was in fact
freed at the last moment (to be repeated in his 'second' death when his attempted suicide also fails), and that the first episode of the narrative does *not*
concern the discovery of ice, which only follows several pages later. But these
are strategies of *narrative*, whereas the description of looking forward-and-
back in the same sentence is a device of *language*. The compounded result is
an impression of drifting in time, of past and future simultaneously invading
the present; or, phrased differently, of a present constantly, and precariously,
exposed to invasions by past and future.

And this becomes a weave in the text as a whole. The first reference to the
Captain facing the firing squad will be repeated many times before it 'actually
happens' (p. 111); and it is entirely in keeping with this weave that, when he is
visited by his mother just before he is to be taken out of his cell for his execution,
he should tell her, 'Don't beg or bow down to anyone. *Pretend that they shot me a
long time ago*' (p. 108, my emphasis). It is also fitting that when he really dies in
the story, he should again relive 'that prodigious afternoon of the gypsies when
his father took him to see ice' (p. 218), but the important point about this event
is that when he finally dies, just after he has watched the sad circus going by, the
reader discovers that this moment, too, has already been narrated:

> He locked himself up inside himself and the family finally thought
> of him as if he were dead. No other human reaction was seen in

him until one October eleventh,[12] he went to the street door to watch a circus parade. (p. 215)

Only three pages later in the text the narrator will describe how Aureliano goes to the door, watches the circus, returns to the chestnut tree in the courtyard where his father used to be tied up, urinates, and dies. On the level of the story it happens *now*; on the level of the text it has already happened.

Had this happened only a few times, it would have been easy to read over it; but it becomes a constitutive factor of the text. Little Remedios's death, soon after she has reached puberty and married Aureliano, is narrated on p. 77, *followed by* an account of events which preceded it, only to catch up with the narrative present two pages later. On p. 84 Aureliano, more or less out of the blue, remarks that, 'These are not times to go around thinking about weddings'; this is followed by a broad-ranging account of events from that period, before the narrative returns to the original statement: 'It was during those days that Úrsula asked him his opinion about the marriage between Pietro Crespi and Amaranta, and he answered that these were not times to be thinking about such a thing' (p. 88). In these cases, as in so many others, language is shown to fold in upon itself, regularly signalling moments in time well ahead of their occurrence in the story, in order to catch up with them later. As many critics have shown, such circles and eddies are characteristic of the text; but it is important that they should also be read as flexions of *linguistic* muscles.

Sometimes this happens in a much more elaborate way. Chapter 6 opens with a remarkable synopsis of Colonel Aureliano Buendía's life as a soldier, beginning with the cryptic statement that, 'Colonel Aureliano Buendía organized thirty-two armed uprisings and he lost them all' (p. 91). Only towards the end of Chapter 9 is this particular loop completed, recapitulating the years of his thirty-two rebellions before he returns to attempt suicide (pp. 149–51)—which clears the scene for the novel's second major movement to begin. In this case, the synopsis serves as a Derridean supplement to the ensuing elaborations which will both consume it and restate its significance.

In numerous other instances this process of complicated prolepsis appears to be orchestrated to achieve an effect of *déjà vu*—by the time Meme's son is brought home (p. 243), we have already learnt about his arrival (p. 239); when Pilar dies in the story (p. 329), she has already been declared dead by the text (p. 322): this is more than what Genette would term iteration in the text, since it is more often than not accompanied by significant variation and deviance. By the time we learn about the conditions in which Aureliano Segundo found Fernanda in her parents' home (p. 172) we already know that they were married (p. 168), but the two accounts of his quest differ quite markedly. The first time it appeared straightforward; in the retelling, as the narrator warms up to his narrative, it becomes immensely complicated.

Ultimately, all these loops serve as a *mise-en-abyme* of the overall narrative situation: the history of the Buendías as the recapitulation of a story already written a hundred years before by Melquíades. This momentous discovery—the coincidence of 'life' and 'text', of 'story' and 'history'—turns out to be cataclysmic, resulting as we have seen in the total annihilation of both the world of the Buendías and the world according to Melquíades, and simultaneously in the eruption of the Márquez text from the ashes of the world which has just been declared destroyed (a 'declaration' as momentous, and as fallacious, as the court's finding that there were no workers in the plantations, or in the official assertion that no-one died in the massacre). As Drechsel Tobin (1978:177) phrases it in the context of a somewhat different argument:

> With this conversion of the past to a visionary future where all is guessed, we are confronted with the probability that our unobtrusive narrator has taken things so calmly because he is one incarnation of the gypsy Melquíades, to whom 'everything is known'.

The text is dead; long live the text.

6

But language connects people and events not only in the time of the narrated world but within its spatial dimensions as well.

When Colonel Aureliano Buendía finds himself in prison, awaiting the firing squad, there is a passage in which he is spatially related to his father in exactly the same way as they are related in time in the novel's opening sentence: 'He thought of José Arcadio Buendía, who at that moment was thinking about him under the dreary dawn of the chestnut tree' (p. 109). The link is more complicated than it might seem at first sight. 'Obviously' the person—the 'him'—referred to in the second part of the sentence, is José Arcadio Buendía whom we know to spend his days under the chestnut tree. But a number of years after this incident, having survived both the firing squad and suicide, Aureliano will return from watching the circus procession to sit down under the same tree and succumb to death. And given the ceaseless uncertainties and ambiguities of the narrative language, it cannot be absolutely sure, in the shadow of death which hangs over the scene, whether it is Aureliano thinking of his father tied up under the tree, or his father thinking of his son who will one day die in the same spot. In both readings there is a spatial connection, established by the language, which carries some of the multiple meanings with which the text abounds.

At the moment when Aureliano pulls the trigger to kill himself, Úrsula discovers that the pot of milk she has put on the stove hasn't boiled yet and is, instead, full of worms; and her first reaction is to pronounce, 'They've killed Aureliano' (p. 149). The connection is inspired by her early discovery, when Aureliano was only three years old, that he had the power of causing objects to move by looking at them (p. 20). The intertwining of time and space is complicated by the fact that in the same instant when she believes Aureliano to be killed, she looks out into the courtyard and sees her husband, 'soaking wet and sad in the rain and much older than when he had died' (p. 149). In other words, when she (wrongly) believes her son to be dead, she finds herself looking at the spot where he will die, years later. Through the intricate ramifications of language time is fully spatialised.

The most spectacular spatial linkage of characters through the manipulations of language occurs at the time of José Arcadio's mysterious death (shot either by himself or by his wife Rebeca). In one of the most famous scenes in the novel (pp. 113–14), the dead man's blood finds its way to his mother, trickling across half the village. She retraces its course in a motion which precisely inverts the meandering sentence in which the trail of blood has been described, until she arrives at the body of José Arcadio. It is a remarkable to-and-fro movement in which the progression of the first sentence is, as it were, devoured by its countermovement in the second—in a brilliant anticipation of the two movements, forward and back, which will explode in the moment of revelation at the end.

7

There is another linguistic force at work in this scene; behind what McMurray (1977:92) calls a technique of 'hyperbole and preposterous distortions' one discerns the workings of metaphor, not only as 'a kind of linguistic unconscious' (Bell 1993:51), but as a form of literalisation through which language in its communal or public form (de Saussure's *langue*) is appropriated for idiosyncratic personal use (*parole*). The notion of kinship, of blood-relationship, specifically the proverb about blood being thicker than water, is here concretised (just as, earlier in the story, the notion of memory is concretised in the form of an ancient galleon discovered in the swamps; or incest in the shape of a child with a pig's tail). The metaphor is turned into a *narrative performance*, theatrical and spectacular, which activates different levels of meaning in the text—most obviously those of the 'magical' and the 'real'. And once again this effect is not derived, in the first instance, from a kind of cultural or symbolical code interpellated by the narrative, but by a manipulation of language.

The text abounds with examples of this functioning, some comparatively brief, like the description of the rain of yellow flowers which marks José Aureliano Buendía's death (p. 120) or the yellow butterflies which accompany the comings and goings of Mauricio Babilonia (pp. 232 ff.), others much more ample, like the magnificent scene of the ascension of Remedios the Beauty. As a metaphorical elaboration of her untouchability, her 'lightness of being', *su impermeabilidad a la palabra de los hombres*, the narrator describes how one afternoon, while helping to fold Fernanda's Brabant sheets in the garden, a delicate wind springs up and Remedios begins to levitate. With delightful 'realistic' detail the scene unfolds:

> Úrsula, almost blind at the time, was the only person who was sufficiently calm to identify the nature of that determined wind and she left the sheets to the mercy of the light as she watched Remedios the Beauty waving goodbye in the midst of the flapping sheets that rose up with her, abandoning with her the environment of beetles and dahlias and passing through the air with her as four o'clock in the afternoon came to an end, and they were lost forever with her in the upper atmosphere where not even the highest-flying birds of memory could reach her. (p. 195)[13]

Perhaps the give-away phrase in the passage is 'birds of memory' in which both the signifying and the signified dimensions of metaphor, tenor and vehicle, are explicitly linked to suggest that the rest of the scene may also be read as metaphor. All the more so as we are directly informed, in the narrator's characteristic dead-pan style, that

> The outsiders, of course, thought that Remedios the Beauty had finally succumbed to her irrevocable fate of a queen bee and that her family was trying to save her honour with that tale of levitation. (p. 195)

Once this practice has been established, it is no longer necessary to alert the reader to its machinations with phrases like 'birds of memory'; and by the time Amaranta Úrsula arrives on the scene, we are prepared for the amplest possible reading of that delightful passage: 'Amaranta Úrsula arrived with the first angels of December, driven on a sailor's breeze, leading her husband by a silk rope tied around his neck' (p. 305).

Once again, language foregrounds itself, in the form of a concretised metaphor ('she keeps her husband on a tight rein'), and by alerting the reader to the various layers of meaning embedded in a seemingly straightforward linguistic and narrative statement, we are prepared to acknowledge the decisive and defining function of language in the text as a whole.

8

This is not merely a powerful function; it is also a function of power—the power, as we have seen, to do and to undo, to create and to destroy. It is demonstrated quite specifically in the episode of old Úrsula's death: after having been turned into a plaything by the children Aureliano and Amaranta Úrsula (in a dramatic reversal of the relationship between generations), the wretched old great-great-grandmother practically reverts to a fetal state and remains lying motionless, but still alive, in her bedroom. From there, the children carry her out by the neck and ankles, pretending to lament her death, while ignoring all her feeble protests (p. 278). And eventually she succumbs—literally killed by language—the language of the children who have proclaimed her dead.

But they are merely adumbrations of old Melquíades, who, a hundred years earlier, already wrote characters into life and out of it; and he, in turn, of course, 'represents' the narrator looming behind him, that other Gabriel Márquez who resumes the narrative when Melquíades and his whole creation are written out of it.

It lies at the heart of storytelling, and this novel is not just a story told but a story about the telling of stories. From the first pages of the first chapter 'the children were startled by [Melquíades's] fantastic stories [. . .] lighting up with his deep organ voice the darkest reaches of the imagination' (p. 13). And when the inhabitants of Macondo are threatened by amnesia, one of their remedies is the telling of stories—even if it is only the senseless, repetitive game of the story about the capon which forms a verbal labyrinth without issue (pp. 44–5). Once they have been restored to the semblance of a normal, or 'real' existence,[14] the most significant irruption into their lives from abroad (apart, that is, from the visits of the gypsies), is that of Francisco the Man who transforms the history and the news of the outside world into song—a language of performance which adds a substratum of knowledge to their lives (p. 49). For many years after his last visit, his narrative songs—in which history has been transmuted into story—are still repeated by Aureliano Segundo (p. 285); and when he, too, disappears from the scene, the songs persist in the performance of 'an accordion group' (p. 333). Language has finally dissolved into music, into songs without words. Which is another form of obliteration, and of new creation; and at the same time, in the persistence of a memory reduced to the mere outline of a tune from which all traces of language have faded away, we discover, perhaps, *that language has always* been, 'essentially', empty and meaningless[15]—except when its power is harnessed in the form of narrative, of storytelling.

At the end, as we have now noted several times, all the stories and their telling are subsumed in the narrative action of the Gabriel who takes over from Melquíades (and who dreamed up Melquíades in the first place): making, unmaking, and then making again. It is the ultimate expression of solitude.

Because this is how language is conceived of in *One Hundred Years of Solitude*, in its functions, and its power, of summoning to life, and then assigning to death, in order to begin again. Text unto text. *Hacer para dehacer.*

NOTES

1. All references to the English text are to the felicitous if flawed translation by Gregory Rabassa in the Picador edition (London, 1978). Reference to the original Spanish text are to the Mondadori edition (Madrid, 1987).

2. 'The ancient Indo-European Sanskrit would seem to represent language in general and thus an appropriate vehicle for recording universal human experiences', writes McMurray (1977:85), but this appears to me to impose an easy symbolism on the novel, in line with McMurray's endeavour to enforce a reading of a 'rounded whole' and of closure.

3. The acts of speech and sex are first associated when in José Arcadio's early encounters with Pilar Ternera 'they reached such a state of intimacy that later, without realizing it, they were whispering to each other' (p. 31). This is confirmed, and emphasised, in his encounter with the gypsy girl where his transport 'burst forth with an outpouring of tender obscenities that entered the girl through her ears and came out of her mouth translated into her language' (p. 35). Later in the novel the language of sex and that of social intercourse significantly tend towards mutual exclusion: on Rebeca's wedding night with José Arcadio she is bitten by a scorpion on the foot, as a result of which 'her tongue went to sleep, but that did not stop them from spending a scandalous honeymoon' (p. 83)—an event repeated to some extent when in her early episodes of lovemaking with Aureliano junior Úrsula Amaranta is obliged to gag herself 'so that she would not let out the cat howls that were already tearing at her insides' (p. 321).

4. The somewhat crude active voice of the English translation is more muted in the original, which refers to 'su impermeabilidad a la palabra de los hombres' (Márquez 1987:263). But the link between language and sex remains obvious.

5. It is curious to note how Macondo retains its sense of isolation through more than a hundred years of narrated time, even though from its earliest days it is visited from abroad: first by the gypsies, then by emissaries from the government, later increasingly by troops and the representatives of commerce. Even after a regular mail service is introduced and a railway link established, it remains strangely intact.

6. See Williamson (1987:59): '*One Hundred Years of Solitude* sets forth two distinct modes of reading history [. . .] Each mode is predicated upon a certain type of consciousness. Aureliano's reading might be termed "incestuous"; it is devoid of objectivity, of reference to external reality and to linear time [. . .] If Aureliano is an

internal reader of the Buendía history, who witnesses his own fate in Melquíades's "speaking mirror", the ordinary reader remains outside the narrated events and is therefore capable of an objective, distanced view of that history.' But since the writer of the second narrative, Gabriel Márquez, is also implicated in the first, as a character, 'he can look back on his experience and write a history of Macondo to rival the interpretation of Melquíades [. . . H]e must construct his account in such a way as to reflect Macondo's history without himself falling prey to the siren-song of nostalgia' (ibid.:61).

7. This is also the ideal envisaged by Beckett's narrator in *Malone Dies*.

8. In this respect Márquez perhaps comes closer than anywhere else to Cervantes who, in the *Don Quixote*, also makes use of a 'fictitious foreign historian' (Bell 1993:61), in the form of Cide Hamete Benengeli, to write his story (see also, *inter alia*, Martin 1987:112). And Cide Hamete in some respects becomes a 'character' in his own story by the time Don Quixote, in Book II, looks back on the first volume of his written adventures.

9. These letters are as 'empty' as her husband's correspondence with his 'partners' in Brussels, about consignments of planes which never arrive (pp. 310, 317).

10. At the appointed hour she awaits their arrival, covered in a sheet and with her head pointing north, and when she wakes up the next morning she discovers 'a barbarous stitch in the shape of an arc that began at her crotch and ended at her sternum' (p. 281). What amounts to a form of crude writing—in which language and sex are once again closely linked—is, in every sense of the word, a *non sequitur*. And then a letter from the invisible doctors arrives, as 'real' or as 'imaginary' as anything else in the narrative, to complain that they could not find anything corresponding to her complaints. This is blamed on 'her pernicious habit of not calling things by their names', and it leads to a diagnosis of a dropped uterus for which pessaries are prescribed. (Fernanda's most common confusion, in writing as in speech, has been that between rectum and vagina.) Another implication of 'barbarous' may also be relevant here, as the term evokes a form of distinction between Self and Other (that is, the Barbarian) which often creeps into descriptions of Macondo and its Others. And in this connection it is amusing to observe that when José Arcadio's penis, that very organ later to be tattooed in foreign tongues, is first observed by Pilar Ternero, she exclaims, '*Qué barbaro!*' (Márquez 1987:37)—a nuance sadly lost, like a number of others, by the limp English 'Lordy!' (p. 28). It is picked up again near the end when Amaranta Úrsula meets Aureliano Babilonia again, once more using the exclamation, '*Qué barbaro!*' (Márquez 1987:306)—this time translated as 'My, my!' (p. 306). It is meant to recall, importantly, the first great virile member of the family; but at the same time it brands *him* as the 'stranger', whereas *she* is the one newly arrived from foreign climes.

11. It is very unfortunate that the key phrase of the novel, *había de* should be translated (correctly) as 'was to' in the first instance and (incorrectly) as 'would' in the second. Many invaluable nuances of the original have been sacrificed by such carelessness. Here it loses the whole notion of a *reprise*, a new cyclic beginning in the narrative.

12. It is another feature of the text, and another 'trick of language', that days of the week or month should be very precisely specified, but without reference to any year, so that the very specificity becomes a marker of vagueness. In *appearing* to signify, language does the opposite; and upon inspection the apparently confident signifier turns out to be empty.

13. The final deft comic touch is added with the subsequent reference to 'the inconsiderate Fernanda [who] was going about mumbling to herself because her sheets had been carried off' (p. 205).

14. Throughout the text the notion of the 'real' is problematised, as innumerable commentators have pointed out. Which makes it piquant, to say the least, to note how persistently characters are described as feeling that 'reality is slipping away' from them: the community as a whole experience it during the sleeping sickness (p. 46); José Arcadio Buendía experiences it when he is tied to the tree (p. 93)—whereas, surely, he of all people has reason to doubt reality from the first visits of the gypsies with their magnifying glasses and their ice and their flying carpets; Colonel Aureliano experiences it during his wars (p. 165); Úrsula feels it in her dotage (pp. 201, 266); Amaranta Úrsula and Aureliano Babilonia break through the final barriers of the real in their lovemaking (p. 326) . . .

15. The 'emptiness' of language as such is illustrated by many episodes in the novel, ranging from the capon story to the endless ramblings and rantings of Fernanda (pp. 262–5), by an acknowledgement of 'hate' which turns out to be 'love' (pp. 222, 228), by Aureliano's disembodied voice giving senseless messages on the telephone (pp. 136, 140), by Úrsula's conversations with the ancestors (p. 266), or by Aureliano Babilonia's (admittedly short-lasting) discovery that all the languages he has learned 'were as useless as the box of genuine jewelry that his wife owned' (p. 329).

JOHN KRAPP

Apathy and the Politics of Identity: García Márquez's One Hundred Years of Solitude and Contemporary Cultural Criticism

The events narrated in Gabriel García Márquez's *One Hundred Years of Solitude* problematize an assumption commonly held by certain critics writing within the arena of contemporary identity politics, to wit: that both individual and collective identity are formed in a site of contestation, wherein a dominant voice eventually and inevitably represents an identity for both itself and for a weaker, subaltern voice. Characteristically relying on generalization to make its case, this strand of critique suggests that the identity of the subaltern is affixed through a process of victimization: the loser in the struggle fights valiantly to represent itself, only to be represented by a hegemonic power with little interest in treating fairly the object of its brutality.[1] Without trivializing or trying to diminish the very real suffering of the victims of the struggle for subjective representation,[2] I wish to argue that García Márquez's novel introduces the possibility that, while the subaltern may indeed be "a figure produced by historical discourses of domination" (Prakash 88), not all subaltern identities are the product of active political struggle. The process of identity construction is an extremely complex phenomenon, and apathy may play a crucial role in it, even among those apparently victimized by a hegemonic discourse.[3]

I am led to my hypothesis about the role of apathy in the politics of identity by two of the novel's most important episodes, both of which in-

From *LIT* 11, no. 4 (Winter 2000): 403–427. © 2001 by Overseas Publishers Association N.V.

volve groups of characters infrequently considered in commentary on García Márquez's text. In the first, a band of Liberals from Macondo and elsewhere, led by Colonel Aureliano Buendía, engage the nation's Conservative government during a prolonged period of civil war. However, despite the commitment of those who fight against the Conservatives, there nevertheless remain a majority of Macondones who do not ally themselves with the Liberal rebels and participate in the wars; rather, they pursue their daily routines in the village as uninterruptedly as possible. In the second, during Macondo's occupation by the Banana Company, several thousand of the banana workers engage in a labor strike that culminates in their being massacred at a train station. However, the workers do not bring themselves to strike on their own; rather, they are inspired to their action by José Arcadio Segundo Buendía, who seems to lead them throughout the strike and who, the novel implies, ultimately provokes the Banana Company's soldiers to fire on the crowd of workers gathered at the station. In both of these episodes, some people ostensibly struggle, indeed at great peril to their own well-being, for the opportunity to represent themselves to a dominant power. But not all people. What about the Macondones who do not follow Colonel Aureliano Buendía into war? Why do they remain behind? What about the Macondones and banana workers who do not stand against the Banana Company, despite the unjust social conditions it establishes in the town? Of those who do, why do they require the leadership of a Buendía, a member of the town's founding aristocratic family, to strike? Can apathy be considered a variable in these sites of identity contestation?

To address these questions, more fully developed accounts of the Civil Wars and the banana workers' strike will be necessary. Moreover, the analysis that follows must be silhouetted against what I take to be the most important, and difficult to clarify, series of questions in any consideration of apathy's role in the politics of identity: is apathy the effective condition of a subaltern group who, after a process of struggle and victimization, have already been represented by others, or, contrary to much critical opinion, may apathy serve as a *precondition* for a subaltern group to be represented by others? That is, how is power implicated in the relationship between nonparticipants and their act of nonparticipation (DeLuca 7)? Put another way, is apathy a *cause* or a *consequence* of a given set of social relations (DeLuca 191)? If it is a choice, is it made consciously? If so can it be called apathy, since the very process of choosing is a display of action, the lack of which is etymologically signified by apathy? If a subaltern identity demonstrates apathy after being represented by a stronger power, and the behavior may be labeled unconscious, can the subaltern subsequently be held accountable for not trying to represent itself more aggressively? These questions have received unsatisfactory attention in the current dialogue on the politics of identity, wherein, if apathy is at all discussed, it is not often figured as a contributing *reason* for why individuals are represented in a particular way.

The Macondones

To this point, I have referred very broadly to the "Macondones," but the term designates a group of people who are at times far from homogeneous. While it would be impossible to delineate every personal or collective identity interest in the novel, the Macondones may be divided into several groups, each of which reveals its own subdivisions based on class, ethnicity, religion, and other demographic codes. There are the founders of the town and the successive generations of their progeny, a class obviously most prominently exemplified by the Buendías, who initially journey to Macondo in search of a place where José Arcadio Buendía can escape his conscience for murdering another man. The newcomers thereafter introduced by Úrsula are first associated with the founders of Macondo and assume an equitable role in the social and political life of the village. Only as the Civil Wars begin to take shape do the newcomers become distinguished from the rebel founders and fill in the population of the vast majority of Macondones, a group that comes to include some founders, who choose to remain behind rather than fight. There are also the Indians, mentioned only on occasion as servants in the founders' homes; within the dynamics of colonialism, these individuals preexist the founders and populate the town in other laboring capacities but are no more concretely categorized.[4] Finally are people who, through the process of natural comings and goings, fill the interstices among these groups and round out the population of the village.

The question of which Macondones are being represented is perhaps never easier to answer than in the beginning of the text, when Macondo is "a village of twenty adobe houses" whose founders are "amazed" (1) at the scientific demonstrations of Melquíades, the learned gypsy. Although these are the same Macondones who will later be cited as owning Indian servants, they believe José Arcadio Buendía to have "lost his reason" (5) when the village's patriarch is the sole citizen to embrace Melquíades's knowledge and instruments as physical tools to be mastered. As a group, the founding Macondones display the kind of ignorance and incredulity that one might stereotypically expect of native servants illiterate in the colonists' language[5] and of lower middle class citizens unable to procure education.[6] Moreover, for years following Melquíades's first visit, these founding Macondones continue to be at turns curious and terrified by the gypsy's demonstrations. As critics of the novel have noted, the founders' inability to understand Melquíades's contributions at the same intellectual level as José Arcadio Buendía makes them easy to manipulate and exploit.[7]

The Macondones' population grows to three hundred during the next several years, at which time José Arcadio Buendía designs the layout of the village, modelling each of the founders' houses in the "image and likeness" (9) of his own and placing them "in such a way that from all of them one could reach the river and draw water with the same effort" and "no house got more sun than another during the hot time of the day" (9). This is prelapsarian Macondo, a communal paradise before the Civil Wars where equity of opportunity and resources governs social life among the founders and their progeny. Throughout the descriptions of the village's early development, there is virtually no direct mention of class or social difference among the founding Macondones. If in fact they are all socially equal, separated from José Arcadio Buendía only by the latter's keen intellect and powerfully disciplined and enterprising nature, why do the other founders concede authority to José Arcadio Buendía during this early stage in the village's history? Nothing in the text suggests that relations between the Buendías and their neighbors are tense, that the Buendías brutalize their neighbors, or that their neighbors feel victimized. Yet what amounts to the Macondones' collective identity as the founding families is the product of only one of these founders. On José Arcadio Buendía's design, the founders become Macondo's bourgeoisie, its ruling class, a status of some import for my considerations on apathy and identity.

Not until Úrsula Buendía returns from a journey with a band of "men and women like them" (39) from a neighboring village do we see the first influx of people who presumably begin to fill the ranks of Macondo's middle class. These newcomers speak the same language and carry with them all things necessary for a comfortable domicile. And like the village's founders, they all acknowledge José Arcadio Buendía's authority over the Macondones' social life, allowing him to apportion land and design their homes. Again, José Arcadio Buendía is put in the position of establishing the Macondones' identity without opposition. He quite literally sets the boundaries whereby the Macondones' status is determined (Chun 195). The newcomers' willing submission to prevailing social protocol might lead one to believe that they are granted the same privileges as the founders, yet they are not among the guests invited to celebrate the inauguration of the Buendías' new house, a party comprised solely of the town's founders. The fact is, social distinctions are evidently being made, but no one voices suffering in their wake. If apathy explains why the founders and newcomers give José Arcadio Buendía license to govern social relations in Macondo, it may be apathy of a very distinct kind, one emerging where no one feels aggrieved by circumstances and subsequently feels no need to alter them (DeLuca 125). Resignation plays no part in the excluded Macondones' reaction to the guest list.

The entire Macondones population's progressive response to the insomnia plague, first the good humor at having more time to enjoy life, then the consolidated effort to retain memory *via* the strategy of Aureliano Buendía, reveals the same kind of dynamic seen during the development of the village. Since the memory of everyone's past is afflicted in the same manner, and there is no question of erasing a specifically chosen individual's or group's identity, any mention of struggle during the insomnia plague amounts to the entire Macondones population's being against something that threatens all of it, not one or more Macondones against others in internecine conflict devolving on class, ethnicity, race, religion, etc. Indeed, the politics of identity as they are contemporarily defined become germane in Macondo only when national power outside the village makes its first uncertain stab at assuming control of the Macondones' social life in the person of Don Apolinar Moscote, who is sent to the village as its new Conservative Magistrate, an event that inevitably facilitates the Civil Wars.

The Moscote Episode and the Civil Wars

When Don Moscote appears, José Arcadio Buendía explains to him how

> they had founded the village [...] no one was upset that the government had not helped them. On the contrary, they were happy that up until then it had let them grow in peace, and he hoped that it would continue leaving them that way, because they had not founded a town so that the first upstart who came along would tell them what to do. (61–2)

The collective pronominal references throughout this declaration deserve attention. They suggest that all of the Macondones, founders and newcomers alike, share José Arcadio Buendía's disapproval of Don Moscote's behavior. However, when the confrontation between José Arcadio Buendía and Don Moscote becomes tense, only "[t]he founders of Macondo, resolving to expel the invaders, went with their older sons to put themselves at the disposal of José Arcadio Buendía" (62). As the first landholders of the village, the founders and their sons would, fulfilling the military expectations of the noble warrior class enshrined throughout feudal history, offer themselves for a fight. But why do the males among the newcomers earlier brought by Úrsula to Macondo not come forth to defend the village as well, since they too hold property?

Heretofore, the novel has implied that the founders and newcomers have all participated to their satisfaction in a communal paradise despite emerging social disparities. This impression enabled my earlier claim that there is no internal conflict among the villagers. Does the failure of some men to stand against Don Moscote at an instance of clear external ideological crisis indicate that there is such conflict? If there is, why do the newcomers not express their disaffection with José Arcadio Buendía's social organization earlier? Sociological discussions of apathy might attribute the newcomers' quietism up to this point to their feeling of political subordination (DeLuca 147), to their comfortable, if not entirely satisfactory, social habits (Thorn 32), or to their assessment of the complexity of society, in which they lack clearly defined goals and purposes (Riesman 1). These explanations treat apathy as a consequence rather than a cause of inaction. The fact that the newcomers do not as a group struggle to establish a distinct identity in Macondo when they first arrive prompts continued suspicions that apathy is the source of their circumstances.

In fairness, I note that if the newcomers' decision not to join the rebellion may be interpreted as an intentional act of contest against the founders, then they are in fact following a precedent that goes at least as far back as the Greek Stoics, who practiced *apatheia* as a meaningful form of commentary on the decay they witnessed in the culture around them; it took the form of a conscientious decision to avoid investing energy in things that they could not control. Ignatius Loyola proposed a similar strategy when confronted with secular distractions to his spiritual reflections, writing in his "First Principle and Foundation" that

> Man is created to praise, reverence, and serve God our Lord, and by this means to save his soul. The other things on the face of the earth are created for man to help him in attaining the end for which he is created. Hence, man is to make use of them in as far as they help him in the attainment of his end, and he must rid himself of them in as far as they prove a hindrance to him. Therefore, we must make ourselves indifferent to all created things [. . .]. Our one desire and choice should be what is more conducive to the end for which we are created. (23–24)

García Márquez's text, however, hardly makes this a compelling possibility, instead suggesting that the founders and newcomers who remain behind are simply indifferent to political events because they do not feel threatened enough to care about political intervention.[8]

Apathy may also figure prominently when Moscote's soldiers arrive and "no one remembered the original agreement not to have armed men in the town" (96). That a matter of such consequence could slip the minds of all Macondones again allows the reader to consider what identity interests are representing themselves in the village. Some among the founders have already elected to identify themselves in conflict with Moscote, yet they too must be included among those who fail to remember the original political principles of Macondo. Why then are they prepared to fight? On what principles do they commit themselves? Perhaps the failure of the newcomers to stand against Moscote, even after he imports armed guards to defend the Conservative stakes in the village, is less difficult to explain: if the newcomers have in fact felt threatened all along by the founders, they may view the Conservative government's efforts to displace the ideology of the founders as the only way to weaken the individuals who they feel immediately dominate them. According to this explanation, apathy never characterized the newcomers, who were shrewd enough to discern the right moment to express their political sympathies in an effort to emerge from beneath the founders' subtle, but surely felt, oppression. Again, the text offers virtually no evidence to support this ascription of passive resistance to the newcomers.

In an ironic turn on the traditional uses of political terminology, Aureliano Buendía assembles a Liberal rebel faction to conserve the Macondones' lifestyle established by his father, while the Conservative government struggles to impress change on the village.[9] Despite the fact that, at their inception, the Civil Wars help to delineate the Liberal and Conservative identity interests in the village,[10] perhaps the most significant thing about Aureliano Buendía's commitment to expelling the Conservatives from the area is his lack of interest in political labels. He tells Moscote that he will be a Liberal simply "because the Conservatives are tricky" (106). Yet he expresses his disgust with Dr. Noguera, a Liberal provocateur, insisting, "You're no Liberal or anything else [. . .] You're nothing but a butcher" (108). As Regina Janes notes, ideology is irrelevant to Aureliano's real justification for rebellion, which is his desire to undercut the brutality of the Conservatives' power (133).

Aureliano Buendía understands that if the Macondones want to represent themselves as they always have, they cannot allow themselves to be dominated by a stronger power that will otherwise represent them. The names assigned to these power groups are far less compelling to Aureliano Buendía than is control over one's identity.[11] Thus his conversation with his friend and fellow rebel, Colonel Gerineldo Márquez:

> "Tell me something, old friend: why are you fighting?"
>
> "What other reason could there be?" Colonel Gerineldo Márquez answered. "For the great Liberal party."
>
> "You're lucky because you know why," he answered. "As far as I'm concerned, I've come to realize only just now that I'm fighting because of pride."
>
> "That's bad," Colonel Gerineldo Márquez said. Colonel Aureliano Buendía was amused at his alarm.

"Naturally," he said. "But in any case, it's better than not knowing why you're fighting." He looked him in the eyes and added with a smile:

"Or fighting, like you, for something that doesn't have any meaning for anyone." (148–49)

Aureliano Buendía calls his conviction pride, which is expressed to the reader in his insistence on thinking, speaking and acting on his own volition, not another's. His insight, that the political struggle over representation means little or nothing to the majority of Macondones who remain behind, appears to be corroborated by the fact that Aureliano Buendía can only assemble "twenty-one men under the age of thirty" (110), all "sons of the founders" (108), to eliminate the soldiers in Macondo and embark on the civil campaign. This is a stunning figure. The remaining founders' sons, who by this point must number over one hundred, their fathers, and all the male newcomers, show no interest at all in joining the revolutionary army. This reaction hardly resembles the kind of Stoic apathy that helped citizens withstand the cruelty of the Empire, since there is no evidence that those who ignore the muster take the Conservative threat seriously. Nor is it the (essentially Stoic) apathy that Christianity preached, advising servants to obey their masters because they have little option to do otherwise, thus preserving the status quo. Rather, a chosen behavior, the remaining Macondones' lack of participation smacks of apathy to political events as long as the domestic situation remains comfortable,[12] a reason borne out by the only instance of their protest when José Arcadio, Aureliano Buendía's brother, takes some of their land and levies contributions against peasants without the government's sanction. Otherwise, the vast majority of the remaining founders and newcomers, who are now categorized in the text as a homogeneous entity, willfully disregard the civil struggle that will ultimately determine how, and by whom, they are represented.

Other examples abound. When Arcadio, Aureliano Buendía's nephew, is placed in control of the town by his uncle and subsequently brutalizes the people, so few contest him that it falls on Úrsula, his grandmother, to discipline him. When the Conservatives begin to regain an authoritative presence in the village, Arcadio can only incite "fifty poorly armed men" (127) to defend the Liberal agenda; though they fight bravely, they are wiped out. The rest of the Macondones go about business as usual. And while there is one reference to the "rebelliousness of the town" (139) that makes the Conservative government reluctant to execute Aureliano Buendía when he is finally captured to bring the first wave of the wars to a close, it is José Arcadio alone, "crossing the street with his fearsome shotgun ready to go off" (141), who prevents his brother's death. The earlier cited rebellious Macondones are conspicuously absent from the rescue. They could be afraid, but of what? Were they not comfortable with the Conservative regime, one suspects they would not have waited until José Arcadio taxed their land to express disapproval with it; they would have acted against the Conservatives sooner. It is much more likely that they do not care, entirely apathetic to the question of who confers their sociopolitical identity as long as their economic success does not suffer.

It might even be too much to claim that the remaining Macondones are attentive enough to political issues to protect the Conservative order, of which they seem to approve, when it is threatened by rebel attack. Consider their estimation of General José Moncada, the Conservative Mayor of Macondo after the first of the Civil Wars comes to a close. Despite the fact that he is not by political sympathy a Liberal, the remaining Macondones respect his authority. Like Aureliano Buendía, he seems more wedded to a perceived standard of fairness and justice than to a political program. Yet, when Aureliano Buendía attacks the village to reestablish Liberal control, Moncada suspects that he will lose the battle because the rebels are "fighting because they want to" (170). From the founders and newcomers who had remained behind at the onset of the war, Moncada receives no support.

Instances like this prompt Gerald Martin to assert that the remaining Macondones "fail to become agents of history for themselves [. . .] they are the echoes of someone else's history [. . .] they are living out their lives in the name of someone else's values" (104), but this is not convincing. The same people who chose not to fight with the Liberals to preserve the founders' original social organization now choose not to fight with Moncada's Conservatives, who have protected their interests thus far. The Macondones who populate Moncada's village choose to do nothing. Moreover, they make their choice with the power to have done otherwise, even to have protected Moncada's government, under which they have thrived. Martin is more accurate in maintaining that these Macondones are "blissfully unaware of historical reality and know nothing of the world which has determined their destiny" (106). Apathetic about who represents them as long as they remain comfortable, the remaining Macondones may also be unaware of the consequences of their actions; they may not realize that their comfort is predicated upon who represents them, and that to this point they have been very fortunate.

As evidenced by their irresolute response to Aureliano Buendía at various stages during the wars, acknowledging him alternately with cheers and scorn, the remaining Macondones are characterized by their lack of principle and foresight. Not one of them protests when Aureliano Buendía is finally willing to surrender and end the war; instead, it is strongly intimated that he had lost the support of the Liberal landowners long ago. It is these same landowners for whom the Liberal rebels engaged the Conservatives in war in the first place. As time passes, the atrocities of the Conservative government accrue, reaching their first peak in the slaughter of revellers gathered at the carnival to watch Remedios the Beauty being coronated queen. The remaining Macondones continue to reproduce their political apathy by refusing to question the official version of the shooting, which relieves the Conservatives of blame. These Macondones are far more interested in Aureliano Segundo's profligacy, in the modernization of the town and its concomitant amenities, in the miracle of the motion pictures introduced to the village. Only Aureliano Buendía foresees the exploitative effects of the railway when it finally arrives; the Macondones are too immersed in wonder at the newness of the changes to their village to think so far ahead (Williamson 54). Sated on bread and circuses, they have no appetite for political struggle to represent themselves. Simply put, the nationalistic struggle, whose most palpable stakes are the identities of the participants (Scheibe 126), completely passes them by.

An instructive, if initially unsettling, parallel may be drawn between the remaining Macondones' behavior up to and during the Civil Wars and the reputed comportment of many German citizens during the Holocaust; such a comparison provides some historical precedent for the theoretical claims I am making about identity politics. In both cases, a coterie of individuals establishes an identity for a much larger group of people. Efforts at explaining why many German citizens did not resist the Nazis run the gamut. Erich Fromm offers the German people's need for authority as a reason why many acquiesced to the Nazis. Fromm has also hypothesized that, assuming their antipathy towards the Nazis' agendum, German citizens' will to represent themselves was impeded by tiredness and resignation (233–34). Norman Geraus recently corroborated this diagnosis, identifying an insidious "contract of mutual indifference" at the core of many Germans' relationship with the Jews (28) and citing Third Reich historian Ian Kershaw that "The road to Auschwitz was built by hate but paved with indifference" (18). Missing from both these accounts is fear. The Nazis had no compunction about exacting tremendously disproportionate reprisals for any injury they suffered and were known to kill many of those who harmed one of theirs. It could thus be argued that, if many Germans appeared indifferent to the brutalities committed against the Jews, they could in part justify this attitude with the suspicion that any of them might meet the same fate if they protested the Nazis' actions.

The Macondones' willingness to be represented, first by José Arcadio Buendía, then by the Conservative government as it inexorably gains political dominance in the village, has no such justification in fear until, if at all,

the Civil Wars are finally over and Aureliano Buendía's opposition to the national government comes to an end. Founders and newcomers alike have in-
ternalized profitable social codes from the moment they arrive (Weigert 39),
and José Arcadio hardly obstructs their process of assimilation; hence, they
have nothing to which to be resigned. In David Riesman's considerations
on apathy, the political impassivity of the Macondones who avoid fighting
during this period is particularly frightening because they are individuals
who could influence public life, who could maintain control over their own
identity, but who nevertheless remain indifferent (189–90). I am not suggesting that, had the Macondones offered collective resistance against the
Conservatives, they would have been able to preserve the ideological stasis
originally established in the village by the founders. Given the resources
of the Conservatives—the sheer number of soldiers, the superior military
arsenal, the national treasury—the Macondones, if they were permitted to
live, would most likely have been forced to accept the terms of sociopolitical
organization dictated by the Conservatives. This is to say that, only if they
offered more collective resistance would their identity be formed through the
process of contestation, brutalization and victimization identified by some
contemporary critics of the politics of identity as lying at the heart of identity
representation. That they could have opted for intervention but chose not to
only strengthens the case for their apathy.

The Macondones who choose not to fight are quite clearly less the victims of others' desire to represent them than they are the product of their
own inertia. Nothing in the text indicates that, prior to the eventual con-
solidation of the Conservative regime, they are disempowered individuals;
instead, they are presented as somewhat disparate but free individuals who
have themselves alone to blame for allowing their interests to wane (De Luca
11, 124). The novel's famous metaphor of solitude, most often discussed as
characterizing the members of the Buendía family, is an active component of
the Macondones' lives as well in so far as they habitually detach themselves
from circumstances that affect them and willingly retreat into their own private concerns until events occur that make it impossible for them to recover
their autonomy. To sum up, in the case of their reaction to the Civil Wars
and the Conservative occupation of the village, the remaining Macondones'
volitional apathy causes them to be represented by others in a manner increasingly at odds with their best interests.

The Banana Company

Aureliano Buendía's assessment of the village *ethos* after the wars is the
litmus of the Macondones' apathy, which prevents them from realizing that
the town is being restructured by the Banana Company:

> When he saw Mr. Brown in the first automobile to reach
> Macondo—an orange convertible with a horn that frightened
> the dogs with its bark—the old soldier grew indignant with the
> servile excitement of the people and he realized that something had
> changed in the makeup of the men since the days when they would
> leave their wives and children and toss a shotgun on their shoulders
> to go off to war. (256)

Witnessing the decapitation of a man whose seven year old grandson accidentally spills a soft drink on a corporal of police, Aureliano Buendía

> suddenly found himself suffering from the same indignation that
> he had felt in his youth over the body of the woman who had been
> beaten to death because she had been bitten by a rabid dog. He
> looked at the group of bystanders in front of the house and with
> his old stentorian voice, restored by a deep disgust with himself, he
> unloaded upon them the burden of hate that he could no longer
> bear in his heart.
>   "One of these days," he shouted, "I'm going to arm my boys so
> we can get rid of these shitty gringos." (257)

No amount of passionate denunciation can rouse the Macondones from their indifference, even as the Banana Company effectively inaugurates the clearest identity disparity yet witnessed in the novel: the Company owners and the banana workers.[13]

García Márquez never specifically identifies which, if any, of the Macondones are employed by the Banana Company as laborers. The novel is also frustratingly silent on the process by which the Macondones who do work for the Company find their way into its labor ranks. It is probably safe to surmise that the founders neither seek labor positions with the Company, nor are they pressed into the Company's service. Because they are conditioned to labor, the Indians might be impelled by the Company to work against their own interests. The newcomers, and whatever other Macondones have filtered into the town over the years to fill in the balance of the population, represent an interest more difficult to classify. It is even possible that no Macondones at all labor in the Company, that the laborers are comprised solely of people brought into Macondo by the Company, "huddled together" in their "miserable huts" (317) separated from the Macondones' homes by an "electrified chicken fence barrier" (295). But the lack of information on the workers' individual identity affiliations before they are made to work for the Banana Company is less important than their collective identity as workers for the Company, for it is their response as workers to the Company's labor practices that prompts consideration of the role of apathy in the formation of their identity.

Some time after the Banana Company operation has been established, José Arcadio Segundo leaves his job as foreman in the Company and takes the side of the workers. His actions single him out as "an agent of an international conspiracy against public order" (320). Thereafter, when the "tension of the people" breaks "with no forewarning," José Arcadio Segundo joins other union leaders and organizes "demonstrations in towns throughout the banana region" (322). The sequence of these events is crucial to the question of whether the workers struggle to represent themselves, or whether they are motivated to action by the example of the leaders who seek to represent them against the Company. Of particular import in addressing this question is the phrase "with no forewarning." Is the prepositional phrase that, by implication, follows this one "to José Arcadio Segundo and the union leaders?" Is it "to the Banana Company?" Is it "to both?" If it is the first, then apathy absolutely cannot figure in the laborers' attempt to represent themselves, which would precede the union leaders' activity on their behalf. If it is the second, then it is possible that the workers act only after José Arcadio Segundo has begun to sow the seed of revolt; in this case, it is equally possible to wonder whether apathy is involved in the workers' failure to represent themselves without a catalyst.

Once their appeals to the courts for better working conditions and medical care are dismissed, a strike does begin, but García Márquez is ambiguous regarding whose power incites it. The same ambiguity marks the workers' reaction to the Banana Company's soldiers, who enter the town and immediately establish martial law: "The workers, who had been content to wait until then, went into the woods with no other weapons but their working machetes and they began to sabotage the sabotage" of the soldiers (326). One possible indication of their continued reliance on José Arcadio Segundo comes as the workers gather at the train station in anticipation of negotiating a settlement with the civil and military leader of the province. José Arcadio Segundo is "commissioned [. . .] to mingle in the crowd and orient it according to how things went" (326). To several official decrees, the crowd spontaneously erupts in response, but at the most crucial moment of the standoff, as the soldiers are preparing to fire into the frozen crowd, José Arcadio Segundo provokes the authorities because he is "convinced that nothing could move that crowd held tight in a fascination with death" (328). Whether José Arcadio Segundo is correct in his assessment of the workers' response to the impending catastrophe is never known. The soldiers subsequently murder nearly everyone gathered in the crowd.[14]

What makes the massacre so significant in a discussion of apathy and identity is the absolute certainty with which the Macondones who had no involvement with the Banana Company come to accept the official version of what happened at the station: "there were no dead, the satisfied workers had gone back to their families, and the banana company was suspending all activity until the rains stopped" (333). No conclusive reason is given for their concession to the authorities' spin on an event that has such an effect on their collective identity. Fear is a possible motive (Penuel 28). Indeed, the entire Banana Company episode could fairly be interpreted as a parable of Latin America's response to dictatorship and the numbing resignation often symptomatic of it; in this view, the description of the banana workers' oppression and murder clearly illustrates the process whereby a dominant power brutalizes a subordinate and determines its identity.

Nonetheless, the novel's remaining scenes suggest the possibility that apathy is still a factor in the behavior of both the banana workers and the remaining townspeople. These scenes proceed quickly in the novel, comprising only approximately one fifth of the narrative. During the fifty nine months of rain that follow the shooting, the Macondones grow impassive to everything around them, so that Aureliano Segundo is convinced that all the citizens are "waiting for it to clear in order to die" (346). After the deluge, "The indolence of the people was in contrast to the voracity of oblivion, which little by little was undermining memories in a pitiless way" (371), so much so that the gypsies who return to Macondo find the town "defeated [, . . .] its inhabitants [. . .] removed from the rest of the world" (371). The post rain torpor even affects the new priest sent to the town to resurrect the faith of the people.

Most alarmingly, the Buendía family, always politically active in the midst of their neighbors' apathy, gradually but inevitably surrender to an indifference about the way in which their past and, subsequently, their future identity is represented. During the rains, Aureliano Segundo mistakes a picture of a Tartar Warrior for his great uncle, Aureliano Buendía (346). When Aureliano Segundo's nephew Aureliano recalls how the Banana Company's army had machine-gunned more than three thousand workers penned up by the station and how they loaded the bodies onto a two-hundred car train and threw them into the sea, Aureliano's own aunt Fernanda is "scandalized [. . .] Convinced as most people were by the official version that nothing had happened" (375). Though Aureliano Segundo recognizes his nephew's version as the same one his brother, José Arcadio Segundo, used to tell, the truth of the slaughter, ignored *en masse* by the rest of the Macondones, irrevocably fades. As the Buendías' grip on historical reality weakens, so does whatever remains of the Macondones' always suspect historical consciousness (Williamson 56). The village inherited by the last generation of Buendías to be born before the whirlwind is a place of utter desolation that cannot even be rehabilitated by the lovemaking of the young Aureliano and his aunt, Amaranta Úrsula.

As suggested by their behavior preceding, during, and after the Civil Wars, the Macondones who remain in the comfort of the village throughout the narrative bring this fate upon themselves. Their volitional apathy, both to the truth of historical circumstances and to the way they are represented by others, simply gains momentum until they interpret the train station massacre the same way they interpret the sociopolitical climate following Aureliano Buendía's surrender to the Conservatives: they ignore the reality of it. The same ascription of apathy as cause cannot be made nearly as felicitously to explain the behavior of the Banana Company workers up to and at the moment of their murder. Of a different socioeconomic class, they are precisely the kind of people to whom contemporary theories of identity politics refer when they maintain that the representation of identity devolves on scenes of violence and victimization. That the workers are victimized requires, I think, little demonstration; however, only a more elaborate consideration of the dynamics of class struggle will reveal whether apathy may nevertheless contribute as either a cause or a consequence of the way the workers are treated by the Banana Company.

Historicizing the ideology of a subaltern group requires at least a preliminary acknowledgement of the possibility that, while social conditions do indeed inform people's thinking, they inform different people's thinking differently (Geraus 109). This rather unstartling observation goes far in helping to explain why workers poised on the threshold of revolutionary behavior do not always catalyze a transformation of their unjust working conditions. Rather, the workers are often prompted from "above," from "outside," towards revolution, just as José Arcadio Segundo leads the banana workers.[15] Lenin's assessment of the role of the proletariat in revolutionary history demonstrates the rhetoric of enactment that characterizes much discussion of the transformative power of the laboring class:

> The doctrine of the class struggle, as applied by Marx to the question of the state and of the Socialist revolution, leads inevitably to the recognition of the *political rule* of the proletariat, of its dictatorship, *i.e.*, of a power shared with none and relying directly upon the armed force of the masses. The overthrow of the bourgeoisie is realisable only by the transformation of the proletariat into the *ruling class*, able to crush the inevitable and desperate resistance of the bourgeoisie, and to organise, for the new economic order, *all* the toiling and exploited masses. (23; emphases in original)

Lenin's vision of the revolutionary consciousness of the proletariat depends on his notion of the proletariat as a consolidated class, in which each member represents the same ideological presuppositions about his or her

place in the dynamic of class struggle.[16] Hence Lenin's generalizing assertion that "[t]he great majority of peasants in every capitalist country where
the peasantry exists (and the majority of capitalist countries are of this kind)
is oppressed by the government and longs for its overthrow, longs for 'cheap'
government" (39). This diagnosis neatly precludes the charge that the peasants are apathetic to their social conditions. But Lenin can no more provide
definitive proof of this collective class "longing" than he can of the laboring
class's potential to revolutionize production. They are themselves ideological
imputations;[17] both are theory, a standard to which practice may, but need
not necessarily, rise. Disputing the premise of a collective class consciousness
introduces the possibility that not all members of the working class feel the
longing to transform their material conditions. Might apathy then be a factor
in some of these members' attitudes towards revolution?

Interpretive ambiguity regarding the latent revolutionary ambition
of the laboring class, an ambiguity faithfully represented in the dynamics
of the banana workers' revolt, is perhaps most famously exemplified in the
discrepant commentary on the proletariat's involvement in Russia's early
twentieth-century revolutionary history. Writing on the 1905 Petersburg
uprising, Richard Pipes alternately undermines and intimates the masses'
transformative power. On the one hand, Pipes maintains that the peasant's
interests "did not extend beyond his own and neighboring villages [. . .] He
was willing to let the world go its own way as long as it left him alone" (109).
Because the peasant lived "at the mercy of nature," which he had to negotiate
every moment for his survival, he was dominated by a mood of "acquiescence
and fatalism" (114). This state of mind resembles the Stoicism of the ancient
Greeks. It could imply victimization, since the peasant might arrive at this
sentiment after assessing his situation and giving in to what he feels are hostile forces. Or it could not, as the peasant might simply choose this attitude
as a way of indicating that this is the way things are. The ambiguity is my
point. Moreover, there was "no evidence that the peasant regarded serfdom,
which so appalled intellectuals, as an intolerable injustice" (116). Rather, it
was the Union of Unions and student activity within the universities that
catalyzed the earliest revolutionary activity, to which the workers were slow
to respond (35–36). In this interpretation, the role of catalyst played by José
Arcadio Segundo is a prerequisite to inciting an otherwise indifferent working class to political action.

On the other hand, according to Pipes, it was not so much apathy as
it was "awe and fear," what I have called resignation, that kept the masses
at bay. Hence for Pipes, apathy caused political inactivity, but apathy was
not freely chosen, as it is by the Macondones who remain in the village
during the Civil Wars.[18] In a section of his *History of the Russian Revolution* aimed at answering the question "who led the February Insurrection?"

of 1917, Trotsky also reveals this analytical ambiguity characteristic of discussions on the potential for the peasants' revolutionary consciousness. He initially comments that the theory of spontaneous revolution has long held sway over popular imagination and cites several participants in the events of 1917 on their surprise when, without warning, "[t]he masses moved of themselves, obeying some unaccountable inner summons" (142–44).[19] However, according to Trotsky, the facts of the matter simply do not corroborate the mystique.

Trotsky instead attributes the revolutionary consciousness of the Petersburg proletariat to the "great revolutionary experience [. . .] in their past" and continues to argue that "in their aggression and self-restraint, in the absence of leadership and in the face of opposition from above, was revealed a vitally well-founded, although not always expressed, estimate of forces and a strategic calculation of their own" (146). It is difficult, of course, to gauge just how well-founded something is prior to its expression. Trotsky subsequently elaborates on the doctrine of "spontaneousness" thus: "[i]n order correctly to appraise the situation and determine the moment for a blow at the enemy, it was necessary that the masses or their guiding layers should make their examination of historical events and have their criteria for estimating them" (150). The sudden shift from the transformative potential of mass consciousness to the emphasis on the inspiriting work of "guiding layers" indicates Trotsky's lack of assurance that the masses might on their own effect a revolutionary change in their material conditions. There is always the fear that they might, like the workers at the train station, stand frozen until someone or something warns them of the bullets about to come their way.

Pipes's and Trotsky's difficulties in accounting for the apparent inability of a subaltern group to represent itself, particularly under opportune conditions, against hostile forces suggest that some theorists of identity politics might be oversimplifying the causal significance of victimization in the process of subaltern identity formation. To reiterate, this does not necessarily mean that no cases exist wherein a subject or group struggles unsuccessfully against a stronger power to represent itself rather than be represented. But when a housewife claims to forswear principles of women's liberation because she is content to remain in the domestic economy and is told that she only thinks the way she does because she has gradually been convinced by oppressive patriarchal hegemonic discourse that this is what she wants, and that if she knew better she would not be happy at all in her present state, can we really be so sure that the housewife is not to be trusted at her word? Must not the theorist on the outside looking in admit that the chance exists that the housewife is truly as content as she says she is, and that her judgment, though incompatible with the theorist's generalizations about housewives, cannot be dismissed as erroneous or benighted?

The indeterminacies of individual and group psychologies make it virtually impossible to characterize the dynamics of human behavior with the kind of certainty often seen in certain writing on identity politics. The example of the founding Macondones and newcomers who choose not to fight illustrates the significant role that apathy might play in the process of identity formation. It is precisely because they function as something of a backdrop against which the exploits of the Buendía family and the Civil Wars take place that these Macondones deserve more attention than they have yet received: when they do have the opening to express their autonomy, they forego it at absolutely crucial junctures. They display what is properly identified as a freely chosen indifference throughout both the founding of the village and the Civil Wars that eventually follow. This indifference, which is not to be confused with conscientious resignation after Stoic or Christian apathy, inevitably allows others to represent their identity against what they only in hindsight realize as their interests.

The banana workers also arguably manifest a benign indifference to their working conditions until they are provoked to rebellion. That the banana workers' apathy is much more difficult to categorize as a cause of their treatment by hostile others is no proof that it without doubt does not contribute to the cause; enough ambiguity regarding the workers' behavior exists to forestall general claims about their collective victimization. Moreover, to find that the banana workers' impassivity is the product of resignation in no way based in apathy would still do nothing to diminish my arguments regarding the majority of Macondones' indifference during the founding of the village and the Civil Wars. This conclusion is, I think, fair enough to validate applying theoretical considerations gleaned from reading García Márquez's novel to the effort to understand individual and group sociocultural behavior. It may then force a reconsideration of one of the most basic, and problematic, claims of an important, influential strand of contemporary identity politics.

NOTES

1. Edward Said, Judith Butler, and Eve Kosofsky Sedgwick are among the most famous critics for whom this assumption serves as a starting point. In *Orientalism*, Said characteristically writes, "because of Orientalism the Orient was not (and is not) a free subject of thought or action (3) [. . .]. The relationship between Occident and Orient is a relationship of power, of domination, of varying degrees of a complex hegemony (5) [. . .]. Evidence of the Orient was credible only after it had passed through and been made firm by the refining fire of the Orientalist's work" (283). Discussing the course of future feminist practice, Butler asserts that "The critical task for feminism is not to establish a point of view outside of constructed identities [. . .]. The critical task is, rather, to locate strategies of subversive repetition enabled by those constructions, to affirm the local possibilities of intervention through participating in precisely those practices of repetition that constitute

identity and, therefore, present the immanent possibility of contesting them" (147). Sedgwick is more general in her speculation that

> most people, especially those involved with any form of politics that touches on issues of identity—race, for instance, as well as sexuality and gender—have observed or been part of many [. . .] circuits of intimate denegation, as well as many circuits of its opposite [. . .]. Such dynamics, the denegating ones along with the consolidating ones—are not epiphenomenal to identity politics but constitute it. After all, to identify *as* must always include multiple processes of identification *with*. It also involves identification *as against*. (61; emphasis in the original)

Linda Nicholson illustrates how generalization is made to serve more concrete ends in her "Introduction" to *Social Postmodernism: Beyond Identity Politics*. Recalling the intellectual currents that attracted her to feminist theory and identity politics, Nicholson explains how her early interest in Marx waned because Marx's radicalism did not speak to the subjective and idiosyncratic nuances of the politics of identity and representation. Thus she became more attracted to feminism. Nicholson's shift, however, inevitably demonstrates the way that much of the work in identity politics evolves: she begins by exploring the specific experiences of a subject or group and at some point comes to speak on behalf of that subject or group. At its worst, this tendency commits the same kind of ideological imperialism—the impression of an identity on a subject or group not able or allowed to represent itself—targeted in the writings of many critics working in the arena of identity politics.

Todd Gitlin synopsizes the logic of this expression of the politics of identity thus:

> identity politics shapes not only the content but also the rhetoric and structure of truth-claims [. . .]. All claims to knowledge are presumed to be addressed from and to 'subject positions' which, like the claims themselves, have been 'constructed' or 'invented' collectively by self-designated groups. Sooner or later, all disputes issue in propositions of the following sort: The central subject for understanding is the difference between X (e.g. women, people of color) and Y (e.g. white males). P is the case because my people, X, see it that way; if you don't agree with P, it is (or more mildly, is probably) because you are a member of Y. And further, since X has been oppressed, or silenced, by Y—typically, white heterosexual males—justice requires that members of X, preferably (though not necessarily) adherents of P, be hired and promoted; and in the student body, in the curriculum, on the reading list, and at the conference, distinctly represented. (152)

Not all writers on identity politics commit themselves to this method of analysis. Joan Scott interrogates Carol Gilligan and Nancy Chodorow on their habit of generalization: "To assume that simply because in some places and in some times women appear to be more morally 'relational' than men in their sense of agency does not in any way support the more general conclusion that *all* women are more morally relational than men [. . .] even assuming the empirical case to be true, is it not a serious mistake to leap from the empirical presence of relational identities to their *normative* valorization?" (Somers 56; emphases in the original). Chandra Mohanty takes issue with critics who erase from their arguments the possibility that women may indeed act, that they are "anything but pure victims" (74). Her perspective is rather exceptional in the field and is typically met with the response that indeed women do act, but they do not act the way they would otherwise choose were they genuinely free to represent themselves.

2. In his 1982 Nobel Laureate address, "The Solitude of Latin America," García Márquez recounts both the sacrifices of those who fought for change in Latin America and the brutalities committed against Latin American peoples in their quest to represent themselves against European imperialism (88, 90). In what is perhaps a testament to his artistic honesty, García Márquez does not univocally foist his political sympathies on his characters. Though he would perhaps be startled by my using his novel in a discussion of apathy and identity, the behavior of the Macondones does permit my observations.

3. Apathy is here defined—on its Greek etymological roots, *a-*, without + *pathos*, emotion—as lack of interest/indifference and/or listlessness.

I do not mean to invest the word with any pejorative connotation. Nor do I mean to make clear distinctions among political, philosophical, or psychological apathy, since they may all be described as manifestations of what I take to be a chosen indifference to a particular situation that could just as appropriately prompt engagement by people empowered to opt either way. A distinction should, however, be drawn between apathy and resignation; the latter does indeed suggest a state of being that evolves as a consequence of brutalization against which an individual or group has little power or opportunity to fight.

4. Kathleen McNerney notes that the Indians employed by the Buendías, for example, are of "royal blood," (30), indicating that the legacy of colonialism in the region of Macondo made little effort to discriminate social and political differences in its business of representing the Indians wholesale as the Europeans' inferiors.

5. Albert Memmi devotes a considerable portion of his study to explaining the capitulative psychology of colonized peoples. In Memmi's account, apathy is the result of victimization, the product of surrender; it is not the cause of the colonized's subalterity (88–127).

6. There is a prevailing modern assumption that apathy is more characteristic of the uneducated; even if this is correct, and the Stoic tradition would suggest otherwise, it is not at all clear whether the uneducated choose their apathy (DeLuca 81–2).

7. See Arnold Penuel (23), and Brian Conniff (170, 172).

8. Nonetheless, the suddenly apparent tension between the values of different groups of Macondones and the social structures of the village is the kind of experience on which both individual and collective identity may be delineated (Fenn 122, Lester 19, John Marx 180–81, Robertson 249).

9. Regina Janes provides a synoptic account of the relationships between Liberals and Conservatives in Latin America ("Liberals" 129–30).

10. The historical events on which García Márquez bases his representation of the Civil Wars are recounted by Gene Bell-Villada (24–29) and Janes ("Political" 70–75).

11. For the historical roots of Aureliano's political affiliation, see Janes ("Liberals" 134).

12. My speculation is encouraged by C. Wright Mills's argument that the more people are able to link their class accoutrements to their personalities, the less likely they are to revolt against class injustices (Sennett 330).

13. See Janes ("Political" 79–80) and McNerney (29) for brief descriptions of the United Fruit Company's operations in Latin America, the events on which García Márquez bases the Banana Company episode in the novel.

14. I say nearly because José Arcadio Segundo manages to lift a small child to safety just before the shooting begins (328). The very fact of this exception compromises José Arcadio Segundo's repeated assurances that the soldiers murdered "everybody who had been at the station" (337), unless of course the child, in his position of safety, no longer counts among that "everybody."

15. See Stanley Aronowitz 137–39, Norman Geraus 109, Lovell 216, and Joseph Schumpeter (in Pipes 121–22).

16. See Richard Pipes: "In order to promote its ideal of comprehensive change, the intelligentsia must [. . .] create an abstraction called 'the people' to whom it can attribute its own wishes" (131).

17. As such, they express a premise that, even according to an ally like Engels, went unrealized at a crucial moment. Of the hopes for a proletariat revolution in 1848, Engels commented, "we and everyone who thought like us were wrong"; the proletariat was simply incapable of catalyzing a transformation of material conditions "by means of a simple and sudden attack" (Medvedev 143).

18. Pipes's evaluation of the cause of the workers' ostensible political indifference reproduces the strategies of Marx and Gramsci before him. As his considerations on the revolutionary potential of the proletariat developed during the course of his career, Marx maintained that the proletariat needed access to politics in order to form itself into a class (Lovell 148). Marx's logic solved the problem of apathy by displacing the responsibility for the workers' perceived indifference on those who set the workers' relations of production. As Gramsci put the relationship in *The Prison Notebooks*, the workers were not apathetic to revolution; instead, the ruling class maintained its hegemony through the ideological mystification of material conditions.

19. See Medvedev: "In 1904–5, it was the working class that emerged as the leader and the driving force of the first Russian Revolution" (97).

WORKS CITED

Aronowitz, Stanley. *The Politics of Identity: Class, Culture, Social Movements*. New York: Routledge, 1992.

Bell-Villada, Gene. *García Márquez: The Man and His Work*. Chapel Hill: U of North Carolina P, 1990.

Butler, Judith. *Gender Trouble: Feminism and the Subversion of Identity*. New York: Routledge, 1990.

Chun, Ki-Taek. "Ethnicity and Ethnic Identity: Taming the Untamed." *Studies in Social Identity*. Ed. Theodore R. Sarbin and Karl E. Scheibe. New York: Praeger, 1983. 184–203.

Conniff, Brian. "The Dark Side of Magical Realism: Science, Oppression, and Apocalypse in *One Hundred Years of Solitude*." *Modern Fiction Studies* 36.2 (Summer 1990): 167–79.

DeLuca, Tom. *The Two Faces of Political Apathy*. Philadelphia: Temple UP, 1995.

Fenn, Richard K. "Religion, Identity and Authority in the Secular Society." *Identity and Authority: Explorations in the Theory of Society*. Ed. Roland Robertson and Burkart Holzner. New York: St. Martin's, 1979. 119–44.

Fromm, Erich. *Escape from Freedom*. New York: Discus, 1941.

Geraus, Norman. *The Contract of Mutual Indifference*. London: Verso, 1998.

Gitlin, Todd. "From Universality to Difference: Notes on the Fragmentation of the Idea of the Left." *Social Theory and the Politics of Identity*. Ed. Craig Calhoun. Oxford: Blackwell, 1994. 150–74.

Gramsci, Antonio. *The Prison Notebooks*. New York: Columbia UP, 1992.

Janes, Regina. "Liberals, Conservatives, and Bananas: Colombian Politics in the Fictions of Gabriel García Márquez." *Gabriel García Márquez*. Ed. Harold Bloom. New York: Chelsea, 1989. 125–46.

———. *One Hundred Years of Solitude: Modes of Reading*. New York: Twayne, 1991.

Lenin, V. I. *State and Revolution*. New York: International, 1932.

Lester, Marilyn. "Self: Sociological Portraits." *The Existential Self in Society*. Ed. Joseph A. Kotarba and Andrea Fontana. Chicago: U of Chicago P, 1984. 18–68.

Lovell, David W. *Marx's Proletariat: The Making of a Myth*. London: Routledge, 1988.

Loyola, Ignatius. *Spiritual Exercises*. Trans. Louis J. Puhl. Bombay: St. Paul Publications, 1962.

Márquez, Gabriel García. *One Hundred Years of Solitude*. Trans. Gregory Rabassa. New York: Perennial, 1992.

———. "The Solitude of Latin America (Nobel Lecture 1980)." *Gabriel García Márquez and the Power of Fiction*. Ed. Julio Ortega. Austin: U of Texas P, 1988. 87–91.

Martin, Gerald. "On 'Magical' and Social Realism in García Márquez." *Gabriel García Márquez: New Readings*. Ed. Bernard McGuirk and Richard Cardwell. Cambridge: Cambridge UP, 1989. 95–116.

Marx, John. "The Ideological Construction of Post-Modern Identity Models in Contemporary Cultural Movements." *Identity and Authority: Explorations in the Theory of Society*. Ed. Roland Robertson and Burkart Holzner. New York: St. Martin's, 1979. 145–89.

McNerney, Kathleen. *Understanding Gabriel García Márquez*. Columbia: U of South Carolina P, 1989.

Medvedev, Roy. *Leninism and Western Socialism*. London: Verso, 1981.

Memmi, Albert. *The Colonizer and the Colonized*. Boston: Beacon, 1965.

Mohanty, Chandra Talpade. "Feminist Encounters: Locating the Politics of Experience." *Social Postmodernism: Beyond Identity Politics*. Cambridge: Cambridge UP, 1995. 68–86.

Nicholson, Linda and Steven Seidman. Introduction. *Social Postmodernism: Beyond Identity Politics*. Cambridge: Cambridge UP, 1995. 1–35.

Penuel, Arnold. *Intertextuality in García Márquez*. York, South Carolina: Spanish Literature Publications, 1994.

Pipes, Richard. *The Russian Revolution*. New York: Knopf, 1990.

Prakash, Gyan. "Postcolonial Criticism and Indian Historiography." *Social Postmodernism: Beyond Identity Politics*. Cambridge: Cambridge UP, 1995. 87–100.

Riesman, David. *The Lonely Crowd*. New Haven: Yale UP, 1950.

Robertson, Roland. "Aspects of Identity and Authority in Sociological Theory." *Identity and Authority: Explorations in the Theory of Society*. Ed. Roland Robertson and Burkart Holzner. New York: St. Martin's, 1979. 218–67.

Said, Edward. *Orientalism*. New York: Vintage, 1979.

Scheibe, Karl E. *Self Studies: The Psychology of Self and Identity*. Westport, CT: Praeger, 1995.

Sedgwick, Eve Kosofsky. *Epistemology of the Closet*. Berkeley: U of California P, 1990.

Sennett, Richard. *The Fall of Public Man*. New York: Knopf, 1977.

Somers, Margaret R. and Gloria D. Gibson. "Reclaiming the Epistemological 'Other': Narrative and the Social Constitution of Identity." *Social Theory and the Politics of Identity*. Ed. Craig Calhoun. Oxford: Blackwell, 1994. 37–99.

Thom, Gary B. *The Human Nature of Social Discontent: Alienation, Anomie, Ambivalence*. New Jersey: Rowman and Allanheld, 1983.

Trotsky, Leon. *The History of the Russian Revolution*. Trans. Max Eastman. New York: Monad, 1980.

Weigert, Andrew J., J. Smith Teitge and Dennis Teitge. *Society and Identity: Toward a Sociological Psychology*. Cambridge: Cambridge UP, 1986.

Williamson, Edwin. "Magical Realism and the Theme of Incest in *One Hundred Years of Solitude*." *Gabriel García Márquez: New Readings*. Ed. Bernard McGuirk and Richard Cardwell. Cambridge: Cambridge UP, 1989. 45–63.

SHANNIN SCHROEDER

"Advancing in the Opposite Direction from Reality": Magical Realism, Alchemy, and One Hundred Years of Solitude

It was as if God had decided to put to the test every capacity for surprise and was keeping the inhabitants of Macondo in a permanent alternation between excitement and disappointment, doubt and revelation, to such an extreme that no one knew for certain where the limits of reality lay.
—*One Hundred Years of Solitude*

Gabriel García Márquez's revision of science in *One Hundred Years of Solitude*, in spite of his radical portrayal of science as both a modern and primal catalyst for the novel's apocalyptic demise, has received only a smattering of critical attention. Some scholars touch on and then dismiss its effects, as when Julio Ortega claims that José Arcadio Buendía's quest for scientific knowledge is "another mythical dream" (87). Yet, as Michael Boccia argues, there is magic in

> the simple technology of the inexplicable. So the magic of technology may range from an ice-making machine to a flying carpet. Even a simple magnet may serve to demonstrate the fine line between magic and technology.... Magic and science are both explanations of some unknown natural phenomenon. And we should not forget that the history of science is little more than each generation disproving the scientific truths of the past. (29)

From *Rediscovering Magical Realism in the Americas*, pp. 39–57. © 2004 by Shannin Schroeder.

Thus, Kenneth Wishnia's treatment of *One Hundred Years of Solitude*, where he revises the book jacket for the science fiction market,[1] is not quite as far-fetched as it might seem.

One Hundred Years of Solitude is a "decodification of the natural order" (Ganguly 176) and of the Western world as well. "This novel is not about 'history-and-myth,' but about the myths of history and their demystification" (Martin, "On 'Magical' and Social Realism" 99); in particular, García Márquez "reveals what is assumed to be natural as praeternatural" and "makes us wonder . . . at the scientific laws of matter and history" (Hart 47). L. Robert Stevens and G. Roland Vela note that "western [*sic*] man's scientific and technological achievements are in great part due to his ability to separate fact from fiction, myth from science, and illusion from reality. It is a paradox of western culture that it draws its psychological strength from a spiritual-mythical well while its muscle is drawn largely from science and technology" (262). Floyd Merrell believes "that the transmutations in José Arcadio [Buendía]'s conception of reality" are "analogous to the development of scientific thought in the Western World." Although Merrell explores the ways in which the novel creates "parallels between the 'scientific paradigms' postulated and implemented by José Arcadio Buendía . . . and the structural history of scientific philosophy in the Western World" (59), García Márquez erects those structures for the express purpose of undermining their authority. The novel "deliberately subverts [the] trend toward rational objectivity [, for] it presents the laws of the universe, and particularly the laws of science and history, not as if they were objective and self-evident facts, but instead as if they were unnatural and strange productions of man's mind" (Hart 47). Stevens and Vela argue that García Márquez's

> view of life, beyond the mythopoeic, is . . . that man is naturally a scientist. The wisdom of the people who live in Macondo is a composite of folk wisdom, hearsay, legend, superstition, and religion—all indiscriminately mixed. And yet [García] Márquez builds into the novel a clear sympathy for a certain quality of knowledge. We might think of this sympathy as an instinct for science. (265)[2]

Yet, though Melquíades and José Arcadio Buendía share with other scientists a "great wonder at the profound mystery of reality" (265), both men's scientific quests are fueled largely by alchemy rather than by modern science.[3] In other words, the worldview of Macondo is arguably one in which scientific facts are external and are the "unnatural and strange productions" for which Stephen Hart argues. Of course, even their quest for ancient scientific "truths" (such as the earth's roundness) *devalues* them in the eyes of the community, since, as Brian Conniff points out, all science seems alternately to mystify and to exploit the other inhabitants of Macondo. Úrsula is convinced that her husband "has lost what was left of his mind" when he dedicates himself to science (172).[4]

One Hundred Years of Solitude also foregrounds the dichotomy that has arisen between science and the humanities and the consequences of the rift between the two (Mosher 89). "José Arcadio Buendía and his neighbors suffer from other numerous failures and disillusions, all of which are linked to science and technology" (90), though "Macondo's ills are not due exclusively to science and technology but rather to a disequilibrium between scientific and humanistic thought" (91). Melquíades, though equally exposed to the sciences, does not illustrate tendencies toward aggression like other characters because he "is an archetype of harmony, one who demonstrates the possibility of reducing, and perhaps even eliminating, the barriers between scientific reasoning and literary artistry" (91).

Melquíades's most meaningful association is with alchemy, a scientific mode that will help (or attempt to help) heal the rift between spirituality and science in *One Hundred Years of Solitude*. R. W. Morrison argues, "The challenge of literature in an age of science and technology is to weave these activities into the tapestry of life as effectively as García Márquez incorporates them into the life of the people of Macondo" (124). García Márquez's "way of seeing things is compatible with both myth and science, but it is neither thing in itself. It has the analytical curiosity of science coupled with the synthetic method of myth" (Stevens and Vela 266). Yet the science García Márquez weaves into *One Hundred Years of Solitude*'s fabric is alchemy, while the "age" of modern or advanced technology stands outside of and is invasive in the magical realist world of the text. Although Melquíades and other characters do attempt to mend the rupture between science and humanity, their attempts rely on the roots (not on the progression) of science, since "[t]he novel's 'apocalyptic closure' is a denial of progress, as conceived by either the scientist or the politician" (Conniff 173). Though Edwin Williamson feels that such pessimistic readings "appear to condemn Latin America to a hopeless condition of historical failure, allowing no scope for change or free human action" (63), García Márquez's own use of literary alchemy redeems, if not this Macondon cycle, then perhaps the next. And García Márquez's own mention of Big Mama's funeral (75) reminds us that there will be a "next time" for Macondo; the experiment will be retried.

One Hundred Years of Science

In *One Hundred Years of Solitude*, Gabriel García Márquez creates a world where truth and fiction are equally strange. Macondo is a realm where reality and the supernatural live side by side; from its very inception, the town seems born of paradox. More importantly, the entire balance of Macondo and its inhabitants—particularly the founding Buendía family—hangs upon the fate of magic and its relationship to realism. Magical realism is more than a way of life for Macondons; it *is* the life of the town. Should reality get out of hand, should the outside overwhelm the solitude of the town and the equilibrium between the supernatural and the "real" world, Macondo's inhabitants would not survive the fall. By refiguring science as incomprehensible and magic as comprehensible, García Márquez also sets the stage within *One Hundred Years of Solitude* for a science that is, like magical realism, at once fact and fiction. Alchemy plays a significant role in the novel because García Márquez's own literary alchemy uses the science as a metaphor for the magical realism in the text. More important, it becomes the driving force for *One Hundred Years of Solitude's* magical realist world; alchemy reconciles the novel's "magical realism as a narrative style with the actual movement of the actions in the novel" (Williamson 46).

Macondo is "advancing in the opposite direction" from almost everything—the town reverts to anarchy from order, to solitude from communality, to the supernatural from the natural, and to alchemy from modern science. By virtue of their roles in that reversion, magical realism and alchemy have much in common within the context of *One Hundred Years of Solitude*. Just as magical realism relies on the juxtaposition of two "realities"—the supernatural and the everyday—so too does alchemy rely on a dichotomy, that is, on its simultaneous physical and spiritual goals. Although alchemy conjures up visions of the ragged scholar locked in his dungeon-like laboratory, doggedly pursuing the transmutation of gold from the base metals—a stereotypical perception that García Márquez intentionally and more than willingly exploits—this typecasting seriously distorts the metaphysical motives behind this ancient science. By referencing alchemy within *One Hundred Years of Solitude*, García Márquez reinforces the two levels of his text, with the ultimate goal of creating a world where Macondo's spiritual and magical demise brings about its physical downfall.[5]

The everyday quality of magical realism can be compared to the physical aspirations of alchemy, as can their respective supernatural and spiritual goals. In other words, both depend on the earthly as well as the "other-worldly." Also, to understand either one, we must accept its duality. Just as alchemy, at its most significant, is at once a spiritual and earthly voyage, magical realism relies on two planes of existence at exactly the same moment. To ignore the "real" in favor of the supernatural or vice versa is to skew magical realism in the direction of such modes as the fantastic or surreal.[6] The magical realist writer, then, is an alchemist of words; he or she metamorphoses both the everyday and the supernatural until they meet on common ground. García Márquez seeks both the real and the supernatural for *One Hundred Years of*

Solitude, just as the true alchemist pursues both a spiritual and a physical height. While supernatural occurrences are frequent in *One Hundred Years of Solitude*, they rarely cause heads to turn. On the other hand, the realistic aspects of life in Macondo seem exotic. For example, in the house of the Buendías, the living are as much ghosts as the dead. Úrsula haunts the house far past her prime or her ability to effect any changes in her home. Fernanda ultimately finds herself living with "three living ghosts—Colonel Aureliano Buendía, Úrsula, and Amaranta" (263). Thus, García Márquez makes into the outlandish or strange what his reader generally accepts as "reality." Reality is by comparison so brutal, and the cruelty of the world (as evidenced in part by the Banana Company massacre) so hard to accept, that levitation or flying, ghosts and spirits seem comprehensible and genuine. The "real" atrocities add a new level of verisimilitude to magical realist fiction,[7] and the brutal interruption of reality in the text softens the effect of the magical or supernatural, even when the dead Prudencio Aguilar is attempting murder or when José Arcadio's blood seeks out his mother at his death.[8] Were García Márquez to make the invasion of the outside world, and science in particular, *less* radical for the characters in his novel, he would undermine his own attempt to create a supernatural that looks so very commonplace.

Alchemy reinforces the sense of a magically real world, stressing that what we know as science, Macondons believe to be magic, and vice versa. As resident but worldly alchemist, Melquíades brings the outside (specifically, modern science) to the attention of Macondo *not* in order to clarify things but rather to mystify. But Melquíades is not alone in his "revision" of reality in Macondo. The book begins with the "discovery" of ice and José Arcadio Buendía's willingness to spend his few pesos so that his sons can experience it. The son who will later be unable to see anything but ruin in Melquíades's room, Colonel Aureliano Buendía, feels the ice and declares it to be hot. His misreading of reality seems both fitting—as a translation of the outside world into the magical one of Macondo—and portentous of his own inability to "handle" the supernatural aspects of his world. Similar "magic" includes the magnifying glass, the daguerreotype (an invention that leaves José Arcadio Buendía "mute with stupefaction" [51]), and the magnets, which Melquíades identifies as the "eighth wonder of the learned alchemists of Macedonia" (2). The inhabitants of Macondo attempt to reconfigure the outside world into something magical as it invades the interior of the text and the town. As long as these attempts work, the town will survive the onslaught of reality. When, however, the outside becomes too powerful, when it invades Macondo and cannot be driven or explained away, then Macondo is doomed.

Thus, *One Hundred Years of Solitude* makes no attempts to codify the magical; rather, in Macondo, it is reality that must be rationalized. Furthermore, something about Macondo itself suggests that it alone is home to magical realism. For example, *when* the wise Catalonian—who is himself "linked with alchemy through a mention of Arnaldo of Villanova, the famed medieval Catalan scholar and alchemist" (McNerney and Martin 110), about whom he knows the intimate detail of his impotence from a scorpion bite (405)—refutes magical realism is perhaps more significant than *that* he shuns it. The wise Catalonian does indeed "[condemn] the effects of magical realism: the fascination with the past, the escape from history into memory, the longing to recover a pristine innocence, and the surrender to mindless erotic desire" (Williamson 60). But he does so *only* after he returns to his homeland:

> Upset by two nostalgias facing each other like two mirrors, he lost his *marvelous sense of unreality* and he ended up recommending to all of them that they leave Macondo, that they forget everything he taught them about the world and the human heart, that they shit on Horace, and that wherever they might be they always remember that the past was a lie, that memory has no return, that every spring gone by could never be recovered, and that the wildest and most tenacious love was an ephemeral truth in the end. (408; emphasis added)

Only after he leaves Macondo does he lose "his customary good humor"; we learn that "his memory began to grown sad" and that, "although he himself did not seem to notice it, those letters of recuperation and stimulation [that he sends back to the Buendías] were slowly changing into pastoral letters of disenchantment" (407–8). The official-looking letter that Aureliano refuses to open near the end of the novel seems to bear the news that reality in fact gets the better of the Catalonian once he is outside the confines of Macondo.

Reality and unreality are equally important aspects of García Márquez's vision of *One Hundred Years of Solitude*. For example, when José Arcadio Buendía finds his "immediate reality . . . to be more fantastic than the vast universe of his imagination, he [loses] all interest in the alchemist's laboratory" (39). This is especially significant when we recall that, earlier, José Arcadio Buendía's imagination is described as "unbridled" and as one that "always went beyond the genius of nature and even beyond miracles and magic" (2). Thus, José Arcadio Buendía's immediate reality is neither natural nor magical—it is beyond that, or at least at this point, both at once. Later in the novel, however, he has "lost all contact with reality" (109). Apparently, the balance of the magical and the real is a necessity in Macondo. To do without reality is to go insane, as José Arcadio Buendía proves; Colonel Aureliano Buendía loses touch with that reality during the war ("Little by little, however, and as the war became more intense and widespread, his image was fading away into a universe of unreality" [165]), but pulls himself out of that unreal world by turning his back on the war entirely and, at the same time, by accepting reality with a passionless embrace that distances him from it. In the last of the war's supernatural effects on him, his coldness becomes a physical as well as mental affliction. His final solitude proves that to forego the supernatural is no less dangerous in Macondo than is José Arcadio Buendía's loss of reality. He is, notably, the only family member who sees the decay of Melquíades's room—the singular symbol of the Buendías' immersion in their magical realist world. The reclusive Colonel Aureliano is so out of sympathy with the delicate balance between magic and reality in the Buendía household that he urinates in the courtyard without knowing he is splattering his father's ghost's shoes (269). His faults, at least for his mother, are summed up by her discovery that Aureliano "had never loved anyone" and "was simply a man incapable of love" (254).

The colonel's insensibility illustrates the most significant connection between alchemy and magical realism in *One Hundred Years of Solitude*: the attitude of characters in relation to the two phenomena. Consider the inventions that the townspeople (and José Arcadio Buendía in particular) interpret as magical, or the fact that the cinema angers the inhabitants of Macondo because of the "fraud" of the actors who die in one film and are "resurrected" to star in the next one. Cinema is "a machine of illusion" in Macondo (230). On the other hand, the residents find the notion that they could come to rely on hand-written signs to remember the names of everyday items during an insomnia plague perfectly acceptable. Similarly, José Arcadio Buendía gives up alchemy because Melquíades's "elixir of life" is actually a set of dentures; ice and magnets, on the other hand, are sources of great wonder. Science is magical in José Arcadio Buendía's eyes, while alchemy can be explained away. Not only does such a view of science reinforce the magical realism of this text; it also demonstrates that science, or at least science interpreted through the lens of alchemy, can be equally magical.

Origins of *Al-kimiya*

The fount of science as we know it today, alchemy has been practiced at least since the time of Christ, and quite possibly since prehistoric times (Burckhardt 11). Alchemy's origins trace back to ancient Egypt[9]; indeed, the Arabic term *al-kimiya* originally meant "the art of the land of Khem." Titus Burckhardt explains that the Arabic *kême* or *khem* refers "to the 'black earth,' which was a designation of Egypt and which may also have been a symbol of the alchemists' *materia prima*" (16).[10] *Materia prima* is the underlying fundamental substance of alchemy. Alchemists assume that within this substance lie secret powers capable of working miracles; alchemical texts may also refer to the *materia prima* as the sea, the seed of things, a virgin, "the hidden stone," an ore deposit, or a flowering tree. Carl Jung believed *materia prima* to be a psychological rather than chemical phenomenon (*Alchemical Studies* 205), but whether taken in the physical or the spiritual sense, this "primary matter" symbolizes the starting place, the illusive first material from whence springs the entire alchemical pursuit of the philosopher's stone (Burckhardt 18). *One Hundred Years of Solitude* emphasizes much the same beginning for Macondo, where José Arcadio Buendía raises the first dwellings in the city out of the earth he discovers.

If the *materia prima* serves as the root of the alchemical process, then the philosopher's stone can be considered the end or product. "The philosopher's stone (with which one can turn base metals into gold) grants long life and freedom from disease to the one who possesses it, and in its power brings more gold and silver than all the mightiest conquerors have between them" (Burckhardt 29). In its literal sense, this stone is a physical object that alchemists attempted to synthesize in their labs, using mercury and sulfur. On the other hand, the stone also represented true spiritual transmutation, the act of making the soul "golden." Gold "corresponds to the sound and original condition of the soul which freely and without distortion reflects the Divine Spirit" (72). The stone itself was indicated in the alchemists' texts in many ways. For example, "the stone that the biblical Jacob used as a pillow, and upon which he poured oil, was an accepted symbol for the Philosopher's Stone" (Powell 70). The stone could also be depicted as a peacock, because the colors in a peacock's tail supposedly appeared during the final stage of formation.

Just as the *materia prima* and philosopher's stone can be represented with word or pictures, so too can all the alchemical processes. Because the representations of the process were encoded in this pictorial language, "an additional barrier [to understanding the texts] was erected in the shape of an extensive structure of pictorial symbolism and allegorical expression" (Glidewell 38). A unique example of this is *The Wordless Book*, a collection of 15 engraved plates that gives the alchemical process in its entirety using symbols and drawings of the alchemists at work (Powell 70).

Reading the works of the alchemists is rather like stumbling upon some bizarre recipe.[11] The alchemist steeped his science in poetic language or symbolism not for the sake of the figurative language itself but rather to fool the foolish. "Gold, for example, was represented at one time or another, in more than sixty different ways" (Glidewell 38). Such obscuring of the meaning behind alchemy was an intentional stumbling block to the "puffers," or those who sought out alchemy only to obtain gold (Powell 19). Therefore, the stereotypes by which the alchemists were judged and labeled were actually nurtured by the alchemists themselves.

Synesios, who most likely lived in the fourth century A.D., wrote, "[A]re you so simple as to believe that we would clearly and openly teach the greatest and most important of all secrets, with the result that you would take us literally?" (qtd. in Burckhardt 28). Many puffers, of course, did just that; they pursued the physical reality of transmutating gold. Those "who sought only worldly goals failed because alchemical success necessarily requires success within the soul" (Powell 19). The adepts, or authentic alchemists, ranked the microcosm *above* the goals of the macrocosm, that is, they placed greater emphasis on transmutating the soul than they did on personal, worldly gain.[12]

Literary Alchemy and *One Hundred Years of Solitude*

We, the inventors of tales, who will believe anything, feel entitled to believe that it is not yet too late to engage in the creation of . . . a new and sweeping utopia of life, where no one will be able to decide for others how they die, where love will prove true and happiness be possible, and where the races condemned to one hundred years of solitude, will have, at last and forever, a second opportunity on earth.

—García Márquez[13]

The Alchemists

Alchemy's rich symbolism makes ripe pickings for García Márquez, who explores much of the lore and symbolism to its fullest through his characters. Among the many alchemists García Márquez creates in *One Hundred Years of Solitude*, Melquíades stands out. Melquíades is actually the "father" of alchemy to Macondo, the first to introduce it to the town. He and his alchemy arrive on the first page, on the heels of the Buendía family, so that Macondo exists only for a very short time without alchemy. His indelible mark on Macondo is ensured by what he leaves behind him:

The rudimentary laboratory—in addition to a profusion of pots, funnels, retorts, filters, and sieves—was made up of a primitive water pipe, a glass beaker with a long, thin neck, a reproduction of the philosopher's egg, and a still the gypsies themselves had built in accordance with modern descriptions of the three-armed alembic of Mary the Jew. Along with those items, Melquíades left samples of the seven metals that corresponded to the seven planets, the formulas of Moses and Zosimus for doubling the quantity of gold, and a set of notes and sketches concerning the processes of the Great Teaching that would permit *those who could interpret them* to undertake the manufacture of the philosopher's stone. (7; emphasis added)

It is no accident that García Márquez places such emphasis on the fact that Melquíades gives José Arcadio Buendía "a gift that was to have a profound influence on the future of the village: the laboratory of an alchemist" (5), since, "like so many pivotal events in the story, the ending takes place in the laboratory" (McNerney and Martin 111).

The future of Macondo is interconnected with the alchemical experiments of the Buendías in much the same way that it relies on the balance of the magical and the real. The home of alchemy in the text—Melquíades's room—is also residence for, or connected with, many of the magical realist events that occur in the novel. The contents of this room are the tools of alchemy, certainly, but the passage also hints at their importance in the final outcome of the Buendías—many of whom will spend the next hundred years attempting to duplicate Melquíades's apparent successes. But "[t]he Buendías experience the solitude of alchemy without achieving its goals; rather than escaping from the tyranny of time, they become its victims, locked in its inexorable repetitive process, until the deciphering of the parchments brings the family chronicle to an end" (McNerney and Martin 111). In other words, Melquíades leaves not only the rudiments for the study of alchemy but also the foundations for the evolution, decay, and ultimate destruction of the family, since the last Aureliano, "who could interpret" the Great Teachings, also deciphers Melquíades's notes on the family history, albeit too late to change the course of that history.

As if to emphasize Melquíades's paternal role in the alchemy of Macondo, García Márquez associates him with numerous alchemical symbols. For example, the hat continuously perched on Melquíades's head looks "like a raven with widespread wings" (6). According to Kathleen McNerney and John Martin, "In alchemical texts, the raven's wing signifies the purification of the alchemist's soul" (106). Moreover, when lead, the most base of all metals, is blackened, the process is "represented by a raven" (Burckhardt 185). This blackening corresponds to the first stage of the alchemical process, while Melquíades, who is represented by black throughout the text, is responsible for first establishing alchemy in Macondo. García Márquez also refers to the ancient alchemist's hands as sparrow-like. Because the sparrow is often associated with Venus (copper), Melquíades symbolizes both beginning and (near) end of the alchemical procedure. That Melquíades is associated with two such alchemically significant birds within the novel seems to indicate that he himself will be responsible for or active in various stages of the history of alchemy in Macondo. Obviously, Melquíades represents more than the father of alchemy to the town; he becomes a *feature* of alchemy's (and therefore, the town's) settlement.

Melquíades's growth from his "leaden" origins surpasses his association with copper. He enjoys two of the legendary benefits of possessing the philosopher's stone—immortality and the ability to cure diseases.[14] After the insomnia plague strikes Macondo, Melquíades's potion saves the entire town from a life without sleep or memory. At the time of his death, Melquíades tells José Arcadio Buendía to burn mercury for 72 hours after he dies. When José Arcadio Buendía questions him he says only, "I have found immortality" (74). In a novel where ghosts are clearly marked as such—consider, for example, Prudencio Aguilar's haunting of José Arcadio Buendía and Úrsula—Melquíades seems more alive than any of the apparently *living* inhabitants of the Buendía home. If Melquíades has indeed successfully reproduced the stone for himself, he ranks as an adept and functions as a symbol of alchemical success in the novel.

Melquíades's influence over the Buendías produces a long line of alchemists; the patriarch of the family, José Arcadio Buendía, is Melquíades's first student. Initially, José Arcadio Buendía seems to have great potential as an alchemist. He certainly begins with a sincere desire to learn the secrets of the science. He willingly devotes hours to working with Melquíades in the lab, where "with shouts [they] interpreted the predications of Nostradamus amidst a noise of flasks and trays and the disaster of spilled acids and silver bromide" (51)—to the point that he ignores and excludes his family. But José Arcadio Buendía does not dedicate himself to alchemy or to his spiritual transformation above all else; instead, he realizes that his family is more important to him, as is monetary gain. When Úrsula returns from her search for José Arcadio, José Arcadio Buendía and the reader both discover his true passion,

> for during his prolonged imprisonment [in the laboratory] as he manipulated the material, he begged in the depth of his heart that the longed-for miracle should not be the discovery of the philosopher's stone, or the freeing of the breath that makes metals live, or the faculty to convert the hinges and the locks of the house into gold, but what had just happened: Úrsula's return. (36)

His neglect of those miracles he supposedly seeks in his lab condemns his entire family, while at the same time it implicates them in his ultimate failure. José Arcadio Buendía's intentions for the magnets Melquíades introduces as alchemical wonders, that is, to extract gold from the bowels of the earth, symbolize the puffer in action. He "seeks practical ends through the methodical exploitation of a nature of which he considers himself no integral part" (Merrell 60). His greed digs up nothing more than a copper locket, perhaps most significant because of copper's close but inferior association with gold, inside "a suit of fifteenth-century armor which had all of its pieces soldered together with rust" (2). Conniff notes, "Searching for gold, José Arcadio finds the remains of Spanish imperialism" (170).[15] Thus, in spite of his potential, José Arcadio Buendía maintains his materialistic world-vision (Merrell 63) and does not credit alchemy's higher purposes, nor does he dedicate himself to his science. Instead, he oscillates between alchemy and his many other pursuits.

José Arcadio Buendía's bout with insanity seems more in keeping with the typical image of an alchemist driven to madness by his search (or, as is medically more likely, by mercury fumes). When he destroys the laboratory, he appears to have reached another plane of thought. His new conscious-ness (proven to be a remarkably lucid state of mind, once Father Nicanor discovers he is speaking Latin) cannot be confused with mastery of alchemy, though, because, in his attempts to destroy the alchemy lab, he denies him-self the success of the adept. José Arcadio Buendía—as if to contradict his own potential—intends to destroy the physical tools of alchemy. Without the physical means for the pursuit of alchemy, he can never achieve the science's spiritual end.

Perhaps José Arcadio Buendía's lost sense of time offers the most telling bit of evidence that he has failed as an alchemist. "Today is Monday, too," he says, because his days refuse to look distinct from their predecessors (80). The seven metals of alchemy each correspond to a day of the week. Monday corresponds to silver, the "little work" of alchemy when compared to the "great work," that is, the progression from silver to gold (Glidewell 28). José Arcadio Buendía is stuck on "Monday," or in the "little work," and is there-fore unable to reach the higher spiritual plane. Silver, the closest to gold of the silver-colored metals, is still one of the lesser works; perhaps this final challenge—the journey back from the depths of his own soul—is beyond José Arcadio Buendía's reach.

While José Arcadio Buendía is distracted from his alchemy by many other interests and desires, his son Aureliano can only be tempted away from the alchemy lab by two things: war and women. When Aureliano is en-gaged with either, his work in alchemy suffers. Conversely, removed from the temptations of women and warfare, he returns to the one comfort he seems to have. Paradoxically, when Aureliano is a young man, José Arcadio Buendía actually attempts to divert his son's interest away from the labora-tory by offering him "money to spend on a woman, but Aureliano spends it on muriatic acid to make aqua regia, a key substance in alchemical research" (McNerney and Martin 107). Thus, even at a young age, Aureliano seems to realize that the laboratory will prove a balm more lasting (if not more heal-ing) than his relationships with women. After Remedios dies, he experiences "a dull feeling of rage that gradually dissolved in a solitary and passive frus-tration similar to the one he had felt during the time when he was resigned to living without a woman. He plunged into his work again" (98). Aureliano's productive periods in the lab coincide with the times he is not involved with either of his other pursuits. Yet Aureliano does not have his father's passion for the work, even if he has the patience José Arcadio Buendía lacked. The gold fish he fashions, melts down, and then recreates in his old age seem to connect Aureliano symbolically to the quest for the philosopher's stone, since "[t]he fish is a most common symbol for Christ, who is in turn frequently used in alchemical texts as a symbol of the philosopher's stone" (McNerney and Martin 107–8). But the Colonel's intricate trinkets are not products of transmutation, and he realizes none of the benefits of alchemy. His tin pail—and not the golden charms it contains—perhaps best represents his inabilities, for he too is held by the lesser works that seem to have plagued his father. Aureliano's name,[16] in the context of alchemy, is ironic rather than prophetic.

When Aureliano dies, other Buendías reopen Melquíades's lab; most of them quickly lose interest. Aureliano Segundo, for one, becomes too lazy. The work that once required his full attention can no longer hold him. Like his namesake, he is distracted by other things—most notably, by Petra Cotes. The two exploit their sexual alchemy, but their animal husbandry, like their affair, has purely physical goals and ultimately burns out. Only Aureliano Segundo's brother, José Arcadio Segundo, comes as close as their great-grandfather to reaching adeptness.

Of José Arcadio Buendía's descendants, José Arcadio Segundo shows the most promise as an alchemist. He is the only Buendía, in fact, to make Melquíades's lab his permanent residence. The sole survivor of the Banana Company massacre,[17] he seeks solace in his work. When soldiers search for him, one looks directly at him from the doorway of the laboratory and yet declares, "It's obvious that no one has been in that room for at least a hundred years." The lab provides a sanctuary for José Arcadio Segundo: "In Melquíades' room, . . . protected by the supernatural light, by the sound of the rain, by the feeling of being invisible, he found the repose that he had not had for one single instant during his previous life" (318). According to Scott Sands, the "alchemists work in solitude because they need to be away from impurity and corruption" (25). The importance of this statement is not lost on a text entitled One Hundred Years of Solitude, in which the Buendías—from José Arcadio Buendía to the last Aureliano—seek out solitude in a town that attempts to shut itself off from the outside (and potentially corrupt) world. Solitude and being an alchemist necessarily go hand in hand in One Hundred Years of Solitude.[18] Consider, for example, how Aureliano awakens out of his solitude when he meets Remedios or how Úrsula's disappearance has a similar effect on José Arcadio Buendía; conversely, José Arcadio Segundo loses himself in the solitude of Melquíades's laboratory as a deliberate response to the "impurity and corruption" of the Banana Company.

As he does for Melquíades, García Márquez describes José Arcadio Segundo through a series of alchemical references. For example, Aureliano Segundo and Santa Sofía de la Piedad note that José Arcadio Segundo has "Arab eyes" (317), associating him with the oldest students of alchemy.[19] The assessment that José Arcadio Segundo's eyes are Arab accompanies his family's fear that he is suffering the "irreparable fate of his great-grandfather" (319). José Arcadio Segundo does not suffer from the insanity that seems to plague José Arcadio Buendía, but both are equally lost to the world. García Márquez does not document any actual experiments in alchemy that José Arcadio Segundo performs, but he does inform us that he "dedicated himself to peruse the manuscripts of Melquíades many times" (318). While we never see the exact content of any of those papers, he seems to be studying both the earlier manuscripts, that is, the transcribed works of the alchemists that Melquíades left for José Arcadio Buendía and the parchments that predict the Buendía family's future. José Arcadio Segundo's devotion is less crazy than it is wholehearted. His reality is "as unreachable and solitary as that of his great-grandfather," but he has no other interest or woman to distract him.

Like his great-grandfather, José Arcadio Segundo does not qualify as an adept. When we see him after the three-year period of rain, he is a massive, green tangle of hair. Green, the color associated with copper or lead (Pachter 263), simultaneously ties José Arcadio Segundo both to the metal closest to gold (in color and in its stage's proximity to gold) and to a base metal—repeating the pattern of association linked with Melquíades through the bird symbolism. José Arcadio Segundo has come close in his quest as an alchemist, as did José Arcadio Buendía, but still does not transmutate the base metal lead into gold, perhaps because he is tainted by the base and vile acts to which he is sole witness. Indeed, the corrupt state of the world is what first drives José Arcadio Segundo into the arms not just of solitude but of alchemy as well. Paradoxically, in spite of his apparently addled state of mind, he is "the most lucid inhabitant of the house" as Aureliano Babilonia is growing up (355).

Aureliano Babilonia deserves mention among the Buendía alchemists because he takes to heart the teachings of Melquíades's manuscripts and holes himself up in the lab, at least for a short time. That Aureliano reaches "adolescence without knowing a thing about his own time but with the basic knowledge of a medieval man" (361) suggests that he would also be conversant in and a student of alchemy. Furthermore, he alone translates the parchments that prophesy his translation of them. Aureliano is the one for whom the untranslated materials Melquíades leaves are intended. Finally, like many before him, including José Arcadio Buendía and José Arcadio Segundo, Aureliano becomes a pupil of Melquíades, whose appearances in the lab provide him with conversation and encouragement. Ultimately, though (and like Colonel Aureliano and the patriarch, José Arcadio Buendía), Aureliano's alchemy is undone by his passion for a woman; his desire for Amaranta Úrsula will tempt him away from his work until the very end of the novel. He is the last in a long line of Buendía men who, for one reason or another, never fully experience complete and total immersion in alchemy. Although he is unique among the Buendías before him in that he has the ability to learn the secrets of the adepts, Aureliano Babilonia lacks the time to fulfill his potential. The Buendías' one hundred years are up.

Macondo as Macrocosm

To consider this novel a macrocosmic alchemy in and of itself, we would need to be able to see the methodology of the science at work within the text itself, and, indeed, García Márquez creates a text in which the literal and fictional worlds are coordinated into one such process. Just as characters in *One Hundred Years of Solitude* attempt transmutations on both the physical and the spiritual planes, García Márquez attempts a dual-level alchemy of his own with the town (and the novel) he creates. The relationship among Úrsula and José Arcadio Buendía, their family, and the town itself becomes an alchemical process—an attempt to produce "gold" out of the marriage of Sulfur and Mercury. By intentionally disrupting the balance between reality and the supernatural, García Márquez ensures that the marriage will result in the destruction of everything the Buendía line first promises to yield. No one and nothing—save the town that García Márquez's later literary alchemy will resurrect—survives this experiment.

The creation and destruction of the Buendía line in Macondo can be considered García Márquez's attempt at one "run-through" of the alchemical process. In this macrocosmic vision of *One Hundred Years of Solitude*, the characters must be the ingredients or "elements." When this town reappears later—during the time of Big Mama's funeral "a century later" (75)—we can assume that new characters (materials) are necessary in order for the cycle to begin again. Alchemists relied on similar repetition in their work to remove impurities—just as many modern chemists repeat their experiments for the same reason. Macondo's impurities—perhaps most evident in the blatantly incestuous Buendía strain—are being filtered out.[20]

Within this particular one hundred years, Macondo and its inhabitants share a noticeably symbolic relationship with alchemy, and several of the characters can be associated with the materials that are important to alchemy. Melquíades can be considered the *materia prima* of alchemy in the text; he does, after all, set the cycle into motion within the town and the novel, and, through frequent association with the color black, also represents the first stage of the alchemical process (Glidewell 28). The many Aurelianos, with gold in their names, are perhaps the most obvious. Yet José Arcadio Buendía, Úrsula, and their entire line of descendants provide more interesting, and more significant, connections with the materials.

Before alchemy can be undertaken, production of the *materia prima* is required, and for that process the alchemist needed sulfur and mercury.[21] More to the point, Melquíades actually requires José Arcadio Buendía and Úrsula in order to set into motion both their line of descendants and his work. Without them, Macondo has no need of his miracles, prophecies, or manuscripts. As the parents of the Macondon strain of Buendías, José Arcadio Buendía and Úrsula serve both Macondo and *One Hundred Years of Solitude* as the sulfur and mercury, respectively. Burckhardt explains that "the marriage of Sulphur and Quicksilver, Sun and Moon, King and Queen, is the central symbol of alchemy" (149). This marriage is vital to the process, and José Arcadio Buendía and Úrsula, through their perpetual roles in the text and through their offspring, provide the symbolic representation of mercury and sulfur. As the basis for their branch of the Buendías, they are perhaps also related to lead, the most base of all metals and the origin from which all transmutation must begin. Úrsula and José Arcadio Buendía become one of the most important aspects of the connection between *One Hundred Years of Solitude* and alchemy, and they set into motion the first of the six "stages" or generations of Buendías.

The alchemical process has six stages that rely on the metals important to alchemy;[22] while Úrsula and José Arcadio Buendía coincide with the first stage of the science, other stages provide interesting parallels with the six generations of Buendías in *One Hundred Years of Solitude*. For example, applying these six stages of alchemy to the Buendía family genealogy explains one of the most bizarre and confusing aspects of the novel: Remedios the Beauty's ascension. According to alchemy, the act of changing base lead into gold requires descent before the alchemist can ascend and reach perfection; the alchemist must journey to the deepest part of his or her own soul in order to purify it. Thus, the first three stages represent a movement downward, especially in the spiritual sense. Ironically, Remedios is born into the fourth of six generations of Buendías. In other words, her "stage" in the family history coincides with the stage of alchemy where metals and the soul begin their ascent toward gold. Her ascension, then, mirrors the progression of the macrocosmic journey of the novel toward some potential, ultimate perfection.

Unfortunately, the Buendías will never achieve the spiritual heights that Remedios's ascent anticipates. Although Gabriel García Márquez creates a nearly ideal setting in which more than one of the Macondons (and particularly the Buendías) could excel at alchemy or reach a "golden" state within the larger context of the novel, only Melquíades seems to find adeptness in the ancient science that he introduces to the town. Though the Buendías provide six generations of offspring, they grow multiplicatively rather than spiritually, proving that, in spite of the prowess Melquíades exhibits as an alchemist, he apparently cannot or does not share his philosopher's stone with his friends. From one Aureliano spring seventeen golden sons; on the surface, then, it looks as though Macondo fulfills the cycle of alchemy. Instead, it is a multiplication that goes nowhere, since only one son will even live into his twenties. When, in fact, children are born to the Buendías, they are almost without exception "tainted" by ancestors, as illustrated by the frequent and confusing repetition of common names of the progeny.[23]

Most significantly, the Buendía line ends just as it begins—with an incestuous couple and their "golden" offspring. "Gold" (Colonel Aureliano), then, is the first thing born in Macondo and, when the red ants carry off the newborn corpse, it is the last thing borne out of it. This final Aureliano, who appears to be "predisposed to begin the race again from the beginning" but who has "the tail of a pig" (417), is not the symbol of alchemical or familial success but rather is false gold. The cycle will grind to a halt for the gold-seeking Buendías. *One Hundred Years of Solitude* produces no more gold than it started with; any impurities are passed from generation to generation, culminating at the end of the novel, where the character Amaranta Úrsula carries out the two greatest fears of her namesakes: she has an affair with her nephew and her child is born with a pig's tail. The final line of the novel tells us "races condemned to one hundred years of solitude did not have a second opportunity on earth" (422). As we already know from earlier in the text, Melquíades has predicted a future Macondo *without* Buendías. To the extent that these characters serve as the "soul" of the text, their failure to make the final alchemical leap suggests that the macrocosmic alchemy of *One Hundred Years of Solitude* will fail as well. In Macondo, at least this time around, the alchemical process and all attempts to master it, fail.

The final generations of the Buendía family open a last ironic chapter in the alchemy of *One Hundred Years of Solitude* with Amaranta Úrsula and Aureliano Babilonia, who "commit incest without fully realizing the true nature of their kinship" (Williamson 51) and who signify both the diametric Adam and Eve and the next José Arcadio Buendía and Úrsula. "They saw themselves in the lost paradise of the deluge," "the paradise of misery" (414, 417). They are not the only humans on earth, but their solitude emphasizes that Macondo maintains its faithfulness to García Márquez's title in spite of outside intervention.

> In that Macondo forgotten even by the birds, where the dust and the heat had become so strong that it was difficult to breathe, secluded by solitude and love and by the solitude of love in a house where it was almost impossible to sleep because of the noise of

the red ants, Aureliano and Amaranta Úrsula were the only happy
beings, and the most happy on the face of the earth. (409–10)

In flouting the failures of past generations, this Edenic state suggests that
the incestuous couple has the power to reverse the apocalyptic spiral of
One Hundred Years of Solitude. Amaranta Úrsula and Aureliano continue
the sexual alchemy their ancestor, Aureliano Segundo, begins with Petra
Cotes. Whereas Western alchemy typically accepts a rather chaste view of
the science, the Eastern tradition required a type of sexual mastery of the
body that ultimately led to the soul's transmutation into gold.[24] In a sense,
then, Aureliano Babilonia and Amaranta Úrsula, (as *materia prima*) have
even more promise of kindling the magical realist potential of the family
line through the alchemy they practice in the bedroom. Moreover, unlike
Aureliano Segundo and Petra Cotes, Amaranta Úrsula and Aureliano are
driven by true love rather than by greed.

By treading on the very taboos that force José Arcadio Buendía and
Úrsula to flee to Macondo one hundred years earlier, Amaranta Úrsula and
Aureliano fall prey to the biological pitfalls of their union and falter as a
result. Williamson argues that they fail because,

> [l]ike magical realism, incest tends towards the fusion of differential
> categories, and as such constitutes a threat to social organization,
> since it weakens the vital distinction that underpins cultural order:
> the difference between self and other. In this sense, incest can
> be taken as a symbolic equivalent of the solipsism that underlies
> magical realism. For, when kinship differences are not properly
> marked, communication or constructive social intercourse are *[sic]*
> rendered ineffective. (47)

Though Williamson argues that science is José Arcadio Buendía's defense
against the threat of incest, "since its basic concern to discover objective facts
about the material world excludes by definition the introverted, solipsistic
mental attitudes represented by incest" (48), in fact, "José Arcadio Buendía's
search for scientific understanding is soon frustrated, not just because his
mentor Melquíades is an alchemist whose knowledge is rooted in occult-
ism and medieval learning, but chiefly and decisively because he chooses to
abandon it and give way to Úrsula's priorities" (49). In spite of the fact that it
is alchemy and not modern science that Melquíades introduces, the primary
reason that the Buendía family line will find science no defense at all is
because they consistently abuse it. At the end of the novel, the Buendía line
cannot be saved because, like the patriarch, Aureliano Babilonia has chosen
Amaranta Úrsula (and therefore, incest) over his scientific pursuits. "In the

Buendía family tree, analogies and parallels override particular differences; the experiences of the various generations conform to stock patterns which repeat themselves with such regularity that the linear sequence of historical events appears to be distorted into cycles of time revolving around a still centre of eternity" (Williamson 52). As Úrsula says earlier in the novel, "I know all of this by heart. . . . It's as if time had turned around and we were back at the beginning" (199). Even apocalypse has "a strange air of eternal repetition" in *One Hundred Years of Solitude* (Conniff 168).[25]

Ultimately, though the Buendía family fails, García Márquez succeeds in his literary alchemy. He creates a world where the believable is unbelievable and where the odd barely causes a stir. Yet García Márquez is working a finer alchemy in *One Hundred Years of Solitude* than is first apparent. His characters, setting, and events frequently mimic the alchemical process itself, and his use of magical realism becomes a tool for his alchemical metaphors. Although the magical realist world cannot save Macondo's founding family—which is, in fact, doomed from the start, just as Melquíades's manuscripts predict—it does not destroy them, either. Magical realism suspends the fate of the Macondons by trapping them in a cyclical web from which they cannot escape. Macondo must, like the alchemists' experiments, be redone, tried again, refined. The one hundred years of solitude announce the failure of the Buendía family alone. Ironically, among the many paradoxes surrounding them on a daily basis, the Buendías suffer from their inability to cope with the juxtaposition of their solitude and the outside world that is so at odds with the world of magical realism in which they live. When the even mixture of magic and reality is tainted by too much reality from the outside world, war, death, and capitalism conspire to reduce Macondo's magic to smoke and its reality to ashes.

NOTES

1. Wishnia renames García Márquez's book *Lonely Century*, touting it as the story of the Gooddays, "A Family Trapped in Time!!!" and asking, "Can the Gooddays decipher [Melquíades's code] before it's too late?" (34).

2. Merrell cites the "mythopoeic" as one of the elements that make up García Márquez's poetic vision of things. "The village of Macondo is a microcosm and the one hundred years recounted in the novel is a compression of the whole history of man" (263).

3. Melquíades and José Arcadio Buendía do not, as Brian Conniff argues, "assume that science is essentially democratizing" (170); alchemy is certainly not a science of democratization, given its privileging not only of metals (the physical) but of spiritual states (the metaphysical).

4. "It is easy from the vantage point of a highly developed technological culture, to think of Melquíades and José Arcadio as being naive, having too many gaps in their learning to be true scientists. There are loose ends in their knowledge

which make them seem provincial. Should we judge them thus, however, we would betray only our own provinciality, for all science has loose ends" (Stevens and Vela 265–66).

5. If magical realism and alchemy share much in common as tools of the fictional inventiveness of García Márquez's *One Hundred Years of Solitude*, though, they evoke even more comparisons within the fictive domain of the novel itself: Melquíades will be responsible for introducing both to the town; both will fail in Macondo; neither will survive (or save the town from) exterior influences.

6. For more on the distinction between magical realism and other literary modes that deal with the supernatural, see Chapter 1 and its discussion of Amaryll Chanady's *Magical Realism and the Fantastic: Resolved Versus Unresolved Antinomy* (NY: Garland, 1985).

7. And, Brian Conniff argues that because these people are "so improbable, and so real . . . a 'resource' like 'magical realism' is needed to depict them" (178).

8. In this respect, we can compare García Márquez and Toni Morrison (see Chapter 5 for more on Morrison's take on brutal reality).

9. Kathleen McNerney's and John Martin's assertion that "the roots of alchemy can be traced back to ancient India" is a claim not substantiated in their article and one directly refuted by the sources on alchemy cited here, though it would suggest a reason that "the manuscript be set down in that tongue [Sanskrit]" (110). Anibal González's argument that Spanish has roots of its own in India, since "Sanskrit is, of course, the *Ursprache* [i.e., the origins for the linguistic genealogy] of Spanish" (73), as well as Melquíades's connection to India through his gypsy roots, are perhaps as convincing a reason for Melquíades's use of Sanskrit.

10. In this way, alchemy shares common bonds with the Hebrew term for Adam, which etymologically may be a wordplay on the word for "earth" (*The Interpreter's Dictionary of the Bible* 42). This is not the only bond *One Hundred Years of Solitude* establishes with Adam, since during the insomnia plague, José Arcadio Buendía functions as a modern-day Adam, who, "[i]n giving things names, . . . also gave them reality." García Márquez "seems to tell us that anything which may be forgotten by man may lose its existence and, perhaps, its *reality*" (Stevens and Vela 264)—a seemingly plausible possibility, given the Banana Company massacre's historical "nonexistence."

11. Melquíades's texts pose a similar challenge—although whether merely through encryption or allegory, only Aureliano knows.

12. "The physical transmutation of metals was a sign which manifested outwardly the inward holiness both of gold and of man—of the man, that is, who had completed the inward work" (Burckhardt 204).

13. From "The Solitude of Latin America," as quoted in Winn, 441. Although Richard Cardwell's translation of García Márquez's Nobel address is included in the references, Winn's version of this particular passage is the more striking translation.

14. Paracelsus, the legendary alchemist, was reputed to have been seen several times after his death in 1541 and declared that "only ignoramuses allege that Nature has not provided a remedy against every disease" (qtd. in Pachter 14).

15. Ironically, the Spanish conquerors themselves might be considered puffers, in that their exploration of the New World was actually an attempt to exploit its gold.

16. The Latin word for gold is "aurum"; "oro" in Spanish.

17. Oddly enough, García Márquez describes the placebo given to the Banana Company workers as "the color of copper sulfate" (306), or royal blue. Alchemically, the color suggests the philosopher's stone, but because this is false medicine, it is also symbolic of false alchemy. The Banana Company does not offer a future to its workers; instead, it seals their tragic fates.

18. McNerney and Martin, who cite alchemy as "a prominent leitmotif" in the novel rather than a major force, nonetheless support the connection between solitude and alchemy when they argue that, although the science is "[i]mportant in its own right, alchemy is also inseparable from the two major themes of the narrative: time and solitude."

19. Perhaps García Márquez intends to reveal that José Arcadio Segundo has the soul of an alchemist, as revealed by his "windows" to the soul.

20. For more on incest and magical realism, see Edwin Williamson, "Magical Realism and the Theme of Incest in *One Hundred Years of Solitude*" (In *Gabriel García Márquez: New Readings*. Bernard McGuirk and Richard Cardwell, eds. Cambridge: Cambridge UP, 1987), a portion of which is discussed elsewhere.

21. Though Melquíades functions as Macondo's *materia prima*, García Márquez also associates him with mercury—in that his immortal state relies on it. His role as the master alchemist who introduces the science to Macondo, though, emphasizes his additional importance to the macrocosmic alchemy of *One Hundred Years of Solitude*. In a way, he uses mercury and sulfur, as represented by José Arcadio Buendía and Úrsula, as the origins of the process.

22. That is, lead, tin, iron, mercury, silver, and copper (Burckhardt 185–93). Gold is the end product rather than a means for transmutation and is therefore not associated with a stage of alchemy.

23. So that, for example, José Arcadio Buendía fathers José Arcadio, who begets Arcadio, who begets José Arcadio Segundo, who begets José Arcadio.

24. This fact is borne out by Chinese historians: "When we hear of alchemy, or read books about it we should always keep in mind that many of these books can also be read as books of sex" (Wolfram Eberhard, *A History of China*, qtd. in Jameson, "Third-World Literature" 87 n. 8).

25. Conniff later adds, "For García Márquez, such an assertion of history's circularity is not merely a matter of philosophical speculation; it is a calculated attempt to make the outrages of oppression, ancient and recent, visible again; it is an attempt to make Colombian history credible" (177).

Chronology

1928	Gabriel José García Márquez born on March 6 in Aracataca, Colombia, to Gabriel Eligio García and Luisa Santiaga Márquez Iguarán. Spends first eight years of his childhood with his maternal grandparents.
1936–1940	When García Márquez is eight, his grandfather dies. The boy goes to live with his parents. Sent to boarding school.
1940	Wins scholarship to the secondary school Liceo Nacional de Zipaquirá, near Bogotá.
1947–1949	Studies law at the National University in Bogotá and at the University of Cartagena. Begins career as journalist.
1950	Quits law school to pursue journalism full time. Begins a number of literary friendships.
1953	Quits journalism temporarily and travels around Colombia working various jobs.
1954	Returns to Bogotá. Writes articles and film reviews for *El espectador*.
1955	Publishes first novel, *La hojarasca* (*Leaf Storm*). Goes to Europe on assignment.
1956	Since military has shut down main paper that García Márquez works for, he stays in Europe. He tours socialist countries in Europe, intrigued by the possibilities socialism offers for political troubles in Colombia.

1957	Military regime steps down in Colombia, and García Márquez returns home. He settles in Caracas and writes for the newspaper *Momento*.
1958	Marries Mercedes Barcha in Barranquilla.
1959–1961	Cuban Revolution. Works in Cuba's Prensa Latina news agency. First son, Rodrigo, born in 1959. In 1961 resigns his post at Prensa Latina.
1961	Publishes *El coronel no tiene quien le escriba* (*No One Writes to the Colonel*). *La mala hora* (*In Evil Hour*) also published, but in censored edition.
1962	Publishes *Los funerales de la Mama Grande* (*Big Mama's Funeral*). Second son, Gonzalo, born.
1967	*Cien años de soledad* (*One Hundred Years of Solitude*) is published. Moves to Barcelona during last years of Franco dictatorship.
1972	*La increíble y triste historia de la cándida Eréndira y de su abuela desalmada* (*The Incredible and Sad Tale of Innocent Eréndira and Her Heartless Grandmother*) published.
1974	Founds *Alternativa*, a leftist publication, in Bogotá.
1975	Publishes *El otoño del patriarca* (*The Autumn of the Patriarch*). Leaves Spain and returns to Mexico.
1977	Publishes *Operación Carlota* (*Operation Carlota*).
1981	Publishes *Crónica de una muerta anunciada* (*Chronicle of a Death Foretold*).
1982	Awarded Nobel Prize for Literature. Publishes *El olor de la guayaba* (*The Fragrance of Guava*), interviews with Plinio Apuleyo Mendoza.
1985	Publishes *El amor en los tiempos del cólera* (*Love in the Time of Cholera*).
1989	Publishes *El general en su laberinto* (*The General in His Labyrinth*).
1992	Publishes *Doce cuentos peregrinos* (*Strange Pilgrims*).
1994	Publishes *Del amor y otros demonios* (*Of Love and Other Demons*).
1999	Purchases *Cambio*, a Colombian news magazine. In June, is hospitalized for fatigue; in September, goes to Los Angeles to undergo treatment for lymphatic cancer.
2001	Publishes first volume of memoirs, *Vivir para contarla* (*Living to Tell the Tale*).

2004   Publishes *Memoria de mis putas tristes* (*Memories of My Melancholy Whores*).

Contributors

HAROLD BLOOM is Sterling Professor of the Humanities at Yale University. He is the author of 30 books, including *Shelley's Mythmaking, The Visionary Company, Blake's Apocalypse, Yeats, A Map of Misreading, Kabbalah and Criticism, Agon: Toward a Theory of Revisionism, The American Religion, The Western Canon,* and *Omens of Millennium: The Gnosis of Angels, Dreams, and Resurrection. The Anxiety of Influence* sets forth Professor Bloom's provocative theory of the literary relationships between the great writers and their predecessors. His most recent books include *Shakespeare: The Invention of the Human,* a 1998 National Book Award finalist, *How to Read and Why, Genius: A Mosaic of One Hundred Exemplary Creative Minds, Hamlet: Poem Unlimited, Where Shall Wisdom Be Found?,* and *Jesus and Yahweh: The Names Divine.* In 1999, Professor Bloom received the prestigious American Academy of Arts and Letters Gold Medal for Criticism. He has also received the International Prize of Catalonia, the Alfonso Reyes Prize of Mexico, and the Hans Christian Andersen Bicentennial Prize of Denmark.

MICHAEL G. COOKE was a professor of English and African American studies at Yale University. He wrote extensively on Romanticism and African American literature, with his work including titles such as *Acts of Inclusion: Studies Bearing on an Elementary Theory of Romanticism* and *Afro-American Literature in the Twentieth Century.*

BRIAN CONNIFF is professor and chair, graduate program faculty, in the department of English at the University of Dayton. He has published *The Lyric and Modern Poetry.*

219

GENE H. BELL-VILLADA is a professor of romance languages at Williams College. He is the editor or author of several titles. More specifically, he edited *Gabriel García Márquez's* One Hundred Years of Solitude: *A Casebook* and *Conversations with Gabriel García Márquez.*

JAMES HIGGINS is a professor of Latin American literature at the University of Liverpool. Among the titles he has authored are *The Literary Representation of Peru* and *Myths of the Emergent: Social Mobility in Contemporary Peruvian Fiction.*

ARIEL DORFMAN is Walter Hines Page Research Professor of Literature and Latin American Studies at Duke University. He is a playwright and also has published a memoir, poetry, and novels.

MICHAEL BELL is a professor in the department of English and Comparative Literary Studies at Warwick University in the United Kingdom. He is the author of *Sentimentalism, Ethics and the Culture of Feeling and Literature, Modernity and Myth*

FLORENCE DELAY has been a professor of comparative studies at the University of La Nouvelle Sorbonne (Paris III) and a researcher in English literature.

JACQUELINE DE LABRIOLLE was a professor of comparative studies at the University of La Nouvelle Sorbonne (Paris III) and a researcher in English literature.

ANDRÉ BRINK is an honorary professor in the department of English Language and Literature at Cape Town University. Nominated for the Nobel Prize in Literature, he has written many novels. Additionally, he has translated works of Shakespeare and others into Afrikaans.

JOHN KRAPP is a teaching fellow of interdisciplinary studies at Hofstra University. He is the author of *An Aesthetics of Morality: Pedagogic Voice and Moral Dialogue in Mann, Camus, Conrad and Dostoevsky.*

SHANNIN SCHROEDER is an associate professor of English and director of the Writing Center at Southern Arkansas University. She is on the editorial board of *The Philological Review.* Her research interests include modern literature of the Americas and non-Western world, magical realism, and writing center theory.

Bibliography

Baker, Robert. "Historical Time, Narrative Time, and the Ambiguities of Nostalgia in *Cien años de soledad*." *Siglo XX/20th Century* 13, no. 2 (1995): 137–159.

Baldo, Jonathan. "Solitude as an Effect of Language in García Márquez's *Cien años de soledad*." *Criticism: A Quarterly for Literature and the Arts* 30, no. 4 (Fall 1988): 467–496.

Bell-Villada, Gene H., ed. *Gabriel García Márquez's* One Hundred Years of Solitude: *A Casebook*. Oxford; New York: Oxford University Press, 2002.

Boldy, Steven. "*One Hundred Years of Solitude* by Gabriel García Márquez." In *The Cambridge Companion to the Latin American Novel*, edited by Efraín Kristal, pp. 258–269. Cambridge, England: Cambridge University Press, 2005.

Cheever, Leonard A. "Fantasies, Enigmas, and Electronic People: Three Types of 'Ghosts' in Modern Fiction." *Lamar Journal of the Humanities* 20, no. 2 (Fall 1994): 17–32.

———. "Orderly Disorder: Chaos in *One Hundred Years of Solitude*." *Publications of the Arkansas Philological Association* 15, no. 1 (Spring 1989): 11–27.

Columbus, Claudette Kemper. "The Heir Must Die: *One Hundred Years of Solitude* as a Gothic Novel." *MFS: Modern Fiction Studies* 32, no. 3 (Autumn 1986): 397–416.

Faris, Wendy B. "Larger Than Life: The Hyperbolic Realities of Gabriel García Márquez and Fernando Botero." *Word & Image: A Journal of Verbal/Visual Enquiry* 17, no. 4 (October–December 2001): 339–359.

Fields, Wayne. "*One Hundred Years of Solitude* and New World Storytelling." *Latin American Literary Review* 15, no. 29 (January–June 1987): 73–88.

Franz, Thomas R. "Mist and Mountain in Three Sagas of Cela, Montero and García Márquez." *Ojáncano: Revista de Literatura Española* 12 (April 1997): 69–80.

Griffiths, Ian. "Gabriel García Márquez and Virginia Woolf." *Virginia Woolf Bulletin of the Virginia Woolf Society of Great Britain* 23 (September 2006): 45–52.

Hardin, Michael. "The Everpresent Past: A Self-De(Con)struction of the Narrative of *One Hundred Years of Solitude.*" *South Eastern Latin Americanist* 37, no. 2 (Fall 1993): 1–7.

Irvine, Dean J. "Fables of the Plague Years: Postcolonialism, Postmodernism, and Magic Realism in 'Cien años de soledad' ('One Hundred Years of Solitude')." *ARIEL: A Review of International English Literature* 29, no. 4 (October 1998): 53–80.

Janes, Regina. One Hundred Years of Solitude: *Modes of Reading.* Boston, Mass.: Twayne Publishers, 1991.

Kateria, Gulshan Rai. "*One Hundred Years of Solitude*: Primordial Man and Modern Civilization: A Study of Márquez." *The Literary Criterion* 22, no. 3 (1987): 17–32.

Landau, Iddo. "Metafiction as a Rhetorical Device in Hegel's *History of Absolute Spirit* and Gabriel García Márquez' *One Hundred Years of Solitude.*" *CLIO: A Journal of Literature, History, and the Philosophy of History* 21, no. 4 (Summer 1992): 401–410.

López Mejía, Adelaida. "Debt, Delirium, and Cultural Exchange in *Cien años de soledad.*" *Revista de Estudios Hispanicos* 29, no. 1 (January 1995): 3–25.

———. "Women Who Bleed to Death: Gabriel García Márquez's 'Sense of an Ending.'" *Revista Hispánica Moderna* 52, no. 1 (June 1999): 135–150.

McGuirk, Bernard, and Richard Cardwell, ed. *Gabriel García Márquez: New Readings.* Cambridge: Cambridge University Press, 1987.

McMurray, George R., ed. *Critical Essays on Gabriel García Márquez.* Boston: G. K. Hall, 1987.

McNerney, Kathleen. *Understanding Gabriel García Márquez.* Columbia: University of South Carolina Press, 1989.

Mellen, Joan. One Hundred Years of Solitude. Detroit, Mich.: Gale Group, 2000.

Minta, Stephen. *Gabriel García Márquez: Writer of Colombia.* London: J. Cape, 1987.

Moore, Pamela L. "Testing the Terms: 'Woman' in *The House of Sprits* and *One Hundred Years of Solitude.*" *The Comparatist: Journal of the Southern Comparative Literature Association* 18 (May 1994): 90–100.

Ortega, Julio, ed., with the assistance of Claudia Elliott. *Gabriel García Márquez and the Powers of Fiction.* Austin: University of Texas Press, 1988.

Pelayo, Ruben. *Gabriel García Márquez: A Critical Companion.* Greenwood Press, 2001.

Penuel, Arnold M. *Intertextuality in García Márquez*. York: Spanish Literature Publications Co., 1994.

Robinson, Lorna. "Latin America and Magical Realism: The Insomnia Plague in *Cien años de soledad*." *Neophilologus* 90, no. 2 (April 2006): 249–269.

Root, Jerry. "Never Ending the Ending: Strategies of Narrative Time in *One Hundred Years of Solitude*." *The Rackham Journal of the Arts and Humanities* (1988): 1–25.

Shaw, Bradley A., and Nora Vera-Godwin, ed. *Critical Perspectives on Gabriel García Márquez*. Lincoln: Society of Spanish and Spanish-American Studies, 1986.

Shaw, Donald L. "Concerning the Interpretation of *Cien Años de Soledad*." *Antipodas: Journal of Hispanic Studies of the University of Auckland and La Trobe University* 4 (December 1992): 121–135.

Spiller, Elizabeth A. "'Searching for the Route of Inventions': Retracing the Renaissance Discovery Narrative in Gabriel García Márquez." *CLIO: A Journal of Literature, History, and the Philosophy of History* 28, no. 4 (Summer 1999): 375–398.

Stanion, Charles. "A Lingering Mystery in *One Hundred Years of Solitude*." *Romance Notes* 36, no. 1 (Fall 1995): 69–73.

Valiunas, Algis. "The 'Magic' of Gabriel García Márquez." *Commentary* 117, no. 4 (April 2004): 51–55.

van Delden, Maarten. "Scenes of Instruction in Gabriel García Márquez." *Hispanofila* 115 (September 1995): 65–79.

Williams, Raymond L. *Gabriel García Márquez*. Boston: Twayne Publishers, 1984.

Wood, Michael. *Gabriel García Márquez:* One Hundred Years of Solitude. Cambridge; New York: Cambridge University Press, 1990.

Acknowledgments

Michael G. Cooke, "Ellison and Garcia Marquez: Nostalgia and the Destruction of 'Text.'" *Yale Journal of Criticism* 1:1 (1987), 87–106. © Yale University and The Johns Hopkins University Press. Reprinted with permission of The Johns Hopkins University Press.

Brian Conniff, "The Dark Side of Magic Realism: Science, Oppression, and Apocalypse in *One Hundred Years of Solitude.*" *Modern Fiction Studies* 36:2 (1990): 167–179. © Purdue Research Foundation. Reprinted with permission of The Johns Hopkins University Press.

Gene H. Bell-Villada, "The History of Macondo." From *García Márquez: The Man and His Work.* © 1990 by the University of North Carolina Press. Reprinted by permission.

James Higgins, "Gabriel García Márquez: *Cien Años de Soledad.*" From *Landmarks in Modern Latin American Fiction*, edited by Philip Swanson. © 1990 by Routledge. Reproduced by permission of Taylor and Francis Books UK.

Ariel Dorfman, "Someone Writes to the Future: Meditations on Hope and Violence in García Márquez." *From Some Write to the Future: Essays on Contemporary Latin American Fiction*, translated by George Shivers with the author. © 1991 by Duke University Press. All rights reserved. Used by permission of the publisher.

Michael Bell, "The Cervantean Turn: *One Hundred Years of Solitude*." From *Gabriel García Márquez: Solitude and Solidarity*. © 1993 by Michael Bell. Reprinted with permission of Palgrave Macmillan

Florence Delay and Jacqueline de Labriolle, "Is García Márquez the Colombian Faulkner?" From *The Faulkner Journal* XI: 1 & 2 (Fall 1995/Spring 1996): 119–138. Copyright © 1996 by the University of Akron. Reprinted by permission of the University of Central Florida.

André Brink, "Making and Unmaking. Gabriel García Márquez: *One Hundred Years of Solitude*." From *The Novel: Language and Narrative from Cervantes to Calvino*. © 1998 by André Brink. Reprinted by permission of New York University Press.

John Krapp, "Apathy and the Politics of Identity: García Márquez's *One Hundred Years of Solitude* and Contemporary Cultural Criticism." From *LIT: Literature Interpretation Theory* 11, no. 4 (Winter 2000): 403–427. © 2001 by Overseas Publishers Association N.V. and by Taylor & Francis Informa UK Ltd—Journals. Reproduced with permission of Taylor & Francis Informa UK Ltd—Journals in the format other book via Copyright Clearance Center.

Shannin Schroeder, "'Advancing in the Opposite Direction from Reality': Magical Realism, Alchemy, and *One Hundred Years of Solitude*." From *Rediscovering Magical Realism in the Americas*. Copyright © 2004 by Shannin Schroeder. Reproduced with permission of Greenwood Publishing Group, Inc., Westport, Conn.

Every effort has been made to contact the owners of copyrighted material and secure copyright permission. Articles appearing in this volume generally appear much as they did in their original publication with few or no editorial changes. In some cases, foreign language text has been removed from the original essay. Those interested in locating the original source will find the information cited above.

Index